Dr Peter Lamont is a Research Fellow ~~~~ University of Edinburgh. He specializes ~~~~ and psychic phenomena, and is a past ~~~~ British history. He has also worked pr~~~~ entertainer, and is a former president of the Edinburgh Magic Circle. He wrote and presented the BBC radio series, *Wizards of the North*, and was the academic consultant on the recent BBC television series, *Magic*. He has performed and lectured across the world.

'An enthralling picture of Victorian Britain and its clash between science and religion, between scepticism and a desire to believe in the existence of an afterlife . . . Lamont brings [Home] to life with a deftness of touch and frequent injections of dry wit' *Sunday Express*

'This shrewd and often very funny book distils the perplexities of an age . . . This is a serious and thought-provoking book about how we witness and interpret the world' Hilary Mantel, *New Statesman*

'Peter Lamont is perfectly placed to write the first balanced biography of one of the most notorious of Victorian gentlemen . . . *The First Psychic* is enchanting' Simon Singh, *Sunday Telegraph*

'Great fun . . . An entertaining, engrossing, provocative portrayal of Victorian society in the mid-1800s' *Irish Examiner*

'A wry and intelligent account . . . Fascinating' *Mail on Sunday*

'A clever book' *Daily Telegraph*

'*The First Psychic* is a wonderful tale, wherever any reader is positioned on the spiritualist spectrum . . . Intriguing' *FT Magazine*

'Peter Lamont reveals the incredible story of this remarkable man's life' *Daily Express*

'The definitive work on the extraordinary life of Daniel Dunglas Home' *Scots Magazine*

'This is fascinating stuff' *Time Out*

Also by Peter Lamont:

The Rise of the Indian Rope Trick

THE FIRST PSYCHIC

The Peculiar Mystery of a Notorious
Victorian Wizard

PETER LAMONT

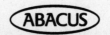

ABACUS

First published in Great Britain in 2005 by Little, Brown
This edition published in 2006 by Abacus

A CIP catalogue record for this book
is available from the British Library.

ISBN-13: 978-0-349-11825-3
ISBN-10: 0-349-11825-6

Typeset in Perpetua by M Rules
Printed and bound in Great Britain by
Clays Ltd, St Ives plc

Abacus
An imprint of
Little, Brown Book Group
Brettenham House
Lancaster Place
London WC2E 7EN

A member of the Hachette Livre Group of Companies

www.littlebrown.co.uk

For Bob
and for Claudia
for quite different reasons

CONTENTS

ACKNOWLEDGEMENTS

Not so long ago, the BBC ran a series entitled *Great Britons*. Its purpose was to elect the greatest Briton in history, as voted for by the British public. The top ten included Darwin and Shakespeare, yet both were beaten by Winston Churchill and Diana, Princess of Wales. I think that speaks volumes for how the British regard their past.

My own candidate was never considered, but that is hardly surprising. Few historians have heard of him, and, in any case, I was never asked. Had I been asked, however, and had I said that my candidate was Daniel Dunglas Home, I suspect I would have been laughed at. Not immediately, of course. At first I would have been asked who he was. Then I would have been laughed at. But most historians, depending upon their research interests, have their particular favourites, people who were great in their particular field. And, in the history of the paranormal, nobody was greater than Daniel Dunglas Home.

If it were possible to go back in time, just once, and witness an event from the past, I would choose to attend a séance with Home. For me, he is the most interesting person who ever lived. He is more interesting than Jesus, Caesar or Napoleon, who immediately spring to mind as interesting dead people. I have studied Home for the last decade, while working at the Koestler Parapsychology Unit, and that would not have happened had it not been for the late Prof.

Bob Morris. Bob was a man of remarkable balance, legendary patience, and dangerous cocktails. He questioned everything, considered all sides, and ruled out nothing as a possible ingredient. He made me think, he made me laugh, and sometimes his cocktails made me feel sick. In short, he provoked a range of emotions, most of which I miss.

Over the years, I have enjoyed discussions (occasionally heated, but rarely violent) with a healthy range of viewpoints about the paranormal in general, and about Home in particular. Concerning the latter subject, which is the most relevant here, I have had fruitful interaction with so many people that I have forgotten most of their contributions. On the one hand, this is rather good, since it allows me to believe that I am naturally balanced in my thinking. On the other hand, it means I will probably upset everyone who is not about to be named. Nevertheless, those who will not be upset (at least for that reason) are Eberhard Bauer, John Beloff, Stephen Braude, Derren Brown, Gordon Bruce, Michael Coleman, Alan Gauld, George Hansen, Walter von Lucadou, Tricia Robertson, Archie Roy, Teller, the late great Marcello Truzzi and the ubiquitous Richard Wiseman, all of whom have made me think about Home (whether or not they intended to). Anyone who knows these individuals will know that they hold quite different views about the paranormal. So, much as I would like to think that they would all like this book, I would settle for all of them being upset in roughly equal measure.

In the historical research that preceded the writing of this book, I was helped by a number of eminent historians (i.e. they have permanent contracts), including Stana Nenadic, Geoff Crossick, Adam Fox, Trevor Griffiths and a quite different Bob Morris (who has never made me feel sick). In recent months, I have enjoyed a most useful correspondence with Doug Harlow, a fellow fan of the first psychic, even if I have not been able to include all of the information he provided because of space constraints. Nevertheless, when we finally meet, I suspect we will have a very long chat. As always, when it comes to the wonderful world of magic history, I have relied at times on the endless wisdom (and almost endless libraries) of Eddie Dawes and Peter Lane. And, when they asked me to go away, I spent many hours delving into various archives at Edinburgh University library, the National Library of Scotland, the British Library, the Magic Circle library, the Harry Price Collection (University of London), the library of the Society for Psychical Research, and the SPR collection (University of Cambridge). My thanks to all the staff at these wonderful institutions.

When it was all done, I sent the manuscript to my editor, Tim Whiting, who told me to do it all again, but this time to make it interesting. It then went to Steve Guise, who told me to do it one more time, but this time without the errors. Throughout all of this, I remained cheerful, upbeat, and never complained, because I respect them both so much. My thanks to Tamsin Barrack and Cecilia Duraes at Time Warner, who are going to make me famous, and to my agent, Peter Tallack, who is going to make me rich (I think that is the arrangement). And finally, to Claudia, who is concerned with neither fame nor fortune, and whose only desire is for me to be happy (I think that is the arrangement). But at least, at the time this book appears, we will both be in employment, and if everything does go pear-shaped, there's always Columbo.

PREFACE

Daniel Home was the world's first psychic. Perhaps he was a charlatan, but that makes him no less mysterious. He convinced countless Victorians that furniture moved without being touched, that musical instruments played on their own, and that he could float in the air. In fact, he performed so many extraordinary feats, for so many witnesses and in such a wide range of circumstances, that he became one of the most famous men of his time. And yet you have probably never heard of him.

You have probably never heard of him because he has largely been written out of the history books. This is not because there are no historical sources relating to him, for there are countless letters, diaries and newspapers that discuss him. It is because historians have not taken these sources seriously. For if they believed that these strange things really happened, Home would be a household name today. It is also because his witnesses, who included many of the most famous and powerful people of the nineteenth century, were reluctant to talk about what they had seen. The feats Home performed were so extraordinary that when witnesses described what they had seen, they were dismissed as foolish, even insane.

Nevertheless, scores of witnesses recorded what they saw, some in private and others anonymously, and a few even had the courage to go public, opening themselves up to derision and abuse. Perhaps they were foolish, even insane, but they provoked a controversy and created a mystery. The controversy went to the heart of Victorian society, because the mystery proved so difficult to solve. It challenged science, disturbed religion and bewildered experts in legerdemain. Poets and politicians, emperors and artists, intellectuals in every field, saw what they could not explain and described what others could not believe. The witnesses may be long dead but their testimony remains, so you can read it for yourself and see if you can explain it, or whether you believe it. As you read, you will learn about the utterly remarkable life of a man who was known to all in his time, and who deserves to be better known today. He may have been a charlatan, but he was certainly mysterious, and the mystery has never gone away.

Dr Peter Lamont
Koestler Parapsychology Unit
University of Edinburgh

PROLOGUE:

The last American séance

14 March 1855, Hartford, Connecticut

A group of respectable, well-educated and unsuspecting New Englanders sat around a table to witness the last American séance of Daniel Home. Daniel was no ordinary spirit medium: he was already regarded as the most remarkable of that remarkable profession, and his career had barely begun. He would be known, in years to come, as the first and greatest psychic in history. For the moment, his fame was limited to Connecticut and its neighbouring states, and now he was about to leave that part of the world. This, his final séance, would have to be memorable. What happened, what *really* happened, we will never know. But a journalist from the *Hartford Times* was there, and this is what he reported.

A small party sat around a large table. A cloth was placed on the table, and a lamp was placed on the cloth. Everyone sat back from the table, the journalist pointed out, 'to prevent the possibility of anyone of the party touching it'. He was quite clear on this point: 'the slightest movement of the kind by any one present would have been instantly detected'. Nevertheless, a moment later:

the table-cloth was plainly *lifted up*, on the side opposite to the medium, and in the full light of the lamp. It presented the appearance of something under it, for it *moved about* under the cloth, first to one side of the table and then to the other . . . the force, (for it was a substantial thing, resembling a hand) reached out and *shook hands* with the company . . . Soon after this, the thing, (whatever it was) again lifted up the table-cloth, moving apparently all about the table . . . it reached forward and *touched* one of the party . . . and presently the hand – if it was a hand, *left* its protection of the table-cloth, and commenced *touching* the party in succession, some in one place, and others in another. But nothing could be *seen*!

Then a nearby guitar, 'large and heavy as it was, was dragged out from its place, and carried away to the door', and there, '*at a distance of five or six feet from the party was played upon exquisitely*, and for several minutes, by some power other than that of any one present'. The guitar then began to move 'by invisible means' and, 'encountering a heavy mahogany chair on its way, *the instrument was laid down and the chair dragged several feet* out of the way; after which the guitar was taken up and carried all *around the circle* by the invisibles . . . In a few moments more the writer saw it *poised in the air*, top upwards, and nearly over his head!' A few moments more, and 'a pencil was thrown from some quarter, and fell upon the table, where the hand again appeared, took it, and *began to write*. This was in plain sight . . . The hand afterwards came and shook hands with each one present. I felt it minutely . . . it was *soft* and slightly *warm*. IT ENDED AT THE WRIST.'[1]

This was what the journalist reported, in italics and occasional capital letters. It was not the most extraordinary of Daniel's séances, however, for stranger things would happen yet. Unlike other spiritualist mediums, who conveyed little more than vague spirit messages through the popular knocking sounds of 'spirit-raps', Daniel was to perform a bewildering range of inexplicable feats – foreseeing the future and curing the sick, elongating his body at will and handling red-hot coals, causing large furniture to move without being touched, and levitating himself up to the ceiling. As the Victorians struggled with their faith amid the growing challenge of scientific discoveries, Christians would acknowledge that Daniel's miracles were better supported by evidence than the miracles of Jesus.

Scientists, of course, were sceptical, but would have difficulty providing an alternative explanation. Some would say Daniel was a master mesmerist, but too many witnesses were convinced that what they saw had really happened, and experts in mesmerism rejected the idea. Others would think him a skilful conjuror, yet the greatest conjurors of the age were unable to explain how such feats could be performed without extensive preparation and large apparatus. Despite all the sceptics and their attempts to catch him out, and while other mediums were gradually exposed one by one, nobody could catch Daniel cheating.

His fame was to grow considerably, and with that fame would come much controversy, as startled witnesses struggled to convince a disbelieving public. Further controversy would surround his personal life, with accusations of theft, suggestions of sexual misconduct, and a high-profile court case that would almost destroy him. But with that his fame would soar even higher, and he would become an international celebrity who divided society at every level. In Britain, he would be attacked by Dickens and defended by Thackeray; Faraday would refuse to meet him while Darwin would be eager to test him. In Europe, he would be a guest of the Pope but later be expelled from Rome on the charge of sorcery, he would be detested by Tolstoy yet become a confidante of the Tsar. Throughout his unique career, he would be hounded by the press and threatened by the public, attacked by scientists and denounced by the Church, accused of every form of dishonesty, delusion and devil-worship. At the age of twenty-two, Daniel had much to look forward to.

Yet he had little choice but to leave New England. He had been told that to stay might be dangerous for his health. And so he booked his passage from Boston to Liverpool, and contemplated another crossing of the Atlantic. Just a fortnight after his last American séance, Daniel was going home. For though he spoke with an American accent, he was not an American. The details of his early years, as with so many of the events that followed, were always somewhat mysterious, but his life had begun in the simplest of worlds, in a cottage by a river in a small Scottish village. As he made the return journey across the ocean, he had nine days to wonder how Britain had changed since his departure as a child, and to consider both his unconventional upbringing, and his reasons for having to return.

I

The birth of a wizard

D aniel's mother was a prophet; his father was a bastard.
Elizabeth McNeill was descended from a long line of
Highland seers, possessed with the gift of second sight. A gift,
some called it, though many regarded it as a curse. These
unwanted visions of tragedy and death had been investigated by
Robert Boyle, that most eminent of chemists, and he had been
convinced by this peculiar, and peculiarly Scottish, phenomenon.
Of Elizabeth McNeill, it was said that she 'saw things which were
afterwards found to have occurred at a distance, just as she had
described them . . . and foretold the passing away of relatives'.[1]
This was how Daniel remembered his mother: with enormous
affection and as the source of his own disturbing powers.

He remembered his father, William, with less affection, so far
as he mentioned him at all. There were suggestions that he was
a 'bitter, morose and unhappy man', a drunkard who treated his
wife badly, though Daniel himself provided no details on this. But
those who knew William said that he was of noble blood, if not
noble birth. They knew him as the illegitimate son of Alexander,
tenth Earl of Home. The details of this encounter were left for
others to imagine, which is precisely what they did. The story

was told that the Earl was a 'wild young fellow' who romanced and eloped with a young girl of 'extreme youth and beauty'. It was said that the couple married privately, and soon gave birth to a son and heir to the family estates. At which point, however, the Earl confessed to his young wife that the marriage was illegal, and 'the shock of this discovery proved fatal [to her]'. This was how the situation and bitter temperament of her son, Daniel's father, was later explained by some, though others doubted the story entirely.[2]

The bastard and the prophet were married at the age of nineteen in the village of Currie, six miles south-west of Edinburgh, where the son of a nobleman worked in a paper mill.[3] Balerno Mill was one of the large paper mills in Currie that exploited the fast-flowing Water of Leith that ran from the nearby Pentland hills to meet the Firth of Forth at Newhaven. The couple lived in one of the small cottages that the mill rented to its workers, and a respectable visitor to Currie at this time recorded that 'this class of inhabitants may be described generally as distinguished for their habits of cleanliness'. Their diet of 'oatmeal, potatoes, wheaten bread, tea and sugar' would have been limited, however, by whatever William may have spent in any of the seven dram-shops and public houses in a parish of fewer than 1800 people.[4] It was in the family's 'simple house, with a river at the back', Daniel later recalled in the briefest of references, that his 'beloved mother suffered so much'.[5]

During the following troubled years, Elizabeth had eight children, six sons and two daughters, most of whose lives would never be recorded. The oldest, John, was to enter what might be called the family trade, and would end up managing a paper mill in Philadelphia. His brother Adam would die at sea en route to Greenland at the age of seventeen, while their sister Mary would never reach her thirteenth birthday.[6] The third of the eight children was born on the 20 March 1833, when the Currie parish register recorded the birth of 'Daniel Home, the lawful son of William Home and Elizabeth McNeill'. Three weeks later he was baptized by the parish minister, the Reverend Mr Somerville, and his infancy was spent in that simple house with a river at the back.

It was, perhaps, the perfect setting for his birth, for what was said of Currie at the time could later be said of Daniel himself. 'Its superficial character', a minister recorded, 'is marked by great irregularity . . . it presents no two portions that can be considered exactly alike [thus preventing] a just and correct picture of it as a whole.' It was also said that Currie enjoyed 'salubrious air', and was 'a favourite place of resort with the citizens of Edinburgh during the summer and autumn seasons'. Its recent drainage improvements had improved the health of the locals – indeed, 'the inhabitants of Currie [were] rather famed for being long-lived' – yet not all the inhabitants had benefited from progress. The river at the back of Daniel's house had once enjoyed an abundance of small trout, 'but the chloride of lime and other chemical substances used by the paper-makers [had] almost entirely destroyed them'.[7] This little world of irregularity, of temporary charm, of survival and death, was one that the infant Daniel would leave before long, but those themes would haunt him throughout his life.

Rejection would haunt him, too, and his first taste of it came at the age of one. 'I was very delicate as a child,' he later recalled, 'and of a highly nervous temperament; so much so that it was not thought that I could be reared.'[8] And so he was taken from his home to be raised in the house of his childless aunt, Mary Cook, and her husband, in the coastal town of Portobello. Like Currie, Portobello had strong winds that produced 'air of salubrity', and became 'a place of great resort . . . for families from Edinburgh'. It was also inhabited by locals deeply concerned with 'domestic cleanliness', and there was even a small river that flowed into the Firth of Forth, just a few miles from where the Water of Leith ended its own journey, along with a handful of fortunate trout. But there the similarities ended. This was plain and level land, a growing symbol of a modernising Scotland. 'There is not a parish in Scotland more highly cultivated', it was boasted, 'nor one which resembles more the rich champaign [sic] of England in its general aspect.' The population around this time was about double that of Currie, recorded precisely at 3587, of whom seventy-six were poor and four were insane.[9] The farmers were 'men of independence', while the one paper mill in the parish was surrounded by makers of tiles and bricks, a 'small iron foundry, and a manufactory of hats'. And it was here, we are told, that Daniel began to experience remarkable events. As an infant, 'his cradle was rocked by unseen hands', and at the age of four he had a vision of the death of his little cousin, even though she died in Linlithgow, several miles west of Edinburgh.[10]

What visions he had of Edinburgh itself, real or imagined, we are not told. The Scottish capital would have been a provocative sight for such a sensitive and delicate child. The Old Town was a mass of overcrowded tenements and narrow closes crammed between Edinburgh Castle and Holyrood Palace. South of the Palace stood the extinct volcano of Arthur's Seat, where Mendelssohn had recently viewed a parade of Highlanders 'with long, red beards, tartan plaids, bonnets and feathers, naked knees and their bagpipes in their hands'.[11] Already, in Edinburgh, this romantic image of the Highlands was coming to represent Scotland as a whole. It was an image that had been created by Sir Walter Scott, whose historical novels, poetry and political influence had made him one of the most famous men in Europe, and had earned him the title 'Wizard of the North'.

The Wizard of the North had also written about Scottish magic. In *Letters on Demonology and Witchcraft*, Scott had recalled the true story of Major Weir, the notorious warlock of Old

Town. This otherwise respectable citizen had been accused of 'vile practices' and 'disgusting profligacies', and of having 'an incestuous connexion' with his sister. Under interrogation, he had admitted all manner of shocking acts, yet maintained that 'he had not confessed the hundredth part of his crimes'. For her part, his sister had given 'a stronger and more explicit testimony of their mutual sins'. She had also told of 'her connexion with the queen of fairies, and acknowledged the assistance from that sovereign in spinning an unusual quantity of yarn'. And having spun her yarn, she had been hanged, and her brother had been burned alive for sorcery.[12]

This had happened 150 years earlier, and Scott was confident that nineteenth-century Edinburgh was no place for wizards, witches and warlocks. 'The most ordinary mechanic', he maintained, had 'learning sufficient to laugh at the figments [of] former times'. It was true, he admitted, that 'every generation must swallow a certain measure of nonsense', but he had no doubt that 'the grosser faults of our ancestors are now out of date'.[13] When Scott died in 1832, the city that had made him a freeman decided to build a great monument in his memory. It would be a grand Gothic construction, symbolic of his fondness for the romantic past, but it would be located firmly in the New Town.

The New Town, unlike the dark, chaotic Old Town, was built upon the straight and ordered lines of the Enlightenment. And Scott, like the Edinburgh in which he spent much of his life, had been a product of the Enlightenment, the movement that had denounced magic and sought to replace superstition with reason. In the year of Scott's death, the Enlightenment's legacy of spreading knowledge was extended by the founding of a great Edinburgh periodical, *Chambers' Journal*. The first page of the first issue, on 4 February 1832, declared its price of threehalfpence with pride. This was a journal that 'the poorest labourer in the country . . . nay, every schoolboy should be able to purchase', 'a meal of healthful, useful and agreeable mental instruction'.[14] Robert Chambers, the main contributor, was a biographer of Scott, and wrote many serious articles on literature, art and science, but he and the other contributors were keen to attract a wider audience of poor labourers and schoolboys. In the same issue one could read about the 'Fecundity of the viper' and the 'Deafness of the aged', of 'Extraordinary shooting exploits', and 'Lord Stanhope's calculation about snuff-taking'.[15] There was, indeed, something for everyone.

One could also find Scott's other interests represented in *Chambers' Journal*. An early article on Major Weir told of the sorcerer's 'dreadful, desperate, and yet deserved death', and how he had died with the immortal words: 'I have lived as a beast, and I must die as a beast.'[16] That same year, a book equally critical of magic (and dedicated to Scott) had also been published in Edinburgh. Sir David Brewster, an expert on optics and the inventor of the kaleidoscope, wrote *Letters on Natural Magic* in order to provide scientific explanations for a range of apparently supernatural phenomena. Concave mirrors, he explained, had been used to make heathen gods appear in ancient temples, and acoustic illusions had allowed the gods to speak. Other supernatural sounds were attributed to ventriloquism, while fire-walking and handling hot coals were explained by the use of chemical preparation. And in this book, the inventor of the kaleidoscope assured his readers that ghosts, spectres and spirits were little more than optical illusions.[17]

This was also the view of *Chambers' Journal*, though it expressed it in more condescending language for the benefit of the poor labourer and the schoolboy. An article entitled 'Can horses and dogs see ghosts?' explained:

Now, this is all nonsense. Horses and dogs have curious *imaginations*. They often *think* they see ghosts, which turn out to be no ghosts at all . . . [But] I have noticed — and it has been noticed thousands of times — that however foolishly dogs behave with regard to ghosts, they always have the sense to know a beggar or a poor man from another person.[18]

This was Edinburgh at the time of Daniel's birth, a city in which wizards were unwelcome, and where spirits did not exist, except in the curious imaginations of horses and class-conscious dogs. But in the years to come, a new wizard would appear, one who would be attended by spirits on a regular basis; and both Brewster and Chambers would have something to say about that.

Meanwhile, Daniel was as unaware of this as he was of the larger changes taking place in Britain. He was born into the so-called Age of Reform, when Britain changed for better and for worse, while for many it made no difference whatsoever. The Great Reform Act of 1832 began the modern process of democracy by widening the franchise, but it was extended only to middle-class men. Portobello was now a burgh, governed by a Provost, two bailies, and six councillors, and it shared with its neighbours a Member of Parliament; yet neither Daniel's aunt nor uncle had the right to vote. The majority, who still lacked any democratic influence, had to look elsewhere for signs of improvement. Robert Owen, for example, had pioneered better working conditions at his New Lanark factory, and had organized the first nationwide trade union movement. Nevertheless, child labour remained commonplace in the paper mills and factories of Currie and Portobello, while those who pledged allegiance to Owen's movement were transported to Australia in 1834. Meanwhile, John Bright argued passionately that the repeal of the Corn Laws would make food cheaper, yet even when the Conservatives finally conceded, it would be a generation before the price of bread was affected. As for the reforming Whig party, their economic adviser, Nassau Senior, was an enemy of trade unions and author of the New Poor Law of 1834. His answer to the growing problem of poverty was to create workhouses in which conditions were deliberately worse than in the outside world, to deter the needy from being a drain on resources by *increasing* the fear and shame associated with poverty. The seventy-six poor of Portobello, being under Scottish law, escaped such harsh realities but not the concerns that created them. When a Church minister observed that reliance upon charity in Portobello was 'not now considered so degrading to the feelings as it was forty years ago', he meant this as a criticism.[19]

Despite all the reforms of the 1830s, it is doubtful that Daniel's family would have noticed. One of the great reformers, the Lord Chancellor Henry Brougham, gave a speech in 1834 not far from Portobello. He had pioneered legal and parliamentary reform, had organized and engineered the passing of the New Poor Law, and had done so for the people. 'I have not deserted the people,' he declared, 'have never feared the people. I rejoice, and delight, and glory . . . in every opportunity of meeting the people.'[20] But he had never visited a workhouse to meet the people there. He had not met the people of Portobello. And he had certainly not met Daniel. Not yet.

These great reformers – Owen and Bright, Senior and Brougham – might have had little effect on the life of Daniel's family, but in the years to come, Daniel would have an effect on theirs. For as the Age of Reform gave way to the Victorian Age of Progress, they would all attend his séances, and some would reform their own ideas. Brougham would be called a convert to spiritualism, and Senior would be unable to provide any explanation other than the supernatural. Bright, the great orator, would say much the same, while Owen, the idealist, would be convinced of the existence of an other-worldly utopia. Meanwhile, Chambers would disseminate the knowledge he had gained, while Brewster would question whether he was seeing an optical illusion. And many more of the great and good of Victorian society would attend Daniel's séances, would see things they thought impossible, and would wonder what extraordinary gifts were possessed by this new wizard of the north.

For now, however, Daniel was a mere child, and his life was about to change dramatically. Having already made the trip from Currie to Portobello, he was to experience a longer journey to a land where many poor Scots hoped to find opportunities that did not exist at home. When he left is uncertain. It was after 1838, when the foundation stone for the Scott monument was laid, and the coronation of Queen Victoria took place. It was before 1841, when Charles Dickens visited Edinburgh, and when the census recorded the population of Portobello, without reference to Mr and Mrs Cook or their adopted son.[21] Their point of departure might have been Liverpool, where the sailing ships began the five-week journey that could take three months or longer in bad weather. Unable to afford a private cabin, the Cooks would have endured cramped and poorly ventilated conditions, surrounded by hundreds of fellow steerage passengers, many suffering from dreadful seasickness. And even for those whose stomachs were stronger, there was always the threat of typhus or cholera, or of the ship's sinking without trace. The experience of such a voyage is difficult to imagine now. Dickens himself described the journey: one of dark nights and deafening winds, of clamorous and fierce voices in the sea, the ship with its 'tall masts trembling and her timbers starting under the strain'.[22]

Daniel, a child of a highly nervous disposition, and one who suffered badly from seasickness, could have endured this journey only by retreating into his lively imagination, or being distracted by fellow passengers. There would have been a mixed bunch: Scots, English, Welsh and Irish; men, women and children of every age, though mostly under thirty; farmers of means and unemployed labourers, men of industry, handloom weavers and doctors; some alone, many with their families. Their reasons for going varied, but they all would have shared the simple hope that, whatever their current circumstances, life in America would be better. And the lives of many of them would indeed be improved, while some would find only disappointment, and others would never live to see their ship arrive in New York.

Mr and Mrs Cook arrived safely, and made their way to Greeneville, near Norwich, Connecticut, along with their adopted son. It was there that he attended school and was, as he would be for the rest of his life, something of an outsider. 'He was red-haired, freckled, not obviously clean', one of his schoolmates later recalled, 'and generally known by the boys as "Scotchy".'[23] It was no doubt a gentle but constant reminder of his alien status. According to a neighbour, he was 'a disagreeable nasty boy', while according to a schoolmate he was 'one of the most joyous, affectionate, and whole-souled boys among my whole circle of acquaintances'.[24] Even at this early age, it seems there was little upon which people could agree.

By the age of thirteen, Daniel was still rather delicate, 'unable to join the sports of other boys of my own age'. He preferred instead to visit the nearby woods, to be charmed by nature and indulge his dreamy imagination. On these rambles, he was usually accompanied by Edwin, an older boy who was similar 'both in character and organization'. It was here in the woods with Edwin that Daniel spent the happiest days of his boyhood, the two of them reading the Bible together and telling each other stories.[25] One April day, Edwin told Daniel a story of two lovers. In this story, a lady and her sweetheart made a pact that, if there were an afterlife, whoever died first would visit the other in spirit form. A few days later, the gentleman died, and appeared to his lover in the form of a spirit, proving both his love and the existence of the afterlife. The boys debated whether such things could be true – could spirits really return to earth and appear to those they loved? And then, 'with the romance of their age, they ended by agreeing to bind themselves by the same promise that the two lovers in the legend had taken; and exchanged vows on the spot, in the most solemn manner they could devise'.[26]

It was an unusual ritual, but Daniel was an unusual boy. He was an outsider not only by birth, but also because of the delicate constitution that prevented him from playing with other boys. He had at least one friend with whom he was intimate, and to whom he was now committed. But that was not to last, as the promise they had made was to be tested sooner than either had imagined.

A few weeks later, Daniel's aunt moved to Troy, almost three hundred miles from Edwin and the woods in which the two boys had made their vows. Shortly after, on a moonlit evening in June, Daniel prepared to go to bed. As he drew the sheets over him, darkness filled the room, then a 'gleam of light' appeared, and there at the foot of his bed stood a figure. It was Edwin, 'in a cloud of brightness, illuminating his face with a distinctness more than mortal'. He seemed unchanged, though his hair was long and 'fell in wavy ringlets upon his shoulders', and he looked at Daniel 'with a smile of ineffable sweetness'. Edwin raised his arm and made three circles in the air with his hand, then 'the hand began slowly to disappear, then the arm, and finally the whole body melted away'. At the sight of this vision, Daniel lost the power of movement, but he soon recognized the meaning of the sign: his friend was dead, and had died three days previously. A few days later a letter arrived that confirmed the tragic truth of Edwin's death from malignant dysentery, exactly three days prior to the vision.[27]

This was how Daniel recalled his own earliest memory of a vision. It was a strange story, but not so different from those reported by the chroniclers of second sight. Such visions might be dismissed as hallucinations, and their accuracy attributed to chance, perhaps a freak coincidence of a vivid imagination and untimely illness. But for Daniel this was an ability that he had inherited from his beloved mother across the Atlantic, a disturbing and unwanted gift that few possessed, and that neither he nor she could control. It was, perhaps, in this reluctant acceptance of being different that he felt closest to her. At some point in the following years, Daniel and his aunt returned to Greeneville, and Elizabeth emigrated to America, along with the rest of Daniel's family. She lived only a few miles away and, for a while at least, his sense of alienation was diluted by her company. But in 1850 that short-lived bond also came to an end.

The tragic event was foreseen by Elizabeth herself, and later confirmed by Daniel in another vision. As he lay ill in bed he heard her voice, though he did not recognize it immediately as hers. After all, he knew her to be in Waterford at the time, twelve miles away. But then he turned and saw 'what appeared to be a bust of my mother'. The lips moved and spoke to him, saying three times: 'Dan, twelve o'clock', and then 'disappeared from sight'. Daniel called his aunt, and told her that his mother had died at noon, and his aunt replied: 'Nonsense, child, you are ill, and this is the effect of a fevered brain.' But it was found to be true, and the death of his mother, like the death of his friend, left Daniel once again alone.[28]

He turned to religion, and sought in vain a theology that might accommodate his visions, and a congregation that might give him a sense of belonging. His immediate choice was that of his aunt, who was a devout Presbyterian and held a Calvinist view that no matter how one lived, one's destiny had already been decided. Perhaps the idea that one's destiny was fixed made sense to a young man who could predict the future. However, Presbyterianism had no place for miracles other than those in the Bible, regarding such powers as the work of the Devil.

So instead Daniel joined the Wesleyans, who held a quite different view, believing that every soul could be saved. Indeed, John Wesley had spent an enormous amount of time riding around Britain, preaching to people, and gathering huge numbers of supporters to whom the ideas of equality and salvation were understandably attractive. His message, however, had never been too successful in Scotland, and Mrs Cook, whatever she thought about equality and salvation, was not fond of Wesleyans. So when Daniel joined them, 'her opposition was so violent that I left them to join the Congregationalists'.[29] Not that his aunt was particularly fond of Congregationalists either, but they were an older Puritan sect, less evangelical, more Calvinist, and she regarded them 'with less dislike'.[30] Perhaps it was a compromise, but neither Daniel's new Church nor his aunt's prejudices were able to accommodate what happened next.

The events occurred, as usual, as Daniel was going to bed, when he heard 'three loud blows on the head of my bed, as if struck by a hammer'. Naturally he wondered whether there was someone in the room, but then the knocking sounds were repeated as if 'sounding in my ears'. It was then that he concluded that 'they were something not of earth', and this thought led to a sleepless night. The following morning, at the breakfast table, he looked so pale that his aunt teased him about having exhausted himself at over-energetic prayer meetings. At that moment, the knocks returned – 'a perfect shower of raps all over the table' – and Daniel was 'terror-stricken to hear again such sounds coming with no visible cause'. At first, Mrs Cook reacted more with anger than fear, accusing him of 'bringing the devil to [her] house'. According to Daniel, she 'seized a chair and threw it at me'. But soon the anger turned to fear, and Mrs Cook realized she would need help. And since there was no Presbyterian minister in the area, she would have to rely on those over-enthusiastic sects she had never liked, perhaps even those evangelical Wesleyans. Such is the perspective she gained that day, when the otherwise insurmountable differences among rival Christian sects faded into insignificance when faced with a common enemy.

And so three local ministers came to visit – a Baptist, a Congregationalist, even a Wesleyan – and each attempted to deal with the problem of the rapping sounds. First came the Baptist, who promptly located the source of the troubling noises. 'It is Satan who possesses you,' he declared with authority, 'let us seek to drive him forth by our prayers.' The Baptist sat down and began to pray, but 'at every mention of the Holy names of God and Jesus, there came gentle taps on his chair', and at each request for God's mercy, there were 'loud rappings, as if joining us in our heartfelt prayers'. Daniel was convinced then of the goodness of these sounds, but the Baptist minister 'was so bewildered by the thought that his prayers had seemed to call forth the sounds, instead of silencing them, that he had little to say'.

Next came the Congregationalist, whose church Daniel attended, and so might be expected to offer more comfort. 'Don't be frightened,' he reassured Daniel, 'if this is the work of Satan, it is your misfortune and not your fault.' Precisely what comfort this was supposed to provide is difficult to say, but he too prayed, and he too failed to prevent the mysterious sounds. As to their origin, he 'would not enter into the subject, saying [only] that he saw no reason why a pure-minded boy should be persecuted for what he was not responsible to prevent or cause'. And, finally, came the Wesleyan, whose Church's enthusiasm had so offended Mrs Cook, who preached that nobody was beyond salvation. When it came to Daniel's soul, however, the minister was less enthusiastic. Daniel was, in the opinion of his former pastor, 'a lost sheep', and 'these wonders were the work of

Satan'. In short, the minister's diagnosis was that the boy was condemned to hell. This was a judgement, Daniel later recalled, from which 'I derived no comfort'. And with that, the three wise men departed, 'astonished and perplexed'.[31]

The rapping noises did not stop but increased over the following weeks, much to 'the continued horror of my aunt'. To make matters worse, 'the furniture now began to be moved without any visible agency . . . to [her] great disgust and surprise'. On one occasion, when a table was moving about by itself, Mrs Cook grabbed the family Bible and placed it on top of the table in order to 'drive the devils away'. Yet the table 'only moved in a more lively manner, as if pleased to bear such a burden'. His aunt, 'greatly incensed, and determined to stop it', placed her whole weight on top of the table, but it refused to stop, and she was 'actually lifted up with it bodily from the floor'. The devout Presbyterian with a short temper would not be dealt with so easily for much longer.

The question of what these sounds were, their origins and meaning, remained unclear to Daniel. And the home of Mrs Cook was clearly no place to experiment. He therefore visited another relative, a widow, who was more sympathetic. It was with her that he tried communicating with the rapping sounds, that he 'first began to ask questions, to which we received intelligent replies'. The first communication was from the spirit of his mother, and it would prove to be the most important message he would ever receive. 'I remember it well,' he wrote many years later. 'I have never forgotten it, and I can never forget it while reason and life shall last.' It was a message that would determine the rest of his life, and it went as follows:

Daniel, fear not, my child, God is with you, and who shall be against you? Seek to do good: be truthful and truth-loving, and you will prosper, my child. Yours is a glorious mission – you will convince the infidel, cure the sick, and console the weeping.

He had yet to discover what this meant: the full implications were still to be determined. But at least he knew that it was a glorious mission, that God was with him, and that his purpose in life was to cure and console, and to convince the infidel.

It did not convince his aunt, who remained suspicious that the Devil was behind it all. To make matters worse, the events that had distressed her so much had attracted the curiosity of their neighbours, who 'were besieging the house in a way that did not tend to soothe [her] religious susceptibilities'. The sounds 'distressed her mind beyond endurance'; she 'saw them to be real, she feared them to be unholy', and if they would not leave, then Daniel would have to. Mrs Cook, who had raised him since an infant and brought him so far, who had taken so much but could take no more, turned her nephew out of the house.[32]

That was how Daniel remembered his childhood, and how he came to begin his glorious mission. It was already a rather remarkable story, and many would later remark that it was not true. His birth and adoption, his travel to America, his subsequent ejection from the home of his aunt, these were not doubted (what reason was there to doubt them?). But the feats of clairvoyance, the visions of the dead, and the mysterious rapping sounds that bewildered and terrified the three holy men were events that begged scepticism. Not least because the only evidence of their having happened is that Daniel later said so. Nobody else recorded the strange events in the Cook household.

It would be easy to dismiss them as the fantasies of a sensitive young man who felt the pain of rejection and loss. His removal from his parents' house as an infant, his move to an alien country, the death of his only friend, and then of his beloved mother – all of these reinforced his sense of being alone. These powers might be imagined, yet they provided an ongoing bond with those he had lost. They represented not only a special gift that he shared with his mother, but also a means to communicate with her at great distance. According to Daniel, she had spoken her final words to him on earth from twelve miles away, and she had continued to speak to him from beyond the grave. These communications might not have been real, but they provided a connection with her that could not be broken by distance, not even by death.

As far as Daniel was concerned, he had been given a glorious mission, and if he was going to convince the infidel, he would require more than his own word. It would not be enough to claim that raps were heard and that tables moved; he would have to demonstrate that such things actually happened. Only then might the infidel be convinced and his glorious mission succeed. And if he could not perform such feats by supernatural means, then he would have to resort to other methods. Indeed, it may be that others had come to a similar conclusion, for it soon became clear that there was more to this than Daniel's imagination. The mysterious raps that had terrified his aunt and perplexed the trio of ministers were already being heard elsewhere. Daniel was about to discover that he was not alone, that others seemed to be responsible for similar sounds, and the source of these communications was the subject of much controversy. The movement that was emerging would provide him with a purpose, a means of discovering a place in this world by demonstrating a link with the next. It would also provide the homeless young man with a means of making a living, though neither his spiritual mission nor his material survival was going to be easy. He would have to overcome the hostility of sceptics, who would refuse to believe what they were told, and would do their best to explain away what they saw as trickery and fraud. If his mission were to succeed, and his career was to prosper, he would have to ensure that these mysterious feats could not be explained by natural means. That was the challenge, and no sooner had he realized this than he was faced with an immediate problem. Not so far away, there were sceptics who thought they knew the secret behind the mysterious raps.

2

The rise of a medium

It was the spring of 1851, and Daniel was about to begin his mission. He was eighteen, tall for his age, with a fair complexion and grey eyes. A female acquaintance at the time described his hair as a mixture of red, brown and auburn, 'like a three-coloured, changeable silk – rather inclining to curl; and beautiful hair it is, as you can imagine'. He was, she observed, 'easy-mannered, very intelligent, perfectly artless and very affectionate'. His nose was 'not remarkable', but his forehead was 'large, broad and well-developed'; his mouth was 'handsome' and so, we are told, were his teeth.[1] A less-impressed neighbour, on the other hand, remembered him as a 'heavy-faced, awkward, reddish-haired stripling . . . with the lost expression of countenance that physicians ordinarily associate with the epileptic malady'.[2]

By his own account, Daniel was 'still a child in body from the delicacy of my health, [and] without a friend'. He maintained, however, that apart from 'being of a highly nervous organization, there is nothing peculiar about me that I am aware of'.[3] In one sense this was true, for despite being friendless, he was not entirely alone. These mysterious raps had been reported elsewhere, about three hundred miles away, near Rochester, New York. Two young girls had also produced these strange sounds, and with them had announced the birth of a new religious movement. The knockings that occurred in the presence of Kate and Margaret Fox had quickly been given a profound meaning. This was partly because Andrew Jackson Davis, the man known as the 'Poughkeepsie Seer', had very recently spoken in trance, seemingly under spirit guidance. He had achieved some fame in the New York area, convincing a number of well-educated gentlemen, and so the notion of spirit communication was already part of regional discourse. When the Fox sisters began to converse with the raps, and an intelligent source seemed to be involved, the idea that it might be a spirit was therefore not such a leap of the imagination. Within days, hundreds had come to witness the scene, to marvel at the banal sound of the other world, and in the process, Modern Spiritualism was born.

It was a peculiar faith, cutting across sects, appealing to Anglicans, Roman Catholics, even non-Christians, and it attracted men and women from all social classes. It was inclusive because of its lack of theology: there was neither scripture nor a hierarchy of priests. Christian spiritualists retained faith in the Bible, Catholic spiritualists remained loyal to the Pope, but spiritualism itself revolved around the curious events that occurred at the séance. It was here that the faithful and the open-minded sat together and communicated with the dead. The sitters asked questions and the spirits replied, the medium being the sensitive vehicle through which conversation took place, but with the raps seemingly independent of her. The code that emerged varied somewhat, but a regular pattern was three raps for yes, two for doubtful, and one for no. Numbers could be indicated by a sequence of raps, and letter cards began to be used, allowing the sitter to point to letters, and the spirit to rap when the correct letter was reached. Words and sentences were thereby constructed, and increasingly complex messages were revealed. Loving messages sounded, and occasionally poetry, but it was information that the spirits knew, that the medium could not have known, that convinced so many that the source of these sounds must be of another world. The demand for such proof, and the desire for communication with deceased loved ones was such that the Fox sisters were very busy, and there soon emerged a host of new mediums who could satisfy the demand. Modern Spiritualism offered what millions sought and could find nowhere else: while it provided comfort, it also provided evidence that the soul survived bodily death – personal proof of an afterlife.

Here, then, was the religious movement within which Daniel's glorious mission would proceed, one that would make sense of his early experiences and give wider meaning to the sights and sounds he would provide. Here was the new Church in which he would become a missionary in the battle to convince the infidel. It was also, at a more mundane level, a chance to make a living, for as growing numbers of spiritualists sought contact with the departed, professional mediums were emerging who could supply that demand for an appropriate fee. Already, there were over a hundred mediums in New York alone, and many hundreds more in the surrounding states. Daniel's poor health meant his career options were limited, so the mystery surrounding spirit communications, and the possibility that they were indeed supernatural, offered him his own best chance of survival. Then, in that same spring of 1851, the mystery of the raps was exploded with the arrival of a somewhat simpler explanation.

The exposure took place in the neighbouring state of New York, where the Fox sisters were giving public demonstrations. In the audience were three professors from the University of Buffalo – Dr Flint, Dr Lee and Dr Coventry – who watched with interest and suspected that they had solved the mystery. On

17 February 1851 they went public with their suspicions in a joint letter to the *Commercial Advertiser*. Mrs Fish, the older sister of Kate and Margaret Fox, quickly responded by challenging the doctors to prove their theory. The doctors accepted, and the test began. The doctor's theory was that the rapping sounds could be made by movement of the knee-joints so at first they asked the sisters to sit on a sofa and, sure enough, the raps soon followed. But then they were made to sit with their legs outstretched, so that the knee ligaments would be tense and pressure could not be applied by the foot. For more than half an hour, the spirits, 'generally so noisy, were now dumb'. The sisters returned to their original positions, and the raps began once more, but when the doctors gripped the knees of the sisters, the raps again fell silent. As Dr Lee, the designated knee-holder, relaxed his grip, faint raps were heard, and he confirmed that the movement of the bone was 'plainly perceptible'. The doctors' conclusion was clear, 'that the Rochester knockings emanated from the knee joint'.[4]

And so the mystery of the raps that had bewildered the three men of God had now been solved by three men of science. They were not the work of the devil, it seemed, but the work of the tibia, though potentially a whole range of other joints might simulate such diabolical sounds, from the ankle to the shoulder, from the fingers to the toes. Perhaps if Mrs Cook had known more about physiology, Daniel would still have had a roof over his head. Spiritualists, however, did not accept these findings, and were quick to point out that the doctors had merely provided a theory that was consistent with the evidence, that they had actually *proven* nothing. Furthermore, the raps were only a part of spirit manifestations; the sounds themselves were less important than the information they conveyed. How could one explain the messages that provided information about those present, demonstrating knowledge behind the raps that the medium could not have known? Perhaps knee-joints could make rapping sounds, but presumably they could not read minds. How could one explain the accuracy of the communications?

Two months after the professors had gone public with their theory, a relative of the Fox sisters went public with a confession. In an article in the *New York Herald*, an in-law by the name of Mrs Culver described how the Fox sisters had confided in her. She first confirmed the theory of the professors, that the raps had been produced by the joints of the knees and the feet, and then she revealed the rest. The messages that appeared were simple enough, spelt out by pointing to letters of the alphabet, the correct letter being identified by a rap. Whatever the information, however esoteric it might be, somebody present clearly had to know the answer. And providing the person pointing knew what they were looking for, it was a simple matter to 'watch the countenance and motion of the person'.[5] An eager sitter, anxious to hear what they wanted, would usually inadvertently pause at the correct letters, thus prompting the timing of the rap. Here, then, was the secret of the spirit messages, as confessed by the young sisters who had started it all.

Yet spiritualists were not convinced by this confession. They pointed out minor inconsistencies in Mrs Culver's testimony, and the fact that the Fox sisters themselves had not admitted anything. There was, however, worse to come. Before the year was over, further confessions emerged. A medium called Beardslee confessed before a Justice of the Peace that he had used precisely the same methods as the Fox sisters over three months. Others admitted alternative methods: it was discovered that special tables had been built (containing a rapping device that could be operated by wires) for mediums with incompetent joints, while some claimed to have found at least seventeen different ways of producing the raps without spirit assistance. Meanwhile, a girl of thirteen appeared in court to explain how the spirits had predicted the death of her infant brother. The prediction had come true, but she admitted that she had been responsible not only for the raps but also for her brother's death, and so she was convicted of murder.[6]

Such was the situation in 1851, as Daniel was about to begin his glorious mission. Spiritualist mediums were being accused of fraud, if not infanticide, and spirit messages were being attributed to clicking joints and gimmicked furniture. It was hardly a good time to embark upon a public career as a medium. Nobody was publicly accusing Daniel of anything yet, but none of this was going to make converting the infidel any easier. He would have to do better if he was to survive the current scandals. He would need to instil genuine mystery if he was to convince anyone that supernatural agency was involved, and he would have to ensure that he was not exposed like so many other mediums. Modern Spiritualism was not about to die, despite all the accusations and confessions, for there remained sufficient numbers of people who wanted it still to be true, and who would resist the sceptical rhetoric of the majority. But reaching a new audience of infidels would require more than raps and messages, it would mean providing them with experiences that were not so easily explained. It would also mean opening himself to the scrutiny of a sceptical press. After all, up until now, there was still no evidence that his strange experiences were anything more than the product of his own imagination. If his mission were to succeed, this sensitive and delicate young man would need to court a wider and more critical audience, and suffer the consequences of notoriety.

The event that brought things to a head was a séance he conducted in March 1851, which was reported in a Hartford newspaper run by W. R. Hayden. Not only were the events recorded by somebody else, but the events themselves were significantly more impressive than raps and messages. According to the report,

The table was moved repeatedly, and in any direction that we asked to have it. All the circle, the Medium included, had their hands flat upon the table, and we looked several times under the table while it was in the most rapid motion, and saw that no legs or feet had any agency in the movement. The table was a large and heavy one, without castors, and could not be moved by Mr. Hayden in the same manner by all his exertion . . . At one time, too, the table was moved, without the Mediums' hands or feet touching it at all. At our request, the table was turned over into our lap. The table was moved, too, while Mr. Hayden was trying to hold it still![7]

No longer could Daniel's earlier stories be dismissed as fantasies, for here was a witness who had verified that such extraordinary things could happen. Whether it convinced anyone else, of course, was another question. As far as Daniel was concerned, these events were manifestations of spirit communication, events that he could not control. But others were more cynical: perhaps the journalist was making it all up, an accomplice to the growing reputation of the young medium, or perhaps he had been tricked. But how? The raps might be clicking joints, the messages the result of careful observation of body language, but how could one explain these movements of a heavy table? Was the furniture specially prepared? And if so, how could it work, how was it placed secretly in someone's home, and why was the secret not discovered upon examination?

As it happens, Hayden was not entirely neutral: his wife was to become one of the most famous mediums of the period, and the authenticity of her own spirit manifestations was soon to be questioned in the most public fashion.[8] But for the moment there was no obvious explanation, and Daniel now had a public statement in support of his extraordinary abilities. It was the beginning of his public career and his glorious mission, yet he later claimed that he had not intended or welcomed this sudden change in fortune. 'On seeing this article which made me so public,' he wrote, 'I shrank from so prominent a position with all the earnestness of a sensitive mind; but I now found myself finally embarked without any volition of my own, and indeed, greatly against my will, upon the tempestuous sea of a public life.' Over the following weeks and months, he travelled around New England, performing wonders for the faithful and the infidel alike. He cured the sick and spoke with the dead, with the result that 'hundreds of persons became convinced of the truth of spiritual communion, and found their sceptical tenets no longer available'.[9] That, at least, is what he tells us. And it seems that, in the process, he began to overcome his shyness, and embarked upon the 'tempestuous sea' of public life by conducting séances for people of note and influence.

In 1852, he was in Springfield, Massachusetts, enjoying the hospitality of a man called Rufus Elmer. Daniel's status at this time, as it would be for many years to come, was that of an invited guest. Unlike other spirit mediums, he refused to accept money for conducting séances, but he was nevertheless without a home, and he became, in effect, an itinerant performer of marvellous deeds in exchange for room and board. And the Elmers, it seems, were keen to display Daniel's talents. Every day, he held six or seven séances for the crowds of curious visitors who travelled long distances in the hope of witnessing some marvel or other. Among these visitors were a Harvard professor, David Wells, and the poet and editor of the *New York Evening Post*, William Cullen Bryant. Along with two other people, they attended a séance on 5 April and witnessed the violent movements of the table. They saw it levitate off the floor, and experienced 'a powerful shock, which produced a vibratory motion of the floor . . . like the motion occasioned by distant thunder'. They were so impressed that they wrote to the

Springfield Republican, stating in the clearest terms that all this happened while 'the room was well lighted, the lamp was frequently placed on and under the table, and every opportunity was afforded us for the closest inspection, and we admit this one emphatic declaration: *We know that we were not imposed upon nor deceived*.'[10] Such was the public endorsement from this group of four that included a Harvard professor and the editor of the *New York Evening Post*.

Others recorded events equally deserving of italics. In one case, five men, 'whose united weight *was eight hundred and fifty pounds*, stood on a table', yet the table still moved. In another, witnesses claimed they saw 'a tremulous phosphorescent light gleam over the walls, and odic emanations proceed from human bodies, or shoot meteor-like through the apartment'. These spirit lights, as they came to be known, bewildered many more observers over the following years, but it would be some time before sceptics could claim they knew how Daniel produced them. Meanwhile, Daniel's mission continued, a curious mixture of religious discourse supported by scientific verification, as he convinced eminent scientific and rational men that behind these movements of tables lay a divine purpose. He was investigated by physicians and chemists, by Professor Hare, the inventor of the oxy-hydrogen blowpipe, and by J. W. Edmonds, a Supreme Court judge. Both Hare and Edmonds started out as sceptics and then publicly stated that they were convinced these feats were the work of spirits.[11]

Of all Daniel's séances at this time, however, there was one that would startle his contemporaries more than any other. It took place in August 1852, in a large house in South Manchester, Connecticut, the home of Ward Cheney, a wealthy silk manufacturer, and it was here that Daniel's rise to fame truly began. According to an eye-witness, Daniel 'was thrown into a spiritually magnetic state, [producing] great rigidity of muscle . . . including a magnetic locking of the jaws . . . He then spelt out (with his eyes closely bandaged) some remarkable and interesting messages . . . with almost incredible rapidity. [One message concerned] two sailors lost at sea, relatives of one of the company.' The spirits caused the table to roll

in the manner of a vessel in a violent tempest [accompanied by an equally] violent *creaking* of the cables of a ship when strained in a gale; then came the loud sound of a prolonged wailing, shrieking blast of wind, precisely such a noise as the wind makes in the rigging of a ship in a storm at sea – and the creaking of the timbers and masts as the vessel surged to one side or the other was distinctly heard by all. Next came the regular, sullen shocks of the waves as they struck the bows of the doomed vessel . . . And now the large table was *capsized* on the floor! All this was done with no one touching the table, as a close and constant scrutiny was kept up by two, at least, of our party.

There were then '*tremendous rappings* all about us. Some of the blows on the walls, floor, and tables, within three inches of myself, were *astounding*. I could hardly produce such violent demonstrations with my fist, though I were to strike with all my might. The very walls shook.'

Yet however dramatic the raps, messages and moving tables, they were already part of an emerging repertoire, and it seems that not everybody was as astounded as this witness. And so he asked Daniel 'that the spirits would give us something that would satisfy everyone in the room'.

Suddenly, and without any expectation on the part of the company, Mr Home was taken up in the air! I had hold of his hand at the time, and I and others felt his feet – they were lifted a foot from the floor! He palpitated from head to foot apparently with the contending emotions of joy and fear which choked his utterance. Again and again he was taken from the floor, and the third time he was carried to the lofty ceiling of the apartment.[12]

According to another witness, Daniel was 'much astonished', while 'the entire circle – prepared, as they doubtless were, for something strange' were filled with 'utter amazement'. Others, it seems, were equally impressed, for word of this remarkable feat soon spread, and the name of Daniel Home began to be spoken of in other countries. Up till now, though he had achieved some degree of celebrity, he had not yet entered the histories of the emergence of Modern Spiritualism that had already begun to appear. But with this levitation his reputation rose, too, and within months, the first chroniclers of spirit rapping were asking if there was a comparable event in 'the entire records of spiritual phenomena'.[13]

It was indeed an impressive performance, even if we cannot be certain what witnesses saw – after all, the levitation took place in a darkened room (it had been darkened in order to see the spirit lights). Yet those present were unable to think of any other explanation as to how Daniel had floated in the air, and so they were left with the one they were given: that this was the work of spirits. He would soon discover, however, that not everyone was so easily convinced, even when they could not think of any other explanation, and then he would realise how difficult his mission was going to be.

But for now, his confidence was growing as rapidly as his reputation, and the shy, small-town boy moved on and up. Soon he found himself in the bustling, fast-developing streets of New York City. Away from the boisterous slum of Five Points, the main thoroughfares were increasingly frequented by horse-carts rather than pigs. Fifth Avenue had just become the most fashionable of residences, and on the site of Bryant Park on 42nd

Street, Daniel might have visited the Crystal Palace Exhibition. Five years later, when it suffered the same fate as its London namesake and burned to the ground, the shanty towns of central Manhattan would be cleared for what became Central Park (the main driving force behind this being one of Daniel's recent converts, William Cullen Bryant). But fires were then a frequent feature of New York life, and the chances are that Daniel was awoken at night by the sound of the bells that accompanied volunteer firemen racing to the scene of the latest burning building. New York was, already in 1853, a city that never slept.

It was November, and one of the more fashionable dinners in the city was being hosted by George Bancroft, former Harvard professor, Secretary to the Navy, American Minister in Britain and author of *History of the United States*. His guests included Washington Irving, William Makepeace Thackeray, and the new star of spiritualism, Daniel Home. Such prestigious company was a sign of how quickly he was becoming known in high society, and his invitation an opportunity to impress highly influential people. But the author of *Vanity Fair* was to prove a stubborn customer. Indeed, Daniel would later recall that Thackeray was the most sceptical inquirer he had ever met.[14] He dismissed the raps as 'some natural unexplained phenomenon', while the very idea of spirit messages was 'dire humbug & imposture. They try to guess at something, and hit or miss as may be. 1000 misses for one hit – It is a most dreary & foolish superstition.' Thackeray was decidedly unimpressed. 'I dodged the Spirit by asking questions in Latin & German,' he recalled, and 'after a while [it told me] its name was Anna Maria Makepeace my dear aunt – only I never had one.' But when the table began to turn Thackeray came round. He saw it 'turn round & round. It is the most wonderful thing.' He also heard about Daniel's more dramatic séances. 'The physical manifestations are undoubted,' he wrote. 'Tables moving lifted up & men even lifted off the ground to the ceiling so some are ready to swear – but though I do not believe in this until I see it; I wouldn't have believed in a table turning 3 weeks ago – and that I have seen and swear to.'[15]

It had not, however, been Daniel's most impressive performance. He had met with scepticism from an international celebrity, who had denounced his mission as a foolish superstition. And Thackeray would soon discover that scientists had a less mysterious explanation for how the table-turning might be achieved. Thackeray confined his comments to private notes, but he would let his views be known soon enough, and Daniel's activities would then be the subject of considerable public scrutiny.

Daniel spent the following months moving between Hartford, Springfield and Boston, and by the summer of 1853 he was staying in Newburgh on the Hudson River. From his vantage point on the hill he could see the city below, and watch the river as it snaked through the rocky hills surrounding West Point, from which George Armstrong Custer would graduate just a few years later. Daniel was based at the Theological Institute, where he now planned to do a course not in theology but in medicine. His training was to be funded by Dr Hull, one of the many spiritualist benefactors Daniel had attracted, and who had discovered that Daniel was choosy about what benefits he would accept. He had first invited Daniel to conduct séances for five dollars a day plus expenses, but Daniel had refused any payment. Perhaps taking money would have been to cheapen the mission his mother had given him, but it distinguished him from other mediums, and convinced many spiritualists that he was sincere. On the other hand, he always accepted room and board, travel expenses and occasional gifts. And when Dr Hull offered to pay for a course of study, and then finance his medical training, Daniel had accepted that as well.[16] This, after all, was an opportunity that was beyond his own financial means, and a chance of a genuine career through which he might earn a legitimate salary. The opportunity was the result of displaying his apparent gift, and thus gaining the confidence of wealthy people. Nevertheless, it might provide him with a way out of his dilemma of trying to survive in the material world through what was supposed to be a spiritual mission. But if that was the hope, it was not to be realized, for Daniel became ill, his studies had to cease, and his chance of a medical career was lost.

When he returned to New York in the autumn, the sensitive medium who had so recently shrunk from public view now felt he 'had no right to conceal the light from any[one]'. His mission was about to seek out new territory, prompted by a growing sense of mortality. In early 1854 doctors discovered disease in his left lung, and he was diagnosed with consumption. That winter was bitterly cold, and the cough associated with his illness became worse. His doctors insisted that his only chance for survival would be to move to Europe, and so he made his final visits to friends and followers, and conducted his final séances. The last of these was the one in Hartford, Connecticut, in March 1855, when the *Hartford Times* recorded the events in italics and occasional capital letters.

His last American séance over, Daniel made his way to Boston, boarded the *Africa*, and sailed for England on the last day of March. His journey back across the Atlantic was more comfortable than the one that had brought him to America, being by steamship and in a private berth that was paid for by a spiritualist friend.[17] The cannon that signalled the end of his transatlantic voyage also signalled the start of his new life. He was now fairly well educated and respectably dressed, with equally respectable references from wealthy American citizens. He also had another name, for he was now known as Daniel Dunglas Home. The middle name referred to the noble Scottish house of Home, and the claim that his father had been the natural son of the tenth Earl. It was a claim that would serve Daniel exceedingly well in the social circles he was about to encounter.[18] From such humble origins, he had already risen to a remarkable position in society, and many would say that it was as a result of deceiving credulous victims. Yet even if this were true, he had been uniquely successful, performing many extraordinary feats for which no explanation had yet been provided. His raps and messages had been more impressive to witness than those of his many rival mediums; he had caused tables to move, spirit hands to appear, and he had convinced some astounded witnesses that he could levitate. And throughout all of this, nobody had caught him cheating.

Perhaps that was not so surprising. His witnesses had been largely sympathetic, initially sceptical but not overtly hostile. Even his most sceptical witness, Thackeray, had been impressed by seeing a table mysteriously turn. As Daniel arrived in London, however, there were already those who felt they knew how tables could be moved without the aid of spirits, and who would go out of their way to expose what they saw as the immoral trickery of spirit mediums. They would attend Daniel's séances not to be converted but to discover his secrets and to catch him in the act. He had left his homeland a poor and lonely child, and he returned a more prosperous and wiser young man, but his success so far was partial and tenuous, and many would say that failure was simply a matter of time. Yet the sheer scale of the controversies to come, the phenomenal fame and unenviable notoriety that he would achieve, could not have been expected. And even during his initial short stay in London he would make some influential friends but also some powerful enemies. The sensitive son of a paper-mill worker had gained social status but he was soon to discover that polite society could be both rude and threatening.

3

The reception in London

Mid-Victorian London was a uniquely mysterious place. It was the largest city in the world, the capital of the most powerful nation on earth, and was regarded by its inhabitants as the centre of technological and scientific achievement. It was, quite simply, at the cutting edge of progress: the most modern of cities in an increasingly modern, urban world. And yet, for all the progress, and London's confidence that it knew how the world worked (and how it should be run), even the most respectable members of London society lived in an atmosphere of mystery.

The sheer scale of the city meant that most of it was invisible to observers, and what could not be seen could only be imagined. Beyond the gas-lit main streets of respectable society lay a darker London: the home of the poor, the drunk, the indecent, and the dangerous. Social commentators such as Mayhew and Booth, the novels of Dickens, the engravings of Cruikshank and Doré, all depicted a London which, in the words of one historian, 'edged beyond reality into the supernatural'[1]. Meanwhile, more explicit literary images of the supernatural were provided by Edward Bulwer-Lytton and Edgar Allan Poe, and real-life horror was soon to be reflected in the dark and mysterious activities of Jack the Ripper.[2]

Scientific advances only added to the air of mystery. In the mid-1800s telegraph lines began to cover London's rooftops, providing a new form of communication that few understood and some viewed as almost magical. Technological developments also offered new ways of seeing, though what they suggested was rather ambiguous. Developments in photography offered an apparently objective portrait of reality, yet the popularity of optical illusions reminded the public that the senses could not be trusted. This point was reinforced by Victorian conjurors, who exploited new and unknown technology to deceive their audiences in London theatres.

New forms of knowledge were inevitably accompanied by new forms of ignorance. On the one hand, there was an increasing recognition that, to paraphrase a quote popular with Victorians, there were more things in heaven and earth than were dreamt of. On the other hand, this was accompanied by a growing and necessary confidence in the authority of science and scientists to know about such things. And, in 1855, few scientists were more authoritative than Michael Faraday, the pioneer of electro-magnetism, who investigated the Thames water supply that year, and officially concluded that it was polluted. Faraday, as one historian has pointed out, 'had shown society that it was the expert who had the right to pronounce upon society's unseen threats'.[3]

Yet, as Londoners came to rely upon expert observers to shed light upon areas of urban darkness, observers who would have been deemed reliable on any other matter began to be challenged about what they had observed in the darkness of the séance room. In a city whose inhabitants must have been uniquely aware of what they could not see, and what they did not know, a debate began about fundamental ways of seeing and knowing. In an environment that surrounded people with evidence of new technology that they did not fully understand, the possibility that another mysterious form of communication had been discovered must have seemed all the more plausible. In the centre of Western materialistic culture, the possibility of a spiritual experience must have been all the more appealing. This was the London into which Daniel entered in 1855.

It was a city to which spiritualism was by no means new: already there had been the table-turning and table-tipping craze of the early 1850s. In countless metropolitan drawing rooms, families and friends had gently placed their hands upon a small table, and watched in wonder as it tipped back and forwards on its legs, or turned around on its wheels. When this was combined with a simple code, much like that used by spirit rappers, questions could be asked of the table and answers could be obtained. It was this table-turning, if not the answers to his questions, that had so impressed Thackeray when he had sat with Daniel in New York. Yet all of this could be achieved without the aid of a medium, in the company of one's trusted friends and family. Most were amazed by what they saw; some said it must be the work of spirits, while others denounced it as the work of Satan, and there had been much talk of mesmeric force, odic force, animal magnetism and electro-biology. So far as these terms meant anything at all, and so far as they did it amounted to much the same thing, they referred to some kind of unknown force for which there existed no adequate theory in science. Indeed, the existence of such a force (what we would now call psychic or paranormal) would have meant a significant reassessment of the laws of physics (as it would still mean today).

Scientists, however, soon came up with an explanation for the table movements that fitted better with their existing theories. According to the physiologist W. B. Carpenter, this was a case of 'ideo-motor action', whereby the mind produced subtle and unconscious muscular movement in the arms. In short, individuals were simply pushing the table, but were entirely unaware that they were doing so, in much the same way that one walks down the road without consciously thinking about moving one's legs. Unlike walking, however, which is a learned habit, table movements were not only new but also communicated intelligent messages, and so, Carpenter explained, there was also the matter of 'expectant attention'. The table-tipper was in a state of expectant attention, i.e., already anticipating the answer from the table, and it was this anticipation that provoked the sitter to unconsciously cause the movement. If the table-tipper knew the answer to the question, he or she simply (but unconsciously) tipped or turned the table to give the correct answer. And what of those instances when an answer was received that was not known to any one present, an answer that, it was only discovered later, proved to be correct? This, Carpenter went on, could be explained by 'unconscious cerebration': the mind could hold information that might be consciously unavailable, but unconsciously retrievable, and so we knew many things that we simply did not realize, learned either unconsciously or consciously and then forgotten.[4] And so, for example, when a table was asked to supply esoteric details – how old was great-grandmother when she died, or who previously lived in this house? – the answers to these questions already lay somewhere in the memories of those present, and their expectations of receiving the answer caused them unconsciously to produce the correct answer.

Such were explanations Carpenter gave, though for most of the public this all sounded a bit complicated. Then Faraday designed a simple experiment to test the theory of unconscious muscular movement. He placed a movable board on top of the table, and had the sitters place their hands upon the board, rather than directly upon the table. As a result, it was the board that moved back and forward, while the table remained where it was.[5] This was sufficient proof that it was all down to unconscious pushing, at least for the majority, who had never taken it too seriously in the first place. But a minority maintained that all Faraday had shown was that 'when he pushed, he pushed', and they continued to talk of animal magnetism, departed spirits and Beelzebub. After all, even if Faraday's table had been moved unconsciously, they were quite sure that their table had not been. And even if it had, they themselves had seen and heard things that could not be explained by unconscious cerebration. Many, in fact, had visited professional mediums, and through them had spoken with the dead.

Spirit mediums were numerous in America, and it had not been long before they sought new territory. The first to arrive in London had been Mrs Hayden, the wife of the journalist W. R. Hayden, who had written so enthusiastically of Daniel's own abilities. Respectable men and women had visited Mrs Hayden in order to commune with the spirits, had received communications from beyond, and had been impressed with what they had heard. But not everyone had been so impressed, and certainly not G. H. Lewes, a philosopher and scientist (and, as it happens, the lover of George Eliot) who attended a Hayden séance in order to expose it as nonsense. He had heard of the theories emerging in America, that raps could be produced by the movement of joints, and that spirit messages were the product of careful observation of body language. Lewes figured that if the medium did indeed reply on behalf of the spirits, and if that reply was prompted by the questioner pausing at a particular letter, i.e. by the questioner's desire for a particular reply, then the spirits should respond exactly as the questioner desired. And so he had gone to see Mrs Hayden, had asked some ludicrous questions, and had sought some equally ludicrous answers by pausing at the appropriate moment. When the spirits were asked whether 'the Ghost of Hamlet's father [had] seven noses?', they replied: 'Yes!' When asked: 'Did [Hamlet's] mother take in washing?', the spirits had replied: 'Yes!' And when asked: 'Is Mrs Haydon [sic], the Medium, an impostor', the spirits had replied: 'Yes!' Then, having got the spirits themselves to confess that their medium was a fraud, Lewes published the whole bizarre conversation in the press.[6]

This had inspired others to mislead mediums, and by the time Daniel arrived in London, the spirits had already informed the public that the building of the Pyramids had cost 'eleven and ninepence', that Noah's Ark had been 'made into snuff boxes', and that the Pope was about to be married.[7] It was hardly science but it certainly made it easier for a sceptical public to sneer at the whole of spiritualism, and it did not help Daniel in his glorious mission to convert the infidel. He had arrived from America with something of a reputation, but spirit mediums had come from America before, and London knew how to deal with them.

He was not, however, without a friend. After all, there was still a minority of people who believed in spiritualism, and were anxious for further proof. One of these was William Cox, who, fortunately for Daniel, owned a hotel. Indeed, Cox's Hotel was one of several fashionable hotels on Jermyn Street, just a block away from Piccadilly. According to Daniel, Cox welcomed him 'more as a father would welcome a son, than as a stranger whom he had never seen' (which meant, among other things, that there was no charge for the room). And it was here, in a comfortable and complimentary Mayfair residence, that Daniel began his British career.

It was a perfect base, for one of his fellow residents was both an international celebrity and sympathetic to the cause. Indeed, Robert Owen was sympathetic to many causes. He had been a successful cotton manufacturer, but had turned from profit to philanthropy and politics, and gone on to practise what he preached. He had pioneered improved working conditions for factory workers, and provided mills in which such conditions were established. He had argued long and hard for better education for children, and had set up the first infant school in Britain. He had formed the first national trade union movement, laid the foundations of the co-operative movement, had set forth a vision of a socialist society, and then spent most of his fortune trying to make it work. By 1855, however, though he continued to write and lecture, his utopian vision was far from a reality, and even a man as optimistic as Owen must have entertained grave doubts that it would ever be realized.

He was, in April 1855, an 83-year-old resident of Cox's Hotel, whose better days were over, whose remaining ones were numbered, and whose mind, in the opinion of one biographer, 'was now feeding on itself'.[8] He had already been converted to spiritualism, had met with Mrs Hayden and other mediums, and through them had conversed with deceased members of his family, who had informed him that they were 'very very happy'. He had also talked with Benjamin Franklin, Thomas Jefferson, and the 'Crowned Angel of the Seventh Sphere', with whom Owen enjoyed personal written correspondence. He was, even for the most apologetic of believers, 'unfortunately one of those devotees who, in public estimation, do a cause more harm than good'.[9]

Nevertheless, Owen was still well connected, and he was, after all, extremely handy. Within a fortnight of arriving in Britain, Daniel had met him, held a séance with him, and left the father of modern socialism in no doubt as to the supernatural nature of the communications. This was a promising start, for Owen would quickly pass on what he had seen to friends and former colleagues.

When Lord Henry Brougham, that most eloquent of Whig reformers, expressed an interest in spiritualism, it was Daniel who was recommended as a medium. Brougham was an old friend of Owen, was almost as old, and nearly as handy. The seventy-six-year-old former Lord Chancellor lived round the corner from Cox's Hotel, and round he came to investigate, though from a somewhat more sceptical position than that of his old friend.

Brougham was a Scot and a lawyer, who had made his remarkably successful career from questioning the status quo, challenging widely held opinions and then winning the argument. His views on spiritualism were more mainstream, since most people approached the subject with a fair degree of scepticism. But Brougham also desired a degree of expertise, and though he possessed an enormous breadth of knowledge on political, economic, legal and social matters, and was more than aware of his breadth of knowledge, he did not feel competent to test a spirit medium. It was, therefore, with an uncharacteristic sense of humility that he invited Sir David Brewster to come along to the séance.

Brewster was also a Scot, though a relative youth of seventy-three. He was also relatively handy, since he was a member of the Athenaeum Club, which was just round the corner from Cox's Hotel. But he was no politician, as was soon to become plain to all. Brewster was a scientist, a Fellow of the Royal Society and a Knight of the Realm. His expertise was in optics: he had written at great length on the refraction of light, and had invented the kaleidoscope for those who preferred something less challenging. But it was probably because he was the author of *Letters on Natural Magic*, which had explained how seemingly supernatural phenomena were nothing more than illusions, that Brougham regarded him as the man for the job. Brougham invited him to attend a séance with Daniel, in the words of

Brewster himself, 'in order to assist in finding out the trick'. And so these two septuagenarian pillars of the British political and scientific establishments popped round to the most respectable of London hotels, and began an afternoon séance with the avowed intention of discovering Daniel's secrets.

Daniel no doubt suspected this. He would have known Brougham and Brewster by reputation, and Brewster's scepticism was a matter of record. But he was in no position to decline such scrutiny, and he knew that his mission depended upon convincing the incredulous as well as the faithful. As for what would happen, however, that he could not have known, as his séances were always unpredictable – Daniel would point out that he was merely a medium through whom the spirits manifested themselves. How, even if, they chose to do so was not in his control. But as many a cynic would later point out, that gave him a considerable advantage: he could monitor conditions, and only produce those phenomena that he felt he could get away with. Either way, as he began a séance, he never quite knew what, if anything, would take place. And so, when Brougham and Brewster met Daniel at Cox's Hotel, it is fair to say that nobody knew what was going to happen.

What did happen was recorded shortly afterwards by Brewster in a private letter to his sister. The politician and the scientist joined Daniel and their host, Mr Cox, and the four sat down at 'a moderately-sized table, the structure of which we were invited to examine'. Before long, 'the table shuddered, and a tremulous motion ran up all our arms . . . The most unaccountable rappings were produced in various parts of the table; and the table actually rose from the ground when no hand was upon it. A larger table was produced, and exhibited similar movements . . . A small hand-bell was then laid down with its mouth on the carpet; and after lying for some time, it actually rang, when nothing could have touched it. The bell was then placed on the other side, still upon the carpet, and it came over to me and placed itself in my hand. It did the same to Lord Brougham. These were the principal experiments', the scientist wrote, 'we could give no explanation of them, and could not conjecture how they could be produced by any kind of mechanism'.[10]

The expert on natural magic, who had attended the séance to 'find out the trick', could 'give no explanation'. Whatever had happened, they had to admit that this was hardly unconscious cerebration. Indeed, Cox recalled how 'both Sir David and Lord Brougham were astonished at what they heard, saw, and felt', and that Brewster had, 'in the fullness of his astonishment', made 'a remarkable and emphatic exclamation . . . [that] this upsets the philosophy of fifty years'. On hearing of Brewster's bewilderment, Benjamin Coleman, a wealthy stockbroker and enthusiastic spiritualist, called on the scientist to hear a first-hand account, and 'Sir David said, that what he and Lord Brougham saw "was marvellous – quite unaccountable".' Meanwhile, Brougham, the politician, remained silent.

But Brewster was a scientist, and wished to see again these inexplicable events, to learn perhaps the secret that had eluded him. And so he attended a second séance, at the house of John Snaith Rymer, a successful lawyer whose office was in Whitehall and whose suburban house in Ealing boasted an extensive household of servants. He had soon been convinced of Daniel's powers, both as a medium and to draw rich and fashionable guests to his home. When Daniel visited, his audience for the evening included Brewster, Coleman the stockbroker, the well-known journalist and writer Fanny Trollope, and her son, the writer Thomas Trollope. Along with Brewster, they heard the raps, and watched as 'a large and very heavy dining-table was moved about in a most extraordinary manner'. But though Brewster watched more intently, he left none the wiser. After all, ideo-motor action might tip or turn a small table, but large and heavy dining tables were not unconsciously moved so easily. According to one Edward Buller, Brewster subsequently gave him 'a very remarkable account of the extraordinary powers of Mr Home'. And when he met the Earl of Dunraven on the steps of the Athenaeum Club, just round the corner from Cox's Hotel, he spoke 'most earnestly, stating that the impression left on his mind from what he had seen was that the manifestations were to him inexplicable by fraud, or by any physical laws with which we were acquainted'.[11]

These were impressive words from such an esteemed scientist, particularly one known as a debunker of the supernatural. It was enough to convince Dunraven to investigate for himself, and it led to further séances at Rymer's house in Ealing that summer, attended by the wealthy and fashionable. These included Sir Edward Bulwer-Lytton, the parliamentarian, novelist and playwright, who witnessed a spirit hand, and, 'believing it to be a bona fide human hand, and determined to trace it to its owner, he retained firm hold of it and was dragged half under the table'.[12] There was also his son, Edward Lytton, himself a diplomat (whom Disraeli would later appoint Viceroy of India) and poet, whose style resembled that of Robert Browning. Browning himself was in Florence with his wife, who was fascinated by what Daniel was doing. 'The American "medium" Hume* is turning the world upside down in London,' she wrote; 'he is the most interesting person in England'; by comparison 'all else in England seemed dull and worthless'.[13] When the couple returned to England it was news of Daniel that Elizabeth Barrett Browning sought. When she heard that Lytton had seen the spirit hands, that he 'saw them

---

*In Scotland, the name 'Home' is pronounced 'Hoom', which led many people to misspell his name.

rise out of the wood of the table . . . [and] saw a spiritual (so called) arm, elongate itself as much as two yards across the table and then float away', she convinced her husband that they had to see this for themselves. Browning was hardly enthusiastic, but he humoured his beloved wife, and the poet couple went to Ealing. He later wrote of a spirit hand, 'clothed in white, loose folds like muslin . . . then another hand, larger, appeared, pushed a wreath, or pulled it, off the table, picked it from the ground, brought it to my wife . . . and put it on her head'. He also described how his wife's dress had been 'slightly but distinctly uplifted in a manner I could not account for – as if by some object inside – which could hardly have been introduced without her becoming aware of it'.[14]

All of these fine and respectable celebrities witnessed young Daniel's remarkable abilities at the house in Ealing. They were precisely the sort of influential people he needed to impress. If he could convert them, the whole of the Victorian world would have to take notice and would be forced to consider whether the movement of tables and the materialisation of spirit hands were earthly proof of a life beyond the grave. Things were going well. Indeed, it looked as if this might be the beginning of Daniel's rise to stardom and an international reputation. And in certain respects it was. But, in certain other respects, it was not. For Daniel's success would always depend upon the word of others, and while Sir Edward Bulwer-Lytton privately expressed to Daniel his admiration for the 'extraordinary phenomena which are elicited by your powers', and continued to attend Daniel's séances, he never gave Daniel a public endorsement. Edward Lytton, on the other hand, was more ambivalent: he was mystified by what he saw in general yet suspicious that the spirit hand felt surprisingly human.[15] And while others discussed privately what they had seen, their views rarely reached an audience beyond that wealthy and fashionable circle. That was no accident, for when such debate became public, controversy soon followed, and few in Victorian society, least of all Daniel, benefited from that. Dunraven's own investigation would lead to the most bizarre of documents being published, describing events so out of the ordinary that, though it was quickly withdrawn, its impact would be felt for generations to come. As for the Brownings, their private views were shared with friends, yet they rarely discussed it between themselves. Their marriage may have been famously cordial, but they did not agree upon Daniel Home.

Mrs Browning was familiar with the writings of the Swedish mystic Swedenborg, and accepted the reality of spiritual phenomena. She had already engaged in spirit writing with her son, for she believed that 'before our children are grown up spiritual manifestations will be among the commonplaces of life, and it is well to have them prepared'. What she saw in Ealing, then, was no more than confirmation of her existing view. 'For my own part,' she told her sister, 'I am confirmed in all my opinions. To me it was wonderful and conclusive; and I believe that the medium present was no more *responsible* for the things said and done, than I myself was.'[16] Her husband, however, was somewhat less impressed. His view of Daniel was of a weak and effeminate man, who 'affects the manners, endearments and other peculiarities of a very little child indeed – speaking of Mr and Mrs Rymer as his "Papa and Mama," and kissing the family abundantly'. For him such behaviour was a sign of 'unmanliness . . . [and] in the worst taste'. As for what happened, he told a friend, 'I don't in the least pretend to explain . . . [but] I think the performance most clumsy and unworthy of anybody setting up for a medium.'[17]

And Browning's negative impression of Daniel got only worse. Shortly afterwards, and despite his wife's utter conviction, he declared that he was 'hardly able to account for the fact that there can be another opinion than his own on the matter – that being that the whole display of "hands", "spirit utterances", etc. were a cheat and imposture. I had some difficulty in keeping from an offensive expression of my feelings,' he told a friend, but 'I have since seen Mr Home and relieved myself.'[18] His relief had come when he was asked, in the company of Daniel, 'to give his frank opinion on what had passed . . . [and he had] declared that so impudent a piece of imposture he never saw before in his life'.[19] As for the wreath that the spirits had placed on his wife's head, Browning threw it out the window at the first opportunity. The couple, who disagreed about very little, were unable to reach any compromise. Mrs Browning begged others not to mention Daniel in her husband's presence: 'Don't say a word on the subject – it's a *tabooed* subject in this house.'[20]

Daniel was unaware of this. Though he had been subjected to Browning's dismissive comments, he had no idea of the tension he had caused in the Browning household. He had encountered sceptical witnesses before, and that was hardly surprising. The events that occurred in his presence were, after all, difficult to believe. But perhaps in time, and after further meetings, Browning might yet be convinced, as others had been. The very idea that the great poet could dislike him personally had, it seems, never occurred to Daniel. And so, in an innocent attempt to smooth over what he thought was no more than an unfortunate outburst, Daniel went to call upon the Brownings. It is difficult to know who was more surprised by the visit. Seeing Browning, he 'advanced with his arm outstretched in amity [to show that he] bore no ill-will'. According to a friend, 'Browning looked sternly at him (as he is very capable of doing) and pointing to the open door, not far from which is rather a steep staircase, said – "If you are not out of that door in half a minute I'll fling you down the stairs."' Daniel, we are told, 'attempted some expostulation, but B[rowning] moved towards him, and the Medium disappeared with as much grace as he could manage'[21]

There have been several attempts to explain Browning's aggression towards Daniel. He was angry because he felt deceived, because he did not know how, and because his wife had been taken in. He may have been insulted when he requested a second séance, and Daniel declined on the grounds that he was ill. It was even said that when the spirit hands placed the wreath upon his wife's head, Browning was insulted that they had not placed it upon his own. Others have reasoned that such hostility could only have been provoked by something that, for Browning, would have been 'very dreadful', a lurking suspicion that Daniel's delicate and unmanly demeanour was evidence that he was 'homosexually inclined'.[22] Whether this is true or not, Daniel, unable to understand Browning's hostility, continued to profess his fondness for the poet, which provoked only further animosity. The result was that Browning developed an intense hatred of him, one that would be expressed in various forms over the following years, some more poetic than others.

For now, however, Daniel's London performances had produced a mixed response. His appearances before some of the most eminent of people had inspired sheer conviction, relative apathy and outright hostility. It was a pattern of things to come. He would continue to provoke contradictory attitudes, but would divide society in greater numbers, and at every level. For while the disagreements were, for the moment, expressed in private, the sensitive and seemingly naive medium was about to be the subject of wider controversy. His enemies, some as yet unknown, were about to reveal themselves in the most public manner, and announce that what he did was not so mysterious after all. Not far from Mayfair, in a theatre in Covent Garden, was a fellow Scot who was something of a wizard himself. He claimed that he knew the real secrets of the séance, and had announced to the public that he would expose them. Daniel was about to discover that his glorious mission, and the reputation on which he depended, were under threat from another 'Wizard of the North'.

4

The Wizards of the North

In the autumn of 1855 there was a sense of anticipation in the London air, more specifically in the area of Wellington Street. The coming of the Wizard had been advertised for weeks, and by the time of his arrival, according to the press, 'the excitement was extraordinary'.[1] Above the Lyceum Theatre, an electric light, placed on the pediment of the portico to declare his presence, lit up half the Strand. The crowds turned up in strength to see what would happen, for they had seen the posters around town: hostile declarations from spiritualists, repudiating any connection with the Wizard, and predicting his ultimate failure. It seemed that the secrets of the séance were about to be revealed, and everyone was welcome, providing they bought a ticket.

The man who was to reveal all was no stranger to the public – he was nothing short of a household name – yet nobody really knew the truth about him. He called himself the Great Wizard of the North, and recalled with pride how he had received the title from Sir Walter Scott himself. 'You take the mantle from my shoulders,' the immortal bard had told him, 'and may, in verity, be styled the Wizard of the North. And when I say this,' the great man had insisted, 'I do not intend it as an idle compliment. You are as much a necromancer as any that have existed in the darker ages. You are superior to them. You may, without stretch of the imagination, be styled the Great Wizard of the North.'[2] And so it was that he had styled himself, though not without a stretch of the imagination. For Scott had never said this; in fact he had never even met him. But as Scott was long dead, there was nobody to deny it. The Great Wizard told this story because it made him sound more interesting, and he called himself the Great Wizard because it sounded more interesting than John.

He was, in fact, the son of a tenant farmer from the north of Scotland. His parents had named him John Henry Anderson, then died a few years later. The young orphan had survived his childhood by assisting the local blacksmith until, one day, a troupe of travelling players had passed through town, and left the local blacksmith without an assistant. So had begun one of the most remarkable careers in Victorian show business, and it had begun, as it would proceed, with difficulty. The tall, handsome youth had soon been on stage where, in the opinion of one critic, he had 'brought bad acting to the greatest height of perfection'. John Henry was determined to become an actor, but decided that he night not be ready yet. And so, at the age of seventeen, he had joined the company of a minor showman called Big Scott, married the man's daughter, and made his debut in Aberdeen as a conjuror. There he demonstrated the dangerous 'gun trick', in which a gun was loaded by a member of the audience and then shot directly at the conjuror.

John Henry had survived, predictably, then had sought success on a grander scale, and his chance came with an invitation to entertain at Brechin Castle. Despite making some embarrassing breaches of etiquette at the dinner table of the aristocracy, the uneducated farmer's son had left with a healthy ten pound fee and a testimonial from Lord Panmure describing him as 'the best necromancer that I ever saw'. Armed with these, John Henry had made his way to the capital city, transformed himself into 'The Great Caledonian Magician', and performed illusions before the great and good of Edinburgh, with what he claimed was 'Gorgeous and Costly Apparatus of Silver', but was actually made of tin. On the side, he had sold a 'magical dye' to 'Any Gentleman with a head of Grey Hair that he wishes changed to a glossy black'. In Glasgow, he had erected a Temple of Magic in order to accommodate the larger audiences of the most populous city in the country, and had astounded the Provost by causing his pocket-watch to fly into a loaf of freshly baked bread. John Henry challenged his rivals to discover his 'impenetrable secrets', and when they discovered them, he denounced them as 'petty imitators'. His native land conquered, he had renamed himself the Great Wizard of the North and headed south to London.[3]

John Henry's magical repertoire had grown accordingly, featuring egg-writing and an incomprehensible guinea pig trick, and he started something of a trend when he had become the first magician to pull a rabbit out of a hat.[4] Never troubled by humility, he also claimed to be the only living person endowed with second sight, though he had never meant that to be taken seriously -- on the contrary, he had published booklets on the 'Science of Magic', had denounced any claims to supernatural abilities, and had scoffed at the superstitious peasants of the Scottish highlands, who had (he assures us) arrested him and put him in jail for suspected murder by witchcraft. All of this had boosted the box office, of course, and his shows expanded to include bell-ringers, ballet and a group of Virginia minstrels. By 1844 he had played his last season, and invested his fortune in the construction of Glasgow City Theatre, where he hoped finally to realize his dream of acting on his own stage without fear of unfavourable reviews. The theatre opened in July 1845; four months later, it was destroyed by fire, and John Henry had lost everything.

John Henry Anderson, the brass-necked
Wizard of the North. (*Mary Evans*)

His theatre and his finances in ruins, John Henry sought out new opportunities for profit in the era of Free Trade. He pioneered publicity techniques with enormous posters declaring 'Anderson is coming!', and large cavalcades announced his arrival in town. An unprecedented approach to advertising had seen whole towns papered with playbills announcing the most extraordinary sounding illusions, such as the 'Grand Metamorphesian Wonder' or the 'Phoenixestocalobian'. He set conundrum contests with a silver trophy as the prize, guaranteeing the attendance of all those who entered, and sold booklets containing the best conundrums for a healthy profit. This alone had required him to carry his own printing press, so that eager contestants could read their meagre attempts at humour in print. Even butter pats were distributed to hotels and inns bearing the news 'Anderson is here'. He toured European cities, became the first conjuror to appear before the Tsar and, on his return, performed for the British royal family. When threatened by the arrival in Britain of the great French conjuror, Robert-Houdin, who captured the imagination of the public with his original illusions, John Henry simply copied them and embarked for America in search of new audiences who, unknowingly, praised the Wizard for his 'entirely original illusions'.[5]

It was only a temporary solution. John Henry realised that he needed a new idea, something truly novel. After all, pulling rabbits out of a hat was hardly likely to amuse the public for very long. Victorian conjuring was a tough business, and rival magicians were quick to appropriate any new trick without permission, as John Henry knew only too well. Originality might give one a head start, but long-term survival generally required superior technique, eloquent patter and fine acting ability, none of which were particular strengths of his. His career had been built on exaggerated claims and sheer brass neck, his real skill being that of a publicist rather than an artist. It was not so much an ability to recognise what the public wanted, as his sheer determination to convince them that, no matter what they wanted, they should come to his show anyway. His tactic, for the most part, was to make the public curious enough to buy a ticket. His tricks might be standard, but the language of his posters promised something quite unique: 'A Grand Ambidexterological Illusion with 12 Handkerchiefs, into which will be introduced the Enchanted Loaf and Learned Bottle, the Animated Orange and the Invisible Pigeon'. Not that anyone had the slightest idea what that was supposed to mean, any more than they would have recognised a Phoenixestocalobian, but that was just the point. Once in the theatre, he presented them with everything he could think of, along with a great deal of what other magicians had thought of, and at the end of the show, even if it had not been quite as advertised, everyone felt they had had their money's worth.

But, in the absence of superior technique, eloquent patter and fine acting ability, there was no substitute for novelty. And as John Henry toured America, he sought the new idea that might bring him success back home. He had been performing in New England during 1851, shortly after the reported exposure of the Fox sisters, and presenting himself as 'Professor Anderson', advertising an evening of scientific illusions: 'Magnificent Entertainment of the most refined and elegant character, comprising Science in all its variety, and embracing the most extraordinary feats in HYDRAULICS, ELECTRICITY, PNEUMATICS and NATURAL PHILOSOPHY'.[6]

This was all part of a wider attempt by conjurors at the time to exploit the growing interest in popular science as entertainment. But the combination of scientific education with the topical controversy over whether trickery lay behind the spirit raps provided John Henry with the idea he so desperately needed. He decided to create a performance around the exposure of spirit mediums, using trickery to demonstrate that spiritualism was a fraud. Alternatively, he may have stolen the idea from Wyman, an American conjuror. But even if that were the case, as John Henry knew only too well, originality could be over-rated. It was novelty that mattered, from the audience's point of view. And new this idea was, at least to everyone outside the towns that Wyman had visited. So John Henry went to New York and announced, in capital letters, that he would expose the secret of the spirit raps; that 'THE RAPPING TABLE WILL BE EXHIBITED, and RAPS PRODUCED, and the whole machinery EXPLAINED'. According to the *New York Daily Tribune*, this had caused 'immense excitement', the performance had 'filled New York Metropolitan Hall to overflowing', and John Henry had 'convinced all of the shallowness of the pernicious and fatal delusion [of spiritualism]'.[7] With that, he returned to London in 1853, set for even greater fame and fortune than he had before.

The spirit-rapping plan was postponed, however, for John Henry had arrived home with another novel attraction, one that he felt demanded immediate public attention: he had discovered the 'Aztec Lilliputians', as he called them, though technically speaking they had been discovered already. According to a highly dubious story, inherited rather than invented by John Henry, they had been found in Central America, living with a secret Mayan-speaking tribe. Of the three valiant explorers who discovered them, one was killed by hostile Indians, another was the victim of a ritual sacrifice, and the sole survivor had fled for his life, but not without bringing the two miniature wonders. They had been exhibited in America, in the interest of scientific and public curiosity, and for an appropriate fee, as 'specimens of an absolutely unique and nearly extinct race of mankind'. The two children were, in fact, mentally retarded microcephalics (they had sloping foreheads and pointed skulls), but despite doctors rejecting the ludicrous notion that this was 'a new race of human beings', the children had been taken seriously and viewed with wonder by representatives of the press, Church and Senate, and even by President Fillmore himself.[8] And all of this had happened before John Henry discovered them in New England. One can only imagine what must have gone through his mind.

Within a month of having brought them to Britain, he was at Buckingham Palace, displaying his new attraction to Queen Victoria and Prince Albert. According to the *Illustrated London News*, 'So interested was her majesty that she remained with the "Aztecs" for nearly an hour, and previous to their departure expressed herself much gratified with their visit.' With royal approval, John Henry had gone on to sell out theatres around the country, despite the occasional expert pointing out that this 'remnant of a strange and wonderful race' was nothing more than 'a pair of severely retarded children belonging to a contemporary people'.[9] Letters to *The Times* debated the ancestry of the human exhibits, the ethics of Aztec culture, and the ethics of human exhibits.[10] Meanwhile, the curious flocked in their thousands (or, if we believe John Henry, in their millions) to see what all the fuss was about, having been bombarded with publicity and unable to resist enticing banner lines such as: 'Extraordinary Cheap Exhibition of Living People with Heads Like Birds'. Yet by 1855 the crowds had begun to dwindle and the novelty had worn off, for novelties cannot last forever. So John Henry returned to conjuring and headed for London to take on the spiritualists and expose their trickery.

This, he declared, was a moral crusade, since spiritualism was a dangerous and blasphemous activity that was damaging for a person's mental health. He presented his high moral stance in a pamphlet, which he sold for a shilling, denouncing spiritualism as an 'absurd and remarkable delusion . . . which has driven ten thousand persons mad in the United States'. Spiritualism, he claimed, had caused many 'to become lunatics, and . . . thousands of poor infatuated victims . . . have become melancholy misanthropes and imbecile self-tormentors'. And if that was not bad enough, the spiritualists were 'now organising for a regular and concerted movement against the Bible and all our religious institutions'. Spiritualism was bad and it made you mad: that was the message that John Henry preached, and though it might provoke the enemy, it was his duty to 'fearlessly communicate his knowledge for the benefit of his fellow-men'.[11]

It was true that a hostile reaction from spiritualists seemed to be reflected in the posters around town, but the fact that they fuelled publicity for John Henry's coming performance might remind one that he had his own printing press. In fact, the reaction of spiritualists was less aggressive. The *Yorkshire Spiritual Telegraph*, the first of several spiritualist journals, merely included in its first issue a poem critical of the Wizard, allegedly communicated by the spirit of Robert Burns.[12] As of yet, there was no real threat, and the Wizard had said nothing of Daniel Dunglas Home, the most remarkable of his remarkable profession. His presence in the capital no doubt made the great exposure much more topical, but there existed no great animosity between the two wonder-working Scots. That was yet to come.

On the night of John Henry's performance, amid extra-ordinary excitement, the crowds arrived at seven-thirty, and the show began at eight. The private boxes were filled with the wealthy and fashionable, while the lesser sort, at sixpence a time, were crammed so tightly into the gallery that they 'began their evening in a somewhat sulky mood'. A Victorian gallery could be an ugly and threatening sight, but the Wizard was not one to be intimidated, and 'after a few words of conversation between the professor and the leaders of the malcontents, all angry feelings subsided'.[13] They were, after all, about to be treated to a full evening show of twelve acts in two parts, including 'The Homological Evaporation', 'The Aqua-avial Paradox', and 'The Mesmeric Couch', all for the price of sixpence.[14] And having discovered what these were, they would be introduced to 'Half an hour with the Spirits'. In thirty minutes, the secrets of the séance room would be known to all – at least to all who had bought a ticket.

The great exposure of spiritualism went as follows: suspended from the ceiling were two glass bells; a table was placed on a platform across the pit, and an automaton figure was set on the stage. The Wizard then asked how many letters there were in a selected word, and how many pips there were on a card drawn from a pack. The bells proceeded to answer by ringing, the table by rapping, and the automaton figure by making signs. The Wizard then revealed that the secret was mechanical, though he did not reveal what the secret was, and claimed that the methods of mediums were also mechanical, though not necessarily the same as his. He concluded by denouncing all spiritualists as impostors, claiming that in America he had defied a medium to produce a rap without being detected in trickery, and the medium, faced with such a challenge, had failed to elicit a sound from the spirits. 'This part of the entertainment', it was later reported, 'was distinguished from the rest by the grave tone with which the conjurer expatiated on the mischief done by pretended spirit media, and was received with applause equally serious.'[15]

This, then, was the great exposure of spiritualism; the secrets of the séance had been revealed, as only John Henry Anderson could have revealed them, which is to say that they were not revealed at all. Presumably the assurance, from such a reliable source, that the secret of the raps was 'mechanical', was intended to satisfy the most curious of enquirers – though if one wished to learn the details a booklet was available at the venue for the price of a shilling. In that booklet the reader would be told of the testing of the Fox sisters, of the theory that the raps were produced by moving joints, and of the confession of Mrs Culver. But this was not the real secret, John Henry explained, for investigators 'have watched the toes and the knees of the Medium in vain. The secret of the mystery is elsewhere.' And with that, having obtained his shilling, he revealed the 'real' details of the mechanical secret of the raps:

A galvanic battery and electromagnet are all that are wanted . . . Hidden beneath the table . . . are the hammer and the machinery connected with it, by which the sound is produced . . . when contact is made at the battery . . . [it causes the hammer] to strike the table sharply. So on, in succession, for any number of raps . . . The individual who works the battery . . . [is] out of sight in an adjacent room, with a small

peephole in the partition, through which he can watch proceedings.[16]

It was not the most extravagant claim John Henry had made (though that, in itself, hardly made it credible), and it was actually workable in certain circumstances. But Daniel worked in the homes of respectable citizens whose furniture would have lacked the necessary equipment, where the table was regularly examined by those present, and where a secret assistant could hardly have spied through a peephole without being noticed by the servants. Spiritualists naturally laughed at the idea, and even the popular press, who regularly sneered at spiritualism itself, found the Wizard's spirit-rapping exposure less than convincing. In the words of the highly popular *Family Herald*, 'there is no more resemblance between his rapping and theirs than there is between the lowing of an ox and the song of a titmouse.' 'His "exposure" of spiritualism', agreed the *Morning Star*, was 'as unlike as possible what most persons have now had an opportunity of witnessing', while his 'shilling pamphlet sold at the doors . . . [was] a gross caricature, and misleading', on account of it 'ignoring the existence of Mr Home, the most celebrated of the Spiritualists'.[17]

But most of the public did not need convincing, their view of spiritualism being instinctively dismissive, and they were quite happy to accept the rhetoric and pseudo-explanations of the Wizard. Perhaps he was wrong, but only in the details, for was it not obvious that spiritualism was a delusion, that spiritualists were fools and mediums charlatans? The very idea that the spirits were responsible was so absurd to so many that few chose to examine the Wizard's claims too closely. And as for the Wizard himself, the crowds had come, the tickets had been sold, and that, at the end of the day, was the main thing. If this dreadful delusion – which, if one believed the Wizard, caused insanity and threatened the Bible – had been damaged, that was no bad thing. Surely a mild exaggeration, a touch of theatrical licence perhaps, were justifiable in defence of sanity and the Word of God?

From Daniel's point of view this was frustrating but not too troublesome. After all, the mystery surrounding his abilities remained unsolved. The public might have had their sceptical view reinforced, but they had not witnessed a Home séance. Those who had, even those who remained unconvinced, were baffled by what they had seen, and the explanations of the Wizard were hardly likely to enlighten them. As for those who had been more impressed – and this included one Browning, two Trollopes and a Brewster – the mystery can only have become that much deeper. Indeed, for an expert scientist such as Brewster, the lack of explanation must have been particularly troubling, for it was to such authorities that the public looked for precisely this kind of information. His *Letters on Natural Magic* had been presented as a dedicated sequel to Scott's *Letters on Demonology and Witchcraft*. In a sense it was Brewster rather than John Henry who had taken the mantle from Scott's shoulders, and might be styled the Wizard of the North. But this was not a title that Brewster would have desired, not least because he was no wiser than John Henry when it came to explaining how Daniel's feats were performed. His only comfort, perhaps, was that few people had asked what he thought, since there were few who knew what he had witnessed. But if that situation were to change, then Brewster would be forced to go public in an attempt to protect his reputation. And that, Daniel would discover, would be a more serious threat to his own reputation than the theatrical licence of John Henry.

It was, in fact, only a few weeks after the Wizard had provided the public with his expert opinions that the Brewster controversy began. How the press got hold of the story remains uncertain, though it seems that Daniel was inadvertently responsible.

Following his séance with Brewster and Brougham, in which the eminent observers had expressed their amazement, the young medium had found it difficult to conceal his pride. He had written to a friend in America, the letter had found its way into the press there, and the story had been picked up by the *Yorkshire Spiritual Telegraph*. From Daniel's point of view this was no bad thing, but that was not the end of the matter, for it was not long before the mainstream British press had noticed, and a story appeared in the London-based *Morning Advertiser*. It claimed that Brewster was 'sorely puzzled' at what he had witnessed, and that Brougham admitted to being 'thoroughly nonplussed'. 'These noted men brought the whole force of their discernment to bear upon the solution of the phenomena,' the *Advertiser* reported, but the 'strength of the Spirits who moved material objects about the room proved too much of a problem for them to master'. This was, of course, a useful public endorsement for Daniel, and provided him with a comforting assurance that his mission remained on track. But this was an embarrassing accusation for Brewster, an eminent scientist who was known as an authority on such matters. And so, though he probably later regretted it, Brewster wrote to the *Advertiser* to explain.

It was true, he admitted, that he and Brougham had attended a séance, that he had attended a second séance, and that he had witnessed some 'mechanical effects . . . but I saw enough to satisfy myself that they could all be produced by human hands and feet, and to prove to others that some of them, at least, had such an origin'. This was something of a development, of course, since he had admitted in a private letter to his sister, in which he had described the events of the séance, that he 'could not conjecture how they could be produced by any kind of mechanism'. Now, it seems, he could conjecture, and in a reference to Daniel's American upbringing, he added:

> Were Mr Home to assume the character of Wizard of the West,
> I would enjoy his exhibition as much as that of other conjurors;
> but when he pretends to possess the power of introducing . . .
> the spirits of the dead, . . . he insults religion and common
> sense, and tampers with the most sacred feelings of his victims.[18]

Needless to say, this provoked a response, as there had been others present whose memory of events was rather different. Cox and Coleman both wrote in to point out that Brewster had been quite bewildered by what he had seen – the floating table, the bell that had moved and rung, and the 'unaccountable' raps – and had told them so at the time. 'It is not generous', they pointed out, 'to raise the cry of imposture in a matter you cannot explain.'[19] This Brewster conceded, yet that was then and this was now, and now he was in a position to explain all.

The mystery, he suggested, would have been solved 'if we had been permitted to take a peep beneath the drapery of Mr Cox's table'. The table, he admitted, 'actually rose, as appeared to me, from the ground', but it had been 'covered with copious drapery, *beneath which nobody was allowed to look*'. And it was beneath this drapery that Brewster believed the real secrets might have been hidden. When the table had risen into the air, it could have been 'by the agency of Mr Home's feet, which were always below it'. Similarly, he conjectured further, the mysterious movements of the handbell might have been 'produced by machinery attached to the lower extremities of Mr Home'. As for the raps, he now remembered details that had so eluded him at the time, that they had 'proceeded from a part of the table exactly within reach of Mr Home's foot, and I distinctly saw three movements in his loins, perfectly simultaneously with the three raps'. Could this be true, that Brewster's scientific mind, along with his improved recollection of events, had managed to discover Daniel's secrets – that they were concealed below the table beneath which nobody was allowed to look?

Not in the opinion of the others who had been there, who suggested that Brewster's memory was far from improved. Cox was adamant that 'no hindrance existed to Sir David looking under the drapery of the table; on the contrary, he was so frequently invited to do so by Mr Home, that I felt annoyed at Mr Home's supposing that he or I could be suspected of any imposition'. Coleman, who had been at the second séance, reminded Brewster not only that he had been free to look, but that 'he did "take a peep beneath" the table, putting his head under for some little time'. And Thomas Trollope, who had also been present, declared that 'Sir David was urged both by Mr Home and [the host] to look under the cloth and under the table; that Sir David did look under it; and that whilst he was so looking, the table was much moved.'

This was followed by accusation and counter-accusation, as Brewster provided conjectures wherever he could, and simply denied that the rest had happened. In a letter to his sister, he had privately admitted that a handbell 'actually rang, when nothing could have touched it', but now his recollection of events was that 'the bell did not ring'. On detail after detail, the others present insisted 'it is true', while Brewster maintained 'it is not true'. Reluctant to concede anything for certain, he had stated that 'the table actually rose, *as appeared to me*, from the ground'. *'Appeared* to rise from the ground?' Coleman responded with frustration. 'Did it rise? Why make a question of so plain a fact?'. This provoked one writer to note wryly that the expert on optics 'placed himself before the public as a person who really could not tell whether a table, under his nose, did or did not rise from the ground'.[20]

What the public made of it is difficult to say. It was the word of a hotelier, a writer and a stockbroker against that of an eminent scientist. For throughout all of this, Brougham, the politician, kept very quiet. As for Brewster's conjectures, they were hardly exhaustive, and it is clear from his letter to his sister that he had flatly contradicted himself. Fortunately for him, however, nobody else apart from his sister knew the letter existed. And so his integrity was not challenged (except by the hotelier, the writer and the stockbroker), his version of events was accepted as truth by many, and his conjectures regarded as reasonable, if not perfect. His reputation safe, Brewster went on to become Principal of Edinburgh University, and no doubt felt that that was the end of the matter – which, of course, it was not.

But the more curious among the public suspected that there was a mystery to be solved, and if scientists were not competent to provide the answer, then perhaps others were better qualified. One concerned *Advertiser* reader, by the name of George, wrote appealing to the expert opinion of 'professors of legerdemain'. And sure enough, the Great Wizard responded, in a valiant attempt to clear up matters. Spiritualism, John Henry reminded George, was the cause of 'mental imbecility, fatalism, lunacy, mind-torture, despondency and suicide'. Indeed, 7500 spiritualists were now in mental asylums, he claimed, and 360 had committed suicide. As for the raps, they were 'mechanical', though he failed to explain what that meant, while the other reported phenomena were merely the result of the 'skilful adjustment of levers and cleverly arranged horsehairs', and he failed to explain what that meant either. When 'the anxious public' wrote in again to 'ask from the objector a solution or explanation', there was no response. When, four days later, they 'again ask[ed] for a straightforward answer or explanation to the cause of the phenomena', no explanation, straightforward or otherwise, was forthcoming. But when somebody claimed that the Wizard's statistics on insanity were inaccurate, he was quick to respond. The statistics were available to anyone who wished to check them, though he failed to explain where they might be found.[21]

Daniel himself did not get involved in the debate, for as Brougham knew, silence was often the best policy. Privately, Daniel regarded Brewster as dishonest, which many would have thought was ironic, and he regarded John Henry as a publicity-hungry blowhard, which many would have thought was fair enough. But while the Wizard might indulge in theatrical licence, if one were to be taken seriously, one had to be careful what one said. In any case, Daniel's own claims were rarely likely to help his cause: as for most of his life, he would have to rely upon actions rather than words, and trust those whom he had convinced to spread the word on his behalf. And so those who had actually witnessed Daniel's séances insisted that the Wizard's performance was a 'foolish exhibition', that at Daniel's séances 'not the least deception or delusion was ever attempted', and they 'caution[ed] the public against being led by Sir David Brewster'.[22] As for Thomas Trollope, he was 'wholly convinced, that be what may their origin, and cause, and nature, [the phenomena] are not produced by any fraud, machinery, juggling, illusion, or trickery, on [Daniel's] part.'[23]

The Wizard, who would have begged to differ, had clearly been unable to convince them, but then he did not need to convince anyone. It had been a good season, an exceptional season, and now he was in a position to consider retirement. Since that disastrous fire in Glasgow, which had destroyed his hopes along with his theatre, he had come a long way, and was close to his dream. He had announced his 'Grand Final Farewell Tour', and had set off round the provinces to allow the public one last chance to see him. It was not the first of his farewell tours, for he had announced several over the years; indeed it had been a standard ploy to attract an audience that otherwise might not attend. But this time he meant it, and people across the country were informed, in no uncertain terms, that this was to be his final week in their town: 'Positively the last

5 Nights of Wonders, Unalterably the Last 5 Nights of Magic, Definitively the last 5 Nights of Incomprehensibilities, Irrevocably the Last 5 Nights of the Wizard of Wizards'.

At the end of his most final of final farewell tours, he announced that his career as a conjuror was over. From this point on he would be a full-time actor, and his new career would begin in the most respectable of theatres. Brimming with optimism, he booked the Royal Opera House at Covent Garden theatre for the Christmas season of 1855-6, and staged a series of entertainments somewhat less highbrow than opera. There would be a Christmas pantomime, some hilarious comic sketches, and he would star in a dramatic production of Scott's *Rob Roy*. Exploiting his skills as a publicist, he raised expectations to fever pitch by what the drama critic Henry Morley called 'a system of puffery little short of the marvellous'.[24] The stage was set, his ambition was close to fulfilment, and the public was eager to sample the Wizard's new show.

It was, however, a less than complete success. The pantomime was denounced as 'the dullest that has anywhere been seen in London for a good many seasons past'. The burlesque involved four extremely tall actresses, dressed as Normandy peasants, performing 'some exceedingly stupid business with warming-pans', while a re-enactment of a medieval tournament looked like 'a lump or two of armour upon hobbyhorses'. When the Wizard staged *Rob Roy*, casting himself in the title role, critics noted, in somewhat sarcastic tones, that he 'acted without a morsel of curtailment . . . He explodes his asides defiantly into the faces of the people who are not to hear them.'[25] Meanwhile, over at Drury Lane, the great comic actor Charles James Matthews had much greater success performing in a farce as the 'Wizard of South-South-West-by-East', much to the frustration of his inspiration.

Yet the Wizard was not one to be beaten, and within a few weeks he had employed Matthews to perform the same farce as part of his own show. This was a 'Grand Carnival Benefit', a twelve-hour marathon soirée involving a pantomime, two dramas, an opera and a Grand Ballet, and which followed Matthew's caricature of the Wizard with a sketch involving the Wizard that caricatured Matthews. At the end of what he no doubt regarded as a hugely successful run, John Henry invited respectable society to a grand masked ball, 'on a similar style to what he had experienced in the Russian tradition at the Bolshoi'. It was to be an extravagant affair, one of fine costumes and fashionable guests. The fashionable guests, however, if they came at all, did not stay very long. According to one critic, it was a miserable affair, with 'not 20 persons in evening dress, decorations discreditable to a bard, [and] the company would have disgraced a dancing saloon . . . a disgrace to everyone connected with it'.[26] By five in the morning it had degenerated into an 'orgy of indecency and drunkenness', and John Henry instructed the orchestra to play the national anthem as a cue for all to leave. It was then that a fire was noticed, the two hundred remaining revellers fled for the exits, and within minutes the growing flames 'lit up the façade of St Paul's'. Less than half an hour later, the Royal Opera House had burned to the ground.

Given the state of his remaining guests, it is rather remarkable that nobody died. That, no doubt, was the optimistic way the Wizard will have interpreted events. But if he was over-optimistic, he was also under-insured, and he now found himself in serious debt. For the second time, his plans had burned to the ground, and he would have to start again. His unalterable final farewell tour would have to be repeated, as once more he attempted to rise from the ashes, like a Phoenixestocalobian. This time he would travel even further afield, but he would continue to battle against the bogus claims of spirit mediums, and when he returned, he would eventually encounter the arch-priest of that delusional faith. And this time, it would be personal.

5

Scandal and loss in Florence

While the Brewster controversy brewed, and the Royal Opera House burned, Daniel went to Florence. It was the end of 1855, and he had been invited to stay with the Trollopes, who owned a villa in this most exquisite of cities. Villino Trollope was a generous home, and a venue for visiting writers of distinction. Regular guests included Dickens, George Eliot, and the Brownings, who met to talk of literature and philosophy, and savour the speciality of the house: iced lemonade. It was not a lifestyle that the Trollopes had always enjoyed, for the family had suffered considerable debt and hardship. Yet Fanny had maintained them through her writing, and particularly through the profits of her best-known work, *Domestic Manners of the Americans*. In this she had accused American ladies of false prudery and American gentlemen of spitting too often, and complained about the Declaration of Independence and of the ubiquity of hogs in Cincinnati. Indeed, the book had so offended Americans that it sold very well in England. Her son, Thomas, had also obtained a degree of recognition as a writer, while the younger brother, Anthony, was then best known for his work at the post office, and for having introduced the letter box to England. But Anthony was about to gain a reputation as a man of letters that would surpass that of both his mother and his brother. That year, he would have his first commercial success, *Barchester Towers*, before going on to establish his reputation as one of the most popular English writers of the century. Meanwhile, his mother would publish her last novel, which would not be so well remembered, though it would include a character based on a certain spirit medium.

Dickens would not be present when the medium arrived, and neither would Eliot, but this was probably just as well, as both disliked him intensely. To Dickens, Daniel was a 'ruffian' and a 'scoundrel', and to Eliot he was 'an object of moral disgust'. As for the Brownings, they were virtually neighbours, as they owned Casa Guidi, a villa they had bought shortly after their marriage, and to which they returned as often as they could. And no doubt Mrs Browning would have loved to be there, but she and her husband were rarely apart, and fortunately for Daniel, her husband was in Paris. The circle into which he was introduced was nevertheless a most respectable one of writers, artists, diplomats and aristocrats, providing a variety of attitudes towards spiritualism. There was Hiram Powers, the renowned American sculptor, whose marble statue of a Greek slave had been shown at the Great Exhibition of 1851, and who was already a believer in Daniel's abilities. And there was Baron Seymour Kirkup, an artist of some celebrity who had known Blake, attended the funerals of Shelley and Keats, and was now known as a local eccentric, keenly interested in the occult, slightly deaf and extremely gullible. On the other hand, William Burnet Kinney was American Minister to the Sardinian Court, and his wife was a close friend of the Brownings, to whom Robert had already written of Daniel's unmanliness. It was, perhaps, for this reason that Mrs Kinney was 'as violent against the spirits as Robert'.[1] Other interested and noble parties included Count and Countess

Orsini, Count and Countess Cotterell Lord and Lady Normanby, and Lady Katherine Fleming, whose husband was elsewhere.

Into this celebrated and fashionable company was to enter the son of a paper-mill worker, and his arrival was anticipated with a level of interest that had not been witnessed in Florence for years. There had been the floods of the River Arno, which had caused so much damage to crops and property. And there had been the political instability associated with Emperor Leopoldo's removal and subsequent return. But for Lady Fleming, Daniel was 'a greater event in Florence than an overflow of the Arno or a revolution. At the Club, in the drawing-room, in the servants' hall – court and town – the first question, before even "Good Morning" is – "Mr Home: have you seen him? What has he done?"'[2] And soon he was seen in the club and the drawing room, though not, of course, in the servants' hall, for the son of a paper-mill worker had risen in society. And soon everybody was talking about what he had done.

The Florentine séances were a remarkable success. Even Daniel himself thought the manifestations 'very strong . . . on one occasion while the Countess O[rsini] was seated at [a grand piano], it rose and balanced itself in the air during the whole time she was playing'.[3] Others reported less extravagant miracles: spirit hands appearing before their eyes and disappearing within their grasp, as Baron Kirkup made drawings of the hands in an optimistic attempt 'to show proof'. Meanwhile in Paris, a curious Mrs Browning was informed of events by Mrs Kinney, who wrote 'to confess that she had been *wrong* . . . [that] she and her husband had come to the conclusion that all trickery, as a solution, was utterly impossible'. Countess Cotterell, Mrs Browning was told, 'had her dead baby on her knee for quarter of an hour', and when she asked the infant 'to give her hand to Papa . . . [the Count] swears he felt and held a baby's hand in his'.

All of this occurred at the Villino Trollope where, we are told, 'young Mrs Trollope's gown was blown out'.[4]

News of Daniel's success spread far and wide, and even in America *Harper's Weekly* reported how Florence was being bewildered by 'the incredible power possessed by this blond young man, and his exhibitions of turning tables, dancing chairs, and peripatetic chandeliers'.[5] The rise in the level of the Arno had not been so fast, nor the revolution that had ousted Leopoldo, but then the waters had retreated, and the Emperor had returned, and fortunes in Florence had been known to reverse.

Daniel's change in circumstances came about, in part, as a result of his success. Lady Fleming, who had been so excited at the thought of meeting him, began to get desperate. She wrote to Hiram Powers: 'I think of nothing but Mr Home, and I have decided to write and ask him to call on me. Do you think he will come! All day and all night I have no other idea.'[6] Daniel did indeed call on Lady Fleming and, much to the consternation of her neighbours and acquaintances, stayed for several weeks. She was a married woman, living apart from her husband, and a close-knit group of expatriates was neither slow to gossip nor indifferent to scandal. It was not long before his friends began to think Daniel was 'leading a most dissolute life'.[7] His new acquaintances, who had so quickly embraced him, began to slip away.

As rumour of Daniel's scandalous behaviour spread, Mrs Browning waited in Paris for details to reach her. She had heard there had been some mysterious event that had put Daniel in a very bad light – 'the mystery of iniquity which everybody raved about and nobody distinctly specified' – and she had heard that 'at Florence everybody is quarrelling with everybody on the subject'. Indeed, she had had 'many letters on the subject', but it was not until she was called upon by the brother of Lord

Normanby, the British Minister at Florence, that details of this and further scandals emerged. It seemed that some of his acquaintances had offered to buy Daniel a greatcoat, and that he had ordered a very expensive fur coat, which Mrs Browning felt was 'an indelicate act on his part'. To make matters worse, however, he had 'induced the tailor to leave the money with him, and then left the bill unpaid (which was a dishonest act) so that his friends had to pay it double'. And then 'he said something deleterious about Mr Trollope – and something very coarse of a lady – and something so bad of somebody else, that he had to sign a paper of recantation under pain of horse whipping'.[8]

We do not know what Daniel said about Mr Trollope, nor even which Mr Trollope he said it about. But the young Mrs Trollope, whose gown had been blown out, 'strongly disliked the man', and the elder Mrs Trollope, who had so offended Americans, deserted him for a 'failure in his moral character'.[9] And when she published her last novel, it included a medium by the name of Mr Wilson, 'a thinly disguised and not very complimentary portrait of Home'. Of Wilson, she wrote: 'The great majority of those whom curiosity led to witness the marvellous phenomenon . . . proclaimed him fraudulent.'[10] We do not know if the lady of whom Daniel said something 'very coarse' was Lady Fleming, nor do we know how coarse it was. And we do not know what was said that was 'so bad', or whom it was said about, or who it was who forced the retraction by threatening Daniel with a beating. Daniel himself was particularly quiet on the matter, with nothing more than a vague complaint that 'some persons there did all they could to injure me'.[11]

Perhaps his success had gone to his head, and the degree of attention in a small but influential community had led to a sense of arrogance. But his conduct upset even his close friends, including young Mr Rymer, who regarded Daniel as a brother, and who had brought him to Florence at his father's expense. As Daniel had entered fashionable society, he had drifted away from Rymer, and when Rymer wrote to him, he answered 'very rudely and showed no sense of gratitude for all that the family had done for him'. On reading these letters, even an admirer of the medium confessed that they made him feel 'chilled and disappointed'.[12] And when Daniel attended a social event and met Count Cotterell, who had attended his séances and believed in the reality of what he had seen, the Count turned his back on him, calling him a 'worthless fellow'.[13]

As his popularity among the Anglo-American community declined, his reputation among the local population provided little comfort. As Daniel said himself, he was both hated by the Church and feared by the peasantry. His enemies, playing upon the superstition of the latter, spread rumours that it was his practice 'to administer the seven sacraments of the Catholic church to toads, in order to by spells raise the dead'. He was even advised, by a clairvoyant friend, not to venture out, for his life was in danger. This advice he declined to follow, and he lived to regret it. One night, as he returned home through the dark and deserted streets of Florence, a man appeared from the shadows of a doorway, and approached from behind. Daniel was hit on the left side with a violent force that knocked him breathless, then hit in the stomach again, and again. The man, as he ran from the scene of the attack, cried out '*Dio mio! Dio mio!*', as Daniel dragged himself indoors. It was then that he discovered he had been stabbed with a stiletto, though somehow he had only received one slight cut. The blade, long enough to reach the heart, had been unable to penetrate the thickness of his new fur coat.

When Daniel recalled this failed assassination, he did so with no sense of irony: the coat that had lost him so many acquaintances had miraculously saved his life; and he had almost died from having declined to believe the prediction of a fellow clairvoyant. Perhaps the entire incident is just one more demonstration of why it can be so difficult to believe what we are told. After all, there were no other witnesses to the assassination attempt. Nevertheless, Daniel seemed now to be convinced that he was in great danger. When advised by the Minister of the Interior that he should not go out on the streets, or even allow himself to be seen by his window when the light was on, he seems to have taken that message more seriously. The local peasants, he believed, 'were fully bent on taking my life, and for that purpose were concealed about the neighbourhood with fire-arms'.[14] One way or another, his stay in Florence was going to be temporary.

But though his social position was undoubtedly damaged, his reputation was not entirely ruined. After all, even those who had deserted him maintained, for the most part, that his powers were nevertheless genuine. There was the literary allusion to fraud made by Mrs Trollope, but she made no attempt to explain what she had seen. And it was only years later that Anthony Trollope would tell Dickens of an incident that suggested how the spirits obtained certain information.[15] But for the moment at least, the general opinion of the Anglo-American community was summed up by Mrs Browning. She admitted that Daniel was 'weak and vain', but declared that 'persons who agree in nothing else except in disliking Home (for the foolish young man has succeeded in making himself universally disagreeable) all agree in considering the phenomena above nature . . . They hate him and believe in the facts.'[16]

Such faith might protect his spiritual mission, but it was of little practical use to a man who survived on hospitality. 'I was left in Florence without money,' he complained, 'and my friends in England having their credulity imposed upon by scandalmongers, refused to send me even money of my own.' He was, therefore, once again reminded of the fragility of his social and economic status. Though he never accepted money for the séances he conducted, it was his abilities as a medium on which he depended, and which provided him with the company and lifestyle that he enjoyed. The same mysterious feats that offended the local clergy, and which had (seemingly) provoked a stranger to try to kill him, were nevertheless his only means of survival. Without them, his fate would be precarious. And while many would say that he performed his feats through ingenious trickery, he always insisted that they were beyond his control. He was a medium, nothing more, an instrument through which the spirits showed themselves to be present. It was in his power to invite them to do so, but it was up to them to reply. That, at least, is how he explained his next, and most sudden, change in fortune. Perhaps he himself no longer felt worthy to continue in his glorious mission, or perhaps the attempt on his life convinced him that it would be safer, for the moment, to cease such activities. Whatever the reason, Daniel tells us that, on 10 February 1856, 'the spirits told me that my power would leave me for a year'.[17]

Word quickly spread that Daniel's last remaining source of comfort had left him.[18] Most of his new acquaintances had also left him, though fortunately not all. When he departed from Florence it was with Count Branicka, a Polish nobleman he had met there, and who remained loyal to him even in the absence of the spirits. Together they travelled to Naples, where Prince Luigi, brother of the Neapolitan king, presented Daniel with a ruby ring, despite not having witnessed a single miracle. They also met Robert Dale Owen, American Minister to the Neapolitan court, and son of Robert Owen. But recent events had taken their toll, Daniel later confessed, and 'life seemed to me a blank'. Emotionally, spiritually and materially weak, he 'wished to shun every thing which pertained to this world'. He therefore decided to abandon his mission, and 'determined to enter a monastery'. With this in mind, he went to Rome, and when in Rome, he conformed accordingly. On Easter Monday, with Count Branicka as his Godfather and Countess Orsini as his Godmother, Daniel became a Roman Catholic.

It was only a few weeks since his blasphemous activities in Florence had provoked both priests and peasants, but no longer could he be accused of being either a devil-worshipper or a Protestant. His rapid repentance was so impressive that he was given an audience with Pope Pius IX, where it was rumoured that he made a solemn promise to His Holiness that he would cease to perform his miracles. It was a rumour that Daniel was keen to reject, not least because he had already ceased to perform them. In any case, it was not as if the Catholic Church was against the idea of miracles, it was merely a question of whether a given miracle was deemed to be the work of God rather than the work of the Devil. Indeed, it was even suspected that the Pope had plans to make Daniel a saint, though that was not the official Vatican position. Instead, Daniel tells us, the Pope gave him 'a large silver medal, which it has since been my misfortune to lose'. He took greater care of another gift from the Pope, however: a document 'guaranteeing to [him] and his relatives an entry into Paradise'. This 'interesting document', a relative later boasted, 'is now in my possession'.[19]

Meanwhile, the British press observed with a mixture of sarcasm and regret that Daniel had 'gone over to the Church of Rome', and that spiritualists, few of whom were Catholics, were divided on the matter. Some spoke of Daniel as 'becoming weak-minded, and a little insane', while others held out 'the possibility of his being the means of making the Pope a spiritualist'.[20] He was neither insane nor about to convert the Pope, but, his afterlife now seemingly guaranteed, he decided against entering a monastery and, in June 1856, made his way to Paris.

This was the Paris of the Second Empire, thriving for the moment under Napoleon III. The Crimean War was over and Baron Hausmann was creating a modern Paris of wide boulevards and elegant apartments. The reconstruction of the city forced many poorer families to move to suburban slums, but it also reduced unemployment and thus the likelihood of another revolution, while the wide boulevards made mob control that much easier should the people prove ungrateful. It was a Paris relatively short of celebrities, for Chopin was dead, Victor Hugo was in exile and Monet was still a teenager. But the Brownings were there, and they received news of Daniel's arrival with anger and anxiety respectively. 'Think of my horror', wrote Mrs Browning, 'on Robert's having heard to-day that Hume the medium is in Paris. I thought he was in Rome. I looked so scared that Robert promised me he would be "meek as maid" for my sake, and that if he met the man in the street he would pass without pretending to see.' Her husband, she told her sister, 'had talked himself into quite a hatred of this Hume . . . Pray never mention his name.'[21]

The Brownings, however, saw nothing of Daniel in Paris. His reason for coming, he maintained, had been to 'acquire a facility in the language', but as his French improved, his social and financial position continued to decline. His brief encounter with papal curiosity now over, his remaining patrons, the Branickas, left him to what appears to have been one of the lowest points in his life. News that the spirits had deserted him for a year had reached the ears of various interested parties; indeed it was said that the whole of Paris was speculating upon their return, but Daniel himself was once again silent. His physical condition seems to have deteriorated, and he was confined to bed. His spiritual power gone, and with no wealthy patrons, his financial position was equally weak: when, in the winter, a doctor advised that he move to a more hospitable climate, he was 'without the means of acting on his advice'.[22] As ever, rumours emerged, some suggesting that he was penniless, others that he was near death. 'The last news of Hume,' according to Mrs Browning, was 'that he is dying or dead in Paris of congestion of the lungs!'[23]

But Daniel was not dead, and though seriously ill, his year without spirits was coming to an end. On 10 February 1857, as the clock struck midnight, it was accompanied, we are told, by a series of punctual raps. According to Daniel, the spirits were back. When Paris awoke the following morning, it immediately enquired as to the situation, through the person of the Marquis de Belmont, chamberlain to Napoleon III. Napoleon himself wished to know whether the spirits had returned, whether Daniel were back to his extraordinary self, and, if he were, he was cordially invited to be a guest of the Emperor and Empress. Thus, Daniel's questionable social status and limited financial means were immediately improved by royal approval and patronage. He took up residence in the Hôtel Vouillemont on the Avenue des Champs Elysées, and immediately he became a regular guest of Napoleon and Empress Eugenie.

From the point of view of spiritualists, this was a timely opportunity to convert one of the most powerful men in Europe. As the act of a charlatan, however, it would have been one of desperation. His situation may have been grim, but a man caught deceiving the Emperor of France would quickly find himself in a significantly more precarious position. Napoleon had been ruthless with his political rivals, and what he might have done to a man caught deceiving him personally can only be imagined.

It seems, however, that it was not Daniel who was nervous at the thought of the encounter. For while the Emperor was anxious to see the young wonder-worker, the Empress was merely anxious. This 'very extraordinary man who makes one see ghosts', she confessed, filled her with dread. When Daniel accepted the royal invitation, the Empress described him as 'thin, pale, 21 years old, in very poor health, and with something very strange in his look'. What happened at the séances was also strange, and was described in a private letter to her sister. The first was relatively quiet, she explained, with a table trembling in a way that 'gives one the impression that one has put one's hand on the back of a dog that is afraid'.[24] At later séances, however, an accordion played 'charming tunes all by itself', and a 'bell was transported into the General's hand'. This was General Espinasse, a veteran of the Crimean War, 'who was not at all inclined to believe in such things. He was so shocked [however] that his face became quite drawn and he said he believed he was going to be sick (although he had faced battle at St. Sebastopol).' And then, the Empress continued, a spirit hand pulled at her dress and seized her cushion, and when she enquired whether the spirit loved her, it replied that it did, and pressed her hand, and she was certain that this was the hand of her father. On one occasion, we are told, another spirit hand appeared, and wrote what was recognized by all to be the autograph of Napoleon Bonaparte himself.[25]

None of this, of course, was revealed to the public, who knew that séances were taking place, but had no idea of the details. Such were the ripe conditions for rumour and gossip, and interested parties soon reported what they had heard. Earl Cowley, the British Ambassador, cheerfully told the story that Napoleon had 'asked Hume to raise the spirits of the first Emperor and of Louis Philippe, and being told that they were present in the room, said that he could not see or hear either of them. "Wait a little," said Hume, "and your majesty will feel their presence." Soon afterwards H. M. experienced a violent kick on an unmentionable part of his sacred person, but could never ascertain which of his predecessors had applied it.'[26] Meanwhile,

Mrs Browning had heard that Daniel 'has been the means of an extraordinary manifestation . . . [and f]ive or six persons (including the medium) fainted . . . It happened in Paris, lately!'[27] In Belgium, the press reported that the medium had been retained on a salary of 40,000 francs, and that the Empress and her entourage had been reduced, by diabolical scenes, to a condition of chronic hysteria. Across the Atlantic, *Harper's Weekly* claimed that Daniel and the Empress were so intimate 'that the wicked tongues of Paris were soon busy with scandal'.[28]

Despite his recent improvement in circumstances, Daniel was becoming increasingly aware that he would always be the target of scandalous rumours. And beneath the more sensationalist claims lay some genuine concerns about his regular visits to the French Court, and his possible influence upon the monarchy. When Lord Granville, who later succeeded Gladstone as Liberal leader, visited Paris in April to discuss Anglo-French relations with Napoleon, he was invited to a séance with 'a certain Mr Hume [who] produces hands, raises heavy tables four feet from the ground with a finger, [and] knocks on the Emperor's hand from a distance. The Emperor', Granville noted, 'is rather pleased at the table coming more to him than the others. But seeing Lady G. and me look incredulous, he broke off saying, "They think us mad, and Lord Granville will report that the [post-Crimean] alliance is on a most unstable footing".'[29] Meanwhile, the British Ambassador was writing to the Foreign Secretary in London about 'a certain charlatan by name Hume . . . [who] had established complete hold over the Emperor and Empress', expressing his dismay that the Emperor 'should be so easily gulled', and stressing that, 'as he receives this Hume at all times, and *alone,* the Police are seriously alarmed'.[30]

If outside observers were concerned, those inside the palace were no less worried. At the very least, Daniel's visits created a 'bad impression'; at worst there were fears that the Emperor's enemies might begin 'spreading the report that they consult spirits upon the direction of the affairs of the Empire. This danger has occurred to a number of the Imperial circle.'[31] At some point, we are told, Count Walewski, the Minister of Foreign Affairs, threatened to resign if Daniel remained, declaring 'that Hume was an impostor, and a spy from the Court of Berlin into the bargain . . . [that] he was getting hold of important information and furthermore gaining a regrettable influence over the mind of the Empress.'[32] He had 'gained such an influence at Court', according to Princess Murat, 'that Ministers at a Cabinet meeting requested that Mr Home should be required to leave France'.[33]

When Daniel left for America, his sudden departure both confirmed existing suspicions and prompted further speculation. The Paris correspondent of the *Atlas* reported that, during a séance at the Tuileries, Daniel had caused a pencil to write some words upon a piece of paper, that Napoleon had turned deadly pale upon reading the message, and that he had burned it immediately afterwards. 'Much curiosity', wrote the correspondent, 'has been elicited by the result of this experiment, as it is a well-known fact that immediately after the séance broke up his Majesty drove in his carriage to the Prefet de Police.'[34] Ordinary Parisians also debated the mysterious circumstances of Daniel's sudden departure, of the shocking events 'at a certain séance' that had provoked the Emperor to send him packing, and of his having to leave a position in which, it was a well-known fact, 'he was paid at a rate of a million francs a year'.[35] The story of Daniel's departure soon spread to the international press, and was repeated from one continent to another with typical inconsistency. He had been 'expelled from France *upon an order of the Emperor*;* he had been 'ordered off by the alarmed Emperor . . . [and] was really penniless'; he had, and this was based on 'the most reliable of sources . . . embezzled $30,000, and was banished from France forever.'[36]

No doubt many believed these stories, for it remained the case that far stranger tales had been told by Daniel himself. And so it was amid rumours of political influence, ministerial jealousy and even suspicions of international espionage that Daniel took his leave. His own reason for leaving was somewhat more mundane: to collect his sister from America and bring her back to France to be educated under the protection of the Empress.[37] Yet the growing rumours and concerns, whether justified or not, no doubt made his departure convenient for all concerned. And while Daniel would return soon enough, and would conduct further séances for Napoleon and Eugenie, they would not again take place at the Court of the Tuileries.

When he returned in May, he continued to enchant the salons of Paris – 'his wonderful production of spirit hands has filled us with awe, and the fact of their appearance is now established beyond doubt'[38] – and he provoked further amusing anecdotes. It was said that, on one occasion, a lady complained of being terrified at the touch of a spirit hand upon her leg. At which point a chivalrous gentleman reassured her that the hand on her leg had been his own.[39] Yet beneath such lighter gossip lay more serious considerations. Was it not possible that the desire to witness (and to boast that they had witnessed) such fashionable phenomena make Daniel's witnesses particularly suggestible, and their observation and testimony that much more questionable? And how many times might one sitter have touched another, for private humour (or titillation), and then subsequently denied it? The spirit hands remained a mystery, but many were convinced that they were simply a trick for which the secret had yet to be discovered. And, as it happens, one man in particular was about to announce that he had discovered it.

It was in the southwest coastal town of Biarritz, the venue

for further royal séances, that Daniel soon came under the watchful eye of Dr Barthez. Barthez was physician to the Prince Imperial, and was deeply worried that the Empress was under Daniel's influence. 'The entire belief she has in him,' he wrote with concern, 'the animation and violence with which she speaks of him, really distress me.' And so Barthez determined to watch Daniel as closely as he could. 'As soon as he entered I disliked him intensely,' the Doctor informed his wife by letter. 'His simple, timid, half-awkward air seemed to me to conceal a very able savoir-faire. I noticed between his eyes and his mouth a contraction of expression which gives him a very disagreeable look of duplicity; in a word, his face calls up a desire to smack it.' At dinner, the Doctor's examination continued: 'I was two places distant. I could see and examined him thoroughly, and I am convinced that his half-simple air hides a real duplicity.' And then, after dinner, a séance was held, and Barthez watched as the table quivered, and listened to raps and scratching sounds. He witnessed ladies' dresses being pulled, a handbell being moved, and an accordion being played, and then Daniel asked him to leave. The reason for this, the Doctor concluded, was 'the incredulous smile which I felt was visible on my face'. After he left, he was later informed, a 'table leapt off its four legs'.[40]

Barthez was confident that Daniel was 'a performer of tricks', but he did not know how the tricks were done. He was hardly the first to feel such frustration, for Browning and Brewster were equally convinced, and equally perplexed, and would dearly have loved to know how Daniel's feats were accomplished. To date, however, they had managed little more than vague accusations and guesswork. But Barthez, it seems, was more persistent, and continued to search for evidence of fraud. It took some time to find any, and it may not have been conclusive, but it was to prove more damaging than any accusation Daniel had suffered so far.

With some satisfaction, not to mention a degree of amusement, Barthez wrote again to his wife in September 1857, informing her that 'one of the means by which Mr Home evokes his spirits has at last been detected'.

6

Diagnosis in Biarritz

According to Daniel, the whole thing was a misunderstanding. His power had not been great, his health had once again been failing, and he had been warned by the spirits that 'trouble was in store'. This combination of ill health and anxiety had made him 'more than usually agitated'. The séance itself had therefore been somewhat uneventful, the only notable manifestation being when a bracelet was mysteriously carried from a lady on his left to a lady sitting opposite. It was at that point, to Daniel's great distress, that 'the gentleman on my right hand declared it to have been transported by my feet'. This was, Daniel claimed, an absurd idea, and even if it were true, 'If my legs were eight feet long it would have still been a miracle'.[1] That was Daniel's version of events – he had not been well, he had known it would happen, and the suggestion itself was ridiculous – and after that he never mentioned the Biarritz affair again.[2] But that was not how others saw it, for according to Barthez, 'The Empress is reduced to saying that the Home of to-day is not the Home of other days; that he has lost his power and is seeking to replace it by subterfuge.'

As for the nature of the subterfuge, Barthez explained: 'The matter is simple enough. Mr Home has thin slippers, easily drawn on and off; he has also, I fancy, cuts in his socks, which leave his toes free. At the proper moment he throws off a slipper, and with his toes tugs at a dress here and there, rings a handbell, gives a rap on this side or that, and the thing once done quickly slips his foot back into its slipper again. This', Barthez went on, was not mere speculation, but 'was seen by M. Morio, who drew up a full signed and written statement, with all the details necessary to establish the genuineness of his discovery'. Alas, this first statement by a witness telling us how Daniel accomplished his feats never survived, leading some to conclude that it was never written, and that the whole story was a fabrication. But Barthez's letter survived, and according to him: 'Home saw that he was found out, and I can tell you he cut a very sorry figure. He went out saying that he was ill, and all night he has had nervous attacks and visions and has been surrounded by spirits.'

Finally, as Daniel was judged to be on the point of death, a priest was sent for, and a doctor. The following day, with no sign of improvement, another doctor was sent for, but as it was Barthez, Daniel received very little sympathy. 'His eyes were red, his face swollen', according to Barthez's diagnosis; 'he was calm and overcome with excitement by turns. And he had the deceitful expression I have mentioned before . . . So I took him by the arm, shook it rather roughly, and said in his ear, "Come, Mr Home, no nonsense; let all the spirits be; you know I don't believe in them." The trance ceased at that, and he looked me straight in the face, and saw plainly enough that I was laughing at him.' And so, reported Barthez, 'The evocation of spirits at the villa has suddenly ceased, and we will hope this unworthy charlatan is revealed in his true colours.'[3]

Fortunately for Daniel, these accusations were not made public at the time, and perhaps more importantly, it seems that the Empress did not believe them. According to Barthez, 'Her

Majesty cannot admit that any one could have the face to play tricks on herself and the Emperor for a whole year.' And even if, in a moment of self-doubt, she had wondered whether it might be true, this was not the sort of thing that the Emperor and Empress of France would have wanted revealed. It was only many years later, when the main parties were dead, that Barthez's letter would be published. When it appeared, it would be denounced by spiritualists as little more than the wishful thinking of a cynic who was not even present at the time. But Daniel had too many enemies for rumours not to emerge more quickly, and so it began to be whispered in certain circles that finally he had been exposed as a fraud.[4] And if this were true, that he had been caught and his methods had been discovered, it would not be long before such knowledge was disseminated. If he was secretly using his feet to move and ring hand-bells, and to simulate spirit contact, further exposures would soon occur. Then both his career and his glorious mission would come to a premature end.

There was, after all, no shortage of those who wanted to expose him, and not only in France. In Holland was a group of rationalists whose hostility to spiritualism was well known, and who 'had expressed their utter disbelief in the authenticity of Mr Home's spiritualistic phenomena'. They had dismissed his abilities without ever witnessing them, but it was hardly the sort of audience that Daniel needed at this point. Yet his position was always that of a dependant, and his patrons had been drawn to him because of his extraordinary talent. However insecure he felt, whatever fears he might have had about further accusations or exposure, he relied upon the faith of his admirers for continued support. And so one of these admirers persuaded him to go to Amsterdam in order to convince these most devout sceptics that they were completely wrong.

This was clearly not going to be easy. By their own admission, 'the only thing [they] desired and thus also wanted to occur was that nothing would happen at the sittings, and this only because we then should be able to print an official denial about Home's powers'. Just weeks after he had been allegedly caught in the act, he was to be scrutinized by the most hostile of observers, men who declared that, in the interest of discovering the truth, they 'would be ready and would dare to descend even to his Infernal Majesty's special domain'.[5] When it was over, Daniel would say very little about what happened, simply dismissing the group as of 'infidel tendencies', and expressing 'a wish that they had seen more'.[6] But as he prepared to meet the infidels, it seems he was not entirely aware of what he was getting into.

The first of the Amsterdam sittings took place in February 1858, in a bleak hotel, in front of an audience of ten hostile sceptics that included a doctor of philosophy, a lawyer, an optician and one Dr Gunst, who reported what happened. They sat round a large mahogany table, which they examined sufficiently to note that the top, column and base were 'directly and immovably fixed' together. Daniel urged them to talk freely, and 'insisted that we should observe him and all his manipulations as closely as possible. This too we did.' On top of the table were four candelabras, with two more below, which 'made it possible to obtain an undisturbed view of what was happening under the table'. Meanwhile, the observers, who included men who had previously resisted the influence of mesmerists, 'convinced themselves that they were not getting into an abnormal mental state by applying various methods and devices to gauge their mental health and saneness'. They 'talked freely' and 'laughed mockingly concerning the matter at hand', and each of the individuals 'gave expression to his disbelief'.

These expressions stopped soon enough. For as they mocked, 'the table started to make a sliding movement', and those towards whom it was moving 'were requested to try to stop this movement; this, however, they could not do'. When the table stopped, raps began, and when raps were requested 'in a certain manner, and as many times as we should indicate, [t]his wish was carried out to the full'. As Daniel's sceptical witnesses watched in characteristic disbelief, the table 'started to rise up on one side . . . so high that all of us were very much afraid that [the candelabras] would fall off'. Meanwhile, 'some of us tried very hard to prevent the table from going up', while the doctor of philosophy, 'with a light in his hand, squatted on his haunches to investigate'. They 'then ordered the table to become as light as possible so that we should be able to lift it with one finger. And so it came to pass.' And 'When the order was reversed (i.e. to increase the table's weight) the table could hardly be lifted at all in spite of our utmost efforts'.

Daniel held a second sitting the next day, in which raps replied to all requests, including one made by thought only, but the sceptics 'refrained from putting questions that could only be answered if such a world of spirits really did exist, a possibility we refused to believe in'. At the third and final sitting there was 'a complete rocking movement of the ceiling which became so violent that, together with the chairs on which we were seated, we felt ourselves going up and down as if on a rocking-horse . . . And now phenomena were produced that would make those who possessed weaker nerves than we had, believe that there indeed existed a world of spirits.' One of the men 'declared that he felt something touching his cheek. The unbelievers loudly laughed at him, and all these men wanted also to be touched.' At once, 'one was touched on his arm, another felt something touching his knee, a third one was contacted on his cheek', and 'one only needed to think of a limb or of some other part of one's body to be touched and at the very same moment this wish would be fulfilled'. One man 'was so violently clutched at all of a sudden that he jumped from his chair'.

'All of us', Gunst declared, 'saw this happening.' Some were watching 'above the table while others were watching under the table . . . Other persons were keeping a constant eye on Mr Home in order to see if he was exercising some influence on the phenomena . . . But all was in vain. We saw the phenomena happening but could not explain them. And nothing could be observed that could give rise to even the slightest suspicion that Mr Home was acting in a fraudulent manner.'[7] Such were the conclusions of a group of hardened sceptics, and this in the aftermath of Daniel's uncomfortable experience at Biarritz. Some would say that this was his most impressive performance yet, but Daniel said nothing of it other than to express 'a wish that they had seen more'. Such humility was not entirely characteristic, and perhaps it was simply relief. Nevertheless, he must have felt a deep sense of satisfaction to be exonerated by such a committee, and few things inspire humility more strongly than the belief that one has nothing more to prove. The next day, he went to The Hague to conduct a séance for Queen Sophia, who was rather less sceptical and sufficiently impressed to give him a 'splendid diamond ring'. He then returned to Paris, and promptly disappeared, provoking further rumours, darker ones than before.

According to *Le Nord*, 'it is whispered both secretly and openly that he is in the prison of Mazas, for we know not what crimes'. Daniel's friends were reluctant to believe such whispers, yet they were informed by officials that they had seen and spoken to him in prison.[8] The whispers grew in volume and detail, and soon were heard as far away as Florence, where the Brownings had returned and were being kept abreast of news, no doubt with mixed emotions. Browning was told by a friend 'that Hume the Medium was in the prisons of Mazas for an unnatural offence!'[9]

And further details gradually emerged: Daniel had been 'accused of theft and unnatural practices'. These 'unnatural practices' involved a respectable gentleman who, 'in order to discover the secrets of [Daniel's] intimacy with the spirits', had 'boasted of having shared a bed with the medium'.[10]

Browning, who had been quick to denounce Daniel's 'unmanliness', would have been disgusted at this idea, but his wife would not have been surprised that Daniel had spent a night with an interested enquirer. 'My friend Mr Jarves', Mrs Browning pointed out, 'spent a night with Hume once (when enquiring into the subject) and a four poster bed was carried into the middle of the room – shadowy figures stood by the pillow, or lay down across the feet of those about to sleep.'[11] As far as she was concerned, there were no sexual connotations involved in the nocturnal investigations of Jarves. As for the respectable gentleman being accused of 'unnatural practices' with Daniel in Paris, his mother assured the curious that her son had merely stayed over 'to observe some of the more startling and spontaneous phenomena' and had left confirmed in his belief 'that Home was a consummate charlatan'.[12] Nevertheless, this may have been a sensitive subject in the Court of Napoleon, where (it was alleged) there had recently been uncovered 'one of the strangest and most abominable pederastic scandals of modern times'.[13] It was all enough to convince one chronicler of fringe interests to add the name of Daniel Dunglas Home, along with that of the respectable gentleman concerned, to his list of 'men accused of sodomy', a list that included William II, King of Holland, and Charles II and III, dukes of Parma.[14]

Amid endless Parisian rumours of theft and sodomy, of Daniel being imprisoned and interrogated, and of his revealing scandalous secrets of the French Court that horrified the police, a letter arrived in Paris bearing an Italian postmark. It was from Daniel, who was in Rome, and blissfully unaware of what was being said about him. The rumours of crime and homosexuality were promptly contradicted with new revelations concerning both his financial and his romantic situation. It seems that an Englishwoman, whom he had converted to a belief in life after death, had died and left him an annuity of £240. 'On coming here,' Mrs Browning later wrote from Florence, 'he paid all his wandering debts, I am glad to hear, and is even said to have returned certain gifts which had been rendered unacceptable to him from the bad opinion of the givers.'[15] Whether this included the infamous though now somewhat damaged fur coat, we are not told. And then Robert Browning was informed – no doubt prompting further disbelief – that Daniel 'was about to be married to a Russian lady with £1,200 a year'.[16]

This time the rumours were accurate, for Daniel was about to be married. Indeed, the marriage was such a match as to bewilder even those who did not doubt his extraordinary powers. His fiancée was Alexandrina de Kroll, the daughter of General Count de Kroll and a god-daughter of the late Tsar Nicholas I. The son of a Scottish paper-mill worker, brought up humbly in America and of somewhat limited means, was about to marry into the Russian aristocracy. This was, as one commentator pointed out, 'a feat inexplicable when we think of the rules of the continental *noblesse*. A duc, or a prince, or a marquis may marry the daughter of an American citizen who had made a fortune in lard. But the daughters of the Russian *noblesse* do not marry poor American citizens with the good will of the Tsar.'

And yet, as in so many other ways, Daniel was doing what simply was not done. His recently improved finances could hardly have impressed his in-laws-to-be, and while he could boast impressive connections, his reputation was hardly without blemish. Perhaps this was evidence of his mesmeric charm – and no doubt his claim to informal descent from Scottish nobility helped – but in less than a fortnight of having met the young lady, and without her having even witnessed a séance, the engagement was announced with the approval of all the necessary parties. Alexandrina, known to most as Sacha, a small, pretty seventeen-year-old who was barely out of convent school, was about to become Mrs Home. 'Certainly her taste must be extraordinary,' Mrs Browning wrote to her sister. 'Think of the conjugal furniture floating about the room at night.'[17]

Before the wedding, Daniel returned to Paris to join Count and Countess Koucheleff, the brother-in-law and sister of Sacha. They were accompanied by Polovski, a Russian poet, and Millelotti, an Italian musician. The extensive entourage, which included a chamberlain, physician, valets, maids, secretaries, and the countess's spaniel, took up the first floor of Les Trois Empereurs on the Place du Palais Royal. Here they played host to members of fashionable Parisian society who had the time, resources and inclination to socialise until dawn on a daily basis. And it was here that one of France's most celebrated literary figures was invited one night, stayed somewhat longer than he had intended, and ended up becoming Daniel's best man.

Alexandre Dumas was fifty-five, was enormously successful and enjoyed the proceeds of his success to the full. *The Three Musketeers* and *The Count of Monte Cristo* had made him extremely comfortable, and *The Man in the Iron Mask* had added further to that comfort, but Dumas' appetite for comfort was rarely satisfied. He had travelled widely, eaten well, drunk considerably, loved freely and talked almost as much as he had written. He had not, however, met Daniel Home, though he had often wanted to, so when the opportunity presented itself, he accepted it with little hesitation. When he met Daniel he thought him 'guileless as a child, of average height, slenderly built, frail and highly strung'. He noted his pale skin, his clear blue eyes, the fact that his moustache hid the sensitive curve of his mouth, and he observed, like others before him, that Daniel had good teeth. His hands were 'white and ladylike, are beautifully kept and covered with rings', his dress was Parisian and elegant, and topped by a Scottish bonnet with a silver crest, on which was written: *Vincere aut mori* ('To Conquer or Die').

On the first night that Dumas joined the Koucheleff entourage, he remained until five in the morning, 'promising myself never again to visit a house where they kept such hours. I went again next day and stayed till six.' The company was so enjoyable that he was persuaded by the Count and Countess to join them on their planned trip to Russia, to attend Daniel's wedding and to be his best man. 'It struck me that the whole idea was crazy, and I rather fear it was this last thought that decided me.' So it was agreed: 'The count shook my hand, Home threw his arms around my neck,' and a few days later, they all set off for St Petersburg: the author of *The Three Musketeers*, along with a Russian poet, an Italian musician, and a Scottish-American medium.

They travelled by overnight express to Cologne and continued on to the north coast of Prussia, where they would sail northeast up the Baltic and turn eastwards at Helsinki into the Gulf of Finland. All of this for only 400 francs, 'inclusive of hotels and food', Dumas noted, 'which is not absolutely ruinous'. En route they endured the accommodation at Stettin [Poland] – 'I advise you strongly not to stay in that town. God! What beds! A badly stuffed sofa, draped in a sheet' – and an occasionally choppy Baltic. For Dumas this was no great discomfort, and when a gale sprang up at two in the morning, he simply closed his eyes and went back to sleep. Daniel, however, was more sensitive to such motions, and the following morning, when Dumas went on deck, 'the first thing I saw was Home, pale as death, having spent the whole night in direct communication with the Baltic'. Things only got worse when they transferred to a smaller vessel at Kronstadt to take them to St Petersburg, as 'the wind reached gale force . . . [it] pitched and rolled in the heavy seas. Poor Home turned from pink to yellow, then to pale green, and clung with both arms to the maestro Millelotti.' At which point Dumas, in a rather insensitive gesture to his new friend, 'started off in the direction of lunch, for a high sea always gives me a good appetite'. The contrary experiences of groom and best man ended on arrival at St Petersburg, when 'suddenly Home, now fully recovered from his generosity towards the fish in the Gulf of Finland, clapped his hands, jumped for joy and threw his arms around my neck'.

Daniel's rapid recovery was not good news for Millelotti, however, who was soon reduced to a nervous wreck. 'Scarcely had I reached my room', Dumas recalled, 'when Millelotti staggered in, pale and trembling to collapse in an armchair.' It seems that he had been awoken at one in the morning by the sound of spirit raps, and 'the maestro [had grown] so alarmed that he ran into Home's room and sat on the foot of his bed'. All night long, Dumas was told, Daniel had communed with the spirits until, at dawn, a new spirit appeared, asking to speak to Millelotti. 'It was the spirit of my aunt who died nine months ago,' the poor man faltered. 'She entered into a small marble-topped bedside table that chased me round all the apartment and tried to throw itself around my neck!' The thought of being embraced by a bedside table had been too much for the musician, Dumas observed, so much so that 'At the cold touch of the marble against his cheek the maestro fainted'. Such were the adventures of the wedding party on their journey from Paris to St. Petersburg, as recounted by Dumas, who claimed that even he did not believe the story entirely.[18]

When the author arrived in Russia he seems to have been disappointed not to receive a personal invitation from Tsar Alexander II. To make matters worse, a royal invitation was extended to Daniel, who nonchalantly declined. But none of this proved an obstacle to the main event, and the marriage of Daniel and Sacha took place in St Petersburg on 1 August 1858, with Dumas in his appointed role and the poet Count Alexis Tolstoy acting as a groomsman. The wedding was conducted first according to the rites of the Greek Church, and then there was a Roman Catholic ceremony. The Tsar provided the groom with a wedding gift of an exquisite diamond-encrusted ring, and the couple honeymooned on the Koucheleff estates on the Crimean coast. It was around this time that the new Mrs Home experienced her first spirit vision: one of Daniel's mother and her own father. And though Sacha said that she was not afraid, Daniel saw that she was 'trembling violently'.[19]

Sacha would come to accept the spirits, if not always with ease. By all accounts she was an amiable and affectionate girl who fluctuated between cheerful enthusiasm and a deeper sensitivity. A friend described her as 'radiant with life and joy', but at times 'her eyes in a moment grew deep and dark, her sweet lips quivered; the girl became the deep-hearted, tender, earnest woman'.[20] Her new circumstances must have been an extraordinary change of fortune, and her wedding was only the beginning. She was still seventeen when she became pregnant, and the spirits were never far from her thoughts. At first, it was 'thought it better that she should not join in séances', for when the raps occurred, the unborn child was said to move 'in unison with the sounds'. There were times when she was awoken by raps, and heard voices that frightened her, but gradually the spirits became her friends, and over time her faith was made secure. On 8 May Sacha gave birth to a son, whom they named Gregoire, and Daniel recalled how a bright light, like a star, appeared above him and remained there for three days.[21]

Daniel was by no means in perfect health, and suffered occasional bouts of intestinal inflammation. These he treated and cured, he tells us, by following the advice of the spirits.

Otherwise, life was as stable as it had ever been. To think that only two years earlier he had been in such dire straits in Paris, and now he was an acquaintance of the Emperor of France and the Queen of Holland, a guest of the Tsar and an in-law of Russian nobility. It remained the case that, if he were caught cheating, indeed if he were even suspected of deceiving the Tsar, his situation might be rather less comfortable. But Daniel was not detected, not even suspected, and his social status had never been higher. His clothes expressed his ancestral roots with an air of flamboyance that suggested true confidence. The international press reported that he 'figures as a lion in the Russian salons. He wears a fantastic dress and a Scotch cap and feather, which he never takes off in any salon – there is magic in it.'[22]

No doubt many people supposed that there was a good reason for his proud claim to noble Scottish blood. If he had been caught cheating the Tsar, the punishment for the son of an aristocrat would have been significantly more lenient than for the son of a paper-mill worker. But Daniel showed no signs that this might happen, for his display of confidence was in his abilities rather than in his aristocratic roots. What nobody would have realized was that the motto on his cap – *Vincere aut mori* – was actually that of the Clan McNeill, his mother's line rather than his father's. She, after all, had been the reason he chose the life he was living. How proud she would have been of him: the delicate boy had grown into a man, and was now a husband and a father. And if his ambition was purely material, he could now enjoy a most comfortable lifestyle, perhaps without any need to hold further séances.

But then, he knew that the spirit of his mother was watching him, observing his progress in his glorious mission, and that mission was far from over. Indeed, it could only benefit from the celebrity and influence provided by his current situation. And so it was in new and vastly improved circumstances that Daniel decided to return to London, where he would mix in polite society on better terms than he had done before. He would not escape controversy, for his mission was inherently controversial. And it was at this time that one of the great controversies of history had just begun, a key battle in the so-called war between science and religion. Daniel would play his own part in that war, and would soon be engaged in a battle of his own, one in which his enemies would launch an attack that sought to explain the mystery he had so successfully created.

7

The Cornhill exchange

On 24 November 1859 a book was published that caused a considerable stir. It contained what has been called the best idea anyone ever had, and the controversy has never really gone away. It was not the first theory of evolution; indeed, there had been one only fifteen years earlier. In 1844, *Vestiges of the Natural History of Creation* had described the evolution of fish to reptiles to mammals, and the descent of man from apes. The reaction had been so predictably sensational that the author did not provide his name, and the book had drawn ferocious criticism. Both the theory and the anonymous author were condemned in the most serious language, some critics even suggesting that the lack of specialist knowledge was evidence that it must have been written by a woman. Its popularity was indisputable – it had been read by Whig and Tory, from mechanics to royalty – but its argument had been rejected by scientists as amateur and flawed. As for the mysterious author, the name was not revealed until long after his death, but Charles Darwin knew who had written it: it had been the work of Robert Chambers, the biographer of Walter Scott and the main contributor to *Chambers' Journal*.

When Darwin published *On the Origin of Species* fifteen years later, his evolutionary theory was not so easy to dismiss, because it was supported by the idea of natural selection. This was what made Darwin, rather than Chambers, the hero of science and the enemy of the Bible in the eyes of so many Victorians. His argument was better, his evidence more substantial, and many of his fellow scientists were quickly convinced. Alfred Russel Wallace was certainly convinced, for he had come up with a very similar theory, but he recognized Darwin's primary claim and gave him the opportunity to publish first. This is why Darwin, rather than Wallace, remains the hero of science and enemy of the Bible in the eyes of many today. Darwin himself did not regard himself in that way, but others, like T. H. Huxley and Francis Galton (Darwin's cousin), were on a mission to offer society a scientific and secular worldview, and they preached Darwin's theory with vigour and enthusiasm. Here was an alternative explanation to the Biblical account of the variety of species, and one in which survival or extinction was determined by purely material processes. And many Christians were forced to consider where, in this harsh and merciless view, there was room for an omnipotent God who cared for all living things. It was enough to provoke, in many Victorians, a crisis of faith from which they would not recover.

There was, however, a potential source of comfort. Spiritualists always maintained that their confidence in an afterlife was based not on faith but on evidence. The inexplicable events that took place in the séance room, the spirit communications that manifested themselves in so many bizarre ways: these were clear and observable facts that offered physical proof on which one's faith could comfortably rest. The art critic Samuel Carter Hall, who had 'confessed to disbelief in all miracles', could now declare that 'I have seen so many, that my faith as a Christian is now not merely outward profession, but entire and solemn conviction.'[1] And one man, more than any other, provided such proof on a regular basis, converting the infidel from materialistic tendencies and giving comfort to those whose beliefs had been shaken. He was, for one convert, 'the most marvellous missionary of modern times in the greatest of all causes'.[2] When, just as Darwin's book was being published, he arrived in London with his new wife, the advocates of evolution and materialism were to be faced with something of a crisis themselves. One by one, Chambers and Wallace, Huxley and Galton, even Darwin himself, would realize that the strange abilities of this new Messiah would have to be dealt with one way or another.

For those, on the other hand, who sought to protect their faith from the growing influence of materialism, Daniel's unique aptitude for demonstrating the reality of a spirit world was of the deepest significance. It was also, at a more mundane level, of enormous interest to almost everybody, and particularly to fashionable London hostesses, to whom nothing was more fashionable than novelty. Everyone had heard of his feats, but relatively few had seen them, and one thing that virtually everyone agreed on was that they had to be seen to be believed. The fact that this wonder-worker was now an international celebrity who enjoyed royal patronage in several countries, and that his wife was a most noble lady from a distant land, made the Homes a uniquely fashionable couple, and precisely the type of guests desired by well-connected, but competitive, hostesses. The possibility of seeing extraordinary phenomena – a spirit hand or floating table – might result in a deeply spiritual experience, perhaps even restore one's faith in an everlasting life; but failing that it would provide an enviable story to be told to jealous and not so fashionable acquaintances. Whether to enrich the soul or to boost the ego, Daniel's company was eminently desirable.

It was not the first time he had enjoyed such attention from wealthy and respectable people. He had been the toast of

Florence, until rumours of immorality had led to his downfall; he had been at the pinnacle of Parisian society, but scandal and gossip had quickly followed. So this time he was determined to avoid such unsavoury notices, since his new bride was of impeccable stock and his new admirers would not suffer impropriety. A man who depended so much upon the favours of the wealthy could not afford to upset their polite world. And the ladies who competed for the Homes' company included the influential Duchess of Sutherland, whose reception of Harriet Beecher Stowe had so greatly publicized *Uncle Tom's Cabin* in Britain. They also included Lady Shelley, daughter-in-law of the poet and the creator of *Frankenstein*. Both these ladies begged to see Daniel, and were successful with their invitations. He and Sacha mixed in the most exclusive circles, and their hostesses enjoyed showing how fashionable they were, while being converted to spiritualism in the process. Such an arrangement clearly benefitted everyone concerned.

The most successful of Daniel's many patrons was Mrs Milner Gibson, wife of Thomas Milner Gibson MP, President of the Board of Trade. Their home at 3, Hyde Park Place, became a regular venue for Daniel's séances and the eager elements of high society who were fortunate enough to be invited. This was something of a social coup for Mrs Milner Gibson, but the séances were a frustration to her husband, who wanted nothing to do with them whatsoever. His fear that such scenes might prove politically embarrassing was soon confirmed. On one occasion he rose in the House of Commons to say that he had been a medium of communication between the government and another body, but he was only able to state: 'I have been a medium—', at which point he was drowned out by laughter in the House.[3] It was therefore at the home of Milner Gibson, but not in his presence, that Daniel conducted séances for the great and good of London society. And though few were able to gain access to such soirées, it was not long before everyone knew what had happened there.

The news spread throughout London society by a new medium of communication. The *Cornhill Magazine* was edited by Thackeray, and the reputation of its editor had ensured both a high quality of writing and a rapid growth in circulation figures.[4] The writing was primarily fiction, but it was an article entitled 'Stranger than fiction' that readers found the hardest to believe. It described séances with Daniel that took place at the Milner Gibson house, though thankfully for Milner Gibson, it did not reveal the venue. But the fact that Thackeray published the article was revealing: he would have known about the explanations for table turning that he had seen in New York, and he had obviously decided they were not the whole story. Sceptical he may have been, but he was clearly not satisfied that ideo-motor action explained what Daniel did. Perhaps this was because there was now another story, which was about to be told in his new magazine. The author of the story admitted that it was stranger than fiction, but he was adamant that, however strange, it was 'a question of fact'.

The author remained anonymous, but had attended several of Daniel's séances. He had not only heard raps and seen tables move, but also witnessed 'large sofas advance from the wall against which they stood; and chairs, sometimes occupied, and sometimes empty, shift their places'. And on one remarkable occasion, though it had been rather dark, he had watched as Daniel floated in the air. 'Through the semi-darkness his head was dimly visible,' the author admitted, but when Daniel had 'said, in a quiet voice, "My chair is moving – I am off the ground" . . . I saw his hands disappear from the table, and his head vanish into the deep shadow beyond.' And when Daniel spoke again, 'his voice was in the air above our heads. He had risen from his chair to a height of four or five feet from the ground . . . We watched in profound stillness, and saw his figure pass from one side of the window to the other, feet foremost, lying horizontally in the air . . . He hovered round the circle for several minutes, and passed, this time perpendicularly, over our heads.' Moments later, he 'had reached the ceiling, upon which he made a slight mark, and soon afterwards descended'. Meanwhile, an accordion had 'played a strain of wild pathos in the air from the most distant corner of the room'. The writer stressed that he was giving 'the driest and most literal account' to avoid 'being carried away into descriptions which, however true, might look like exaggerations'.[5]

The *Cornhill* article was the most public account yet of Daniel's strange abilities, and Daniel himself was more than content. It had not been so long ago that he had shrunk from publicity 'with all the earnestness of a sensitive mind'. But since those innocent days he had been the object of such scandal and gossip that he was now more than grateful for positive coverage. He praised the anonymous writer of 'Stranger than fiction' for his 'accuracy and intelligence', for 'such masterly observation, and ability of description'.[6] Fellow spiritualists entirely agreed, and complimented the author for his astute and balanced narrative. Even Thackeray assured his readers: 'As editor of this magazine, I can vouch for the good faith and honourable character of our contributor, a friend of twenty-five years' standing.'

Thackeray, however, was no spiritualist, and he pointed out that as 'he would refuse to believe such things upon the evidence of other people's eyes, his readers are therefore free to give or withhold their belief'. And so, while Daniel regarded the account as the product of masterly observation, most of the public felt quite free to withhold their belief. Others admitted that they believed the facts that had been described, but attributed Daniel's floating in semi-darkness to fraud.[7] For the vast majority of readers, the *Cornhill* article was either dismissed as too strange to be other than fiction, or else the description was taken as given, but the events dismissed as conjuring tricks. The only problem was that nobody seemed able to explain how, if it was trickery, it might be done. Some guessed that it depended upon Daniel preparing the venue in advance, though details of such preparations were never provided, while others claimed such feats required an accomplice, despite all of this having been explicitly ruled out in the *Cornhill* article.[8] It was even suggested that Daniel's levitation had been facilitated by a gas-filled balloon. Meanwhile, the *News of the World* optimistically suggested that John Henry Anderson, the Great Wizard of the North, would be able to explain it all.[9]

The failure to explain how Daniel levitated was certainly another intriguing mystery, but for some it suggested a far more serious problem. It was a particular problem for Victorian scientists, for it concerned the relationship between facts and theories. On the one hand, extraordinary facts had been reported; on the other, there were no theories to explain them. And if the facts could not be explained, perhaps they were not true. This was a growing theme among Victorian scientists, and it posed something of a dilemma; one that got to the very heart of Victorian science.

The general Victorian view of science was that scientists observed facts and, from these, constructed theories. It was these theories that explained how the world worked; they were what constituted scientific knowledge. The problem was that facts and theories did not always match, and sometimes certain theories were rather unpopular, and it was at times like this that the facts would be disputed, and controversy would ensue. When critics of Darwin attacked his theory, they appealed more to scientific than religious authority, claiming that the theory was based upon insufficient facts and was, therefore, not truly scientific. The survival of Darwinian theory itself depended upon a growing body of supporting evidence that made it seem increasingly valid, yet Creationists today are always eager to point out that it remains only a theory. And so it is, though many would say it is the one best supported by the facts.

There were also times when facts and theories were in more direct confrontation, and no more so than in the case of miraculous phenomena. Such feats had been reported for centuries, yet they contravened existing scientific knowledge. Naturally, Victorian scientists were keen to provide a theory that might explain such problematic evidence, and the most common argument was that observation was unreliable. In 1859, an anonymous writer complained that scientists were continually undermining the worth of human testimony because of reported miracles. The anonymous writer was, once again, Robert Chambers, who argued: 'The scientific scepticism of our age professes to spring from a sense of the extreme fallaciousness of the human senses, and the liability besetting us all to deceive ourselves into a belief which gratifies the faculty of wonder.'[10] In short, if witnesses reported facts that sounded unbelievable, their observations were simply dismissed as unreliable.

This theme could be found in Brewster's *Letters on Natural Magic*, which described how various optical illusions could deceive the observer into believing he had seen what he had not really seen, and which presented the eye as 'the principal seat of the supernatural'.[11] The popularity of optical devices such as the zoetrope, the stroboscope, and Brewster's own kaleidoscope, simply reinforced the notion that the senses could not be trusted. The theme was also prevalent in the developing area of mental science, where various forms of hallucinations illusion and delusion were thought to be surprisingly common, and quite consistent with a sane mind. In cases of monomania, for example, it was thought that 'the individual affected is rendered incapable of thinking correctly on subjects connected with the particular illusion, while in other respects he betrays no palpable disorder of the mind'.[12] One did not have to read specialist medical texts to be aware of this, for it was disseminated through the popular press.[13] And then there was the matter of mesmerism, where subjects could be induced to have the most extraordinary experiences, to see what did not exist and to ignore pain. In scientific journals and the popular press, in mass-produced optical toys and at public demonstrations, the public was being told (and, paradoxically, shown) that the senses were untrustworthy and that observations were unreliable.

This was all well and good, as far as it explained away the evidence for miracles, and so defended natural law from observations of floating mediums. The dilemma for scientists, however, was that science itself was based on observation. If observations were so untrustworthy, then why should one trust the facts observed by scientists? Scientists who felt they had to deal with this dilemma argued, quite simply, that they were more reliable observers of facts than others. This may sound odd, but it was not so surprising, since Victorian scientists were increasingly distinguishing between themselves and non-specialists. Clearly demarcated scientific disciplines were emerging, as were establishments responsible for specialist scientific training. As science became increasingly professionalized and specialized, so the authority of the scientist as expert observer grew. And so it could be argued at this time that 'the evidence of Prof Faraday was of more value in reference to Table Turning and Knocking than is the testimony of large numbers of persons not so well practised in observing'.[14] Needless to say, spiritualists found this view arrogant. Benjamin Coleman, a good friend of Daniel, resented being told that people like him were 'not qualified to judge of plain matters of fact made patent to our senses, because, forsooth, we are deficient in scientific training! You insult our practical common sense, and earn our contempt for your scientific nonsense.'[15] But the contempt of spiritualists did not prevent most scientists from denying the facts, for they did not accept them as facts at all, merely the product of unreliable testimony.

Even if one could not provide an explanation for the events, scientists argued, one could always explain the testimony. There was the possibility of optical illusion, of delusion or hallucination, or of the witness having been mesmerized into imagining the whole affair. Observers who lacked proper scientific training were all the more vulnerable, and therefore that much less reliable. All of this was perfectly consistent with existing scientific knowledge and was, therefore, more plausible than the theory that it was the work of spirits. Such was the argument that Victorian scientists used to explain the otherwise inexplicable, and thereby defended the laws of nature from reports of spirit hands and floating tables.

The argument was quite logical, and perhaps it was true, but it soon became clear that Daniel's feats could not be dismissed so easily. After all, Brewster was about as expert an authority on optical illusions as one could find, and he had personally witnessed Daniel's feats (and even attempted to explain how they were done), but he had never suggested they were an optical illusion. As for the various psychological conditions described by experts in mental science, they did not explain Daniel's feats, according to Dr Charles Lockhart Robertson, Commissioner for Lunacy and the editor of the *Journal of Mental Science*. Robertson at first dismissed the testimony of Daniel's witnesses, but then had the opportunity of witnessing events for himself. Rather than conclude that they were the result of hallucination, delusion, illusion or any similar theory, he actually declared his complete conviction that what he had seen was real.[16] As for mesmerism, which was so often raised as a possible cause of these extraordinary observations, it was true that individuals could be mesmerized – though precisely what that meant was still being debated – but experts on mesmerism did not regard this as an explanation for Daniel's feats. Dr John Elliotson was probably Britain's foremost expert on the subject (as well as being the man upon whom Thackeray based the character of Dr Goodenough in *Pendennis*, and to whom the book was dedicated). Elliotson, like Robertson, had begun by publicly condemning spiritualist phenomena as nonsense: he had even fallen out with a close colleague who had been impressed by Mrs Hayden, and had exposed her methods in a journal he edited, denouncing his colleague as a fool. But when he witnessed one of Daniel's séances, he too declared that what he saw was real.[17] If scientific experts were the most reliable observers, then these scientific experts were in total agreement: whatever theory might explain such facts, the facts themselves were real.

But if the facts were real, then what of existing scientific theories? If they were real, the immutable laws of nature upon which scientific thought depended were at risk, because, as the contemporary press expressed with concern: 'Unless such laws are absolute . . . all confidence in cause and effect vanishes. . . . Chaos has come again.'[18] It is doubtful that many scientists were quite so intimidated, but the threat was real enough. For every time a witness claimed that they had seen the laws of nature upset, it chipped away at the authority of scientific theories, and of scientists themselves. It was for this reason that scientists accused Thackeray of having failed in his duty as an editor. Thackeray's reply was simple enough, yet it encapsulated the central problem that, by any scientific measure, facts came before theories. 'Had you seen what I have witnessed,' the author told them, 'you would hold a different opinion.'[19] And the fact that certain scientific authorities had seen what he had witnessed, and did indeed hold a different opinion, only made matters more difficult for critics of spiritualism.

It was particularly difficult because the Victorians were busy negotiating what counted as science and, in the process, what did not. And when facts did not fit with existing theories, the line between science and pseudo-science became more blurred. This was also the case with hydropathy, the water cure involving cold baths and brisk walks. It was pioneered by Dr Gully of Malvern, whose patients included Dickens, Tennyson, Carlyle, George Eliot and Florence Nightingale. Even Darwin went to see Gully, to take both the water cure and homeopathic medicine. Despite being sceptical about the worth of either, he left almost fully recovered. It is now thought that the 'cure' was probably the result of the patient avoiding other treatments, many of which were more damaging than helpful. Yet the fact remained that the patient was cured, and that seemed to validate the hydropathic theory – and that did not fit with the rest of science.

Daniel's feats posed a similar problem, for they pointed up the gap between observed events and the ability to reconcile them with existing scientific theories. And Gully knew this only too well, for he had been at the same séance described in the *Cornhill* article. He therefore lent his reputation and credentials to the debate that it provoked. He wrote to the press to confirm the reality of the facts that had been reported, and he did so as an experienced practitioner of scientific observation. He was a medical doctor, a man of science, 'working in a calling in which matters of fact, and not of fancy, especially come under observation'. The idea that he had been the victim of delusion, illusion or hallucination was swept aside. 'We were neither asleep, nor intoxicated, nor even excited,' he declared. 'We were complete masters of our senses.' Gully was not convinced of the spiritual theory; indeed he believed 'we are very, very far from having accumulated facts enough upon which to frame any laws or build any theory', but 'I obstinately stand up for the integrity of my senses during my observation of the wonders above related'.[20] Facts were facts, and the absence of a theory to explain them did not make them any less real.

Chambers would have agreed heartily, not least because he too had been present at the *Cornhill* séance, and had seen the very same facts. He had already written about séance phenomena, though he had done so anonymously. But, having seen Daniel, he began a process of conversion that would lead him to spend many years trying to reconcile the evolutionary theory of *Vestiges* with the extraordinary facts of spiritualism. And though he would never reveal his authorship of *Vestiges*, he was soon to make public his belief in Daniel Home. From that time on, more eminent scientific authorities would also state publicly that they had seen such facts. And when that happened, it would become that much more difficult to dismiss Daniel's feats as the result of unscientific observations. In the words of Professor Challis, Chair of Astronomy at Cambridge University: 'The testimony has been so abundant and consentaneous, that either the facts must be admitted to be such as are reported, or the possibility of certifying facts by human testimony must be given up.'[21]

The mystery surrounding Daniel was therefore of much wider significance than even he realised. For him, this was a glorious mission to convince the infidel of the existence of an afterlife. This, in itself, was hardly a petty subject, but Daniel had underestimated the stubbornness of the infidel. The reluctance of the majority to be converted, along with their inability to explain the reported facts, challenged not only the laws of nature, but also the authority of scientists and the worth of human testimony. If Daniel had truly defied gravity, scientific knowledge was clearly in trouble. On the other hand, if individuals with scientific training could be so wrong in their observations, how could one trust the testimony of anyone again?

For some, the very foundations of knowledge were in question, and in such a serious predicament, the public put their trust in a most unlikely group of people.

After all, Victorian conjurors were not necessarily known for being entirely trustworthy, but they were adamant that magic was a science, and that the most impossible feats could be accomplished by scientific principles. John Henry Anderson was only the most famous advocate of this view, believing that Daniel's miracles were nothing more than tricks. And while he had singularly failed to explain how they were done, there were many others who did their best to expose the deception of the séance room. In the aftermath of the *Cornhill* article, a piece appeared in *Once a Week* entitled 'Spirit-rapping made easy'. The author, who described himself as 'One who is in the secret', explained how one might produce spirit raps (by clicking the toes as one does with the fingers). He also described how one could make a small card table float (by surreptitiously lifting it with one's legs). And then 'One who is in the secret' informed his readers that he was in possession of other secrets: 'I am confident I could tell, with a little further trouble, the means by which Mr Home astonished the writer of a recent article in the "Cornhill Magazine", and, possibly, I may do this hereafter, if it should be wished for.'[22]

This was not only wished for but demanded, and not only by concerned sceptics. For when it came to the claims of conjurors, spiritualists could be rather sceptical themselves. William Howitt, a well-known writer and a spiritualist friend of Daniel, simply did not believe that 'One' was in the secret. He therefore decided to call his bluff, and publicly challenged him to 'go on and explain how Mr Home floated about the top of the room, as mentioned in the *Cornhill Magazine*'. The gauntlet had been thrown and, much to the surprise of Howitt, it was quickly taken up. That same month, 'Spirit-rapping made easy, no. II' appeared.

Daniel must have read it with interest, if not with apprehension, for the author declared that he was 'about to answer Mr Howitt's challenge, and to explain how Mr Home floated about the top of the room . . . and all the other wonders mentioned in the "Cornhill" narrative'.[23]

8

Versions of events

'I think the floating, and all the other business, [were] manageable by means of some very simple contrivances,' wrote the man who was in the secret. 'I find them very easy to construe, and will take them in succession.' He began with some of the business that had occurred 'when Mr Home was not present', repeating that raps could be obtained by the toes, and that a small table could be raised surreptitiously with one's legs. Along the way, he provided a few more details on how a table might be moved in a variety of ways through the agency of a medium's hands and feet. As for 'the performances of Mr Home, which I am about to examine, there is a little more art and a little more adroitness, [but the secret] when I have explained it, will be found to be ridiculously simple in proportion to its effects on the bewildered and mystified spectators'. And with that, his bewildered and mystified readers encountered the words '(to be continued)'.[1] Curious readers (and this must have included Daniel) were left to scour the rest of the page for further enlightenment, only to be faced with the next article, which discussed propellers used by warships.[2] For the moment at least, Daniel's secrets were safe – but the final instalment was yet to appear.

It was a week later that 'One who is in the secret' finally revealed all, when a growing number of eager readers encountered the words: 'I now come to the performances of Mr Home.' By way of an introduction, he challenged Daniel to invite him to a séance, predicting with confidence that he would expose his methods. However, as he had not had this opportunity, he would rely upon the *Cornhill* narrative, and so he went about explaining the reported events. The feats that had been reported included spirit touches and the movement of a hand-bell (which, elsewhere, Dr Barthez had claimed were the work of Daniel's feet). But 'One who is in the secret' rejected this explanation, since such a method would have been easily detected. The real secret, he explained, was an odd though somewhat versatile instrument called a lazy-tongs. This was an extendable tongs with

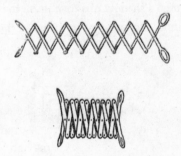

a scissors-like grip, used for reaching objects at a distance. With such a device covered in a velvety covering, 'One' assured his readers, Daniel could have touched, scratched, pulled and grabbed at sitters from several feet away. He also could have moved the curtains, the hand-bell, and the accordion. He could hardly have used it to play the accordion, of course, but One had another secret. The music need not have come from the accordion, but could have come instead from a 'mouth-harmonicon' (an early mouth organ or harmonica). The sound would have been similar, and the instrument would not have been seen in such darkness. This was a particularly interesting theory, though the provider of secrets did not rule out the possibility that Daniel had used a special self-playing accordion. Indeed, he advised all cautious investigators to '*impound the accordion*'.

And then, of course, there was the matter of Daniel's horizontal levitation in front of the window-blind. This was One's final hurdle, and so he tackled it with perseverance. There had been vague gossip about dummies of Daniel and gas-filled balloons, but One was clear that such machinery would be discovered. However, he had thought of an alternative solution that did not require such grand apparatus. The illusion of the levitation could have been achieved by a 'little compact portable magic-lantern, with the simple addition of one phantasmagoria slide'. This device was rather like an early slide projector, and could have projected a shadow of a man upon the background of the window-blind. According to One's theory, Daniel's

movement back and forward in front of the sitters was nothing more than the projection of the slide being moved in one direction and then the other. The fact that his voice was heard above the sitters could have then been a simple matter of ventriloquism, while the mark upon the ceiling could have been made by the ever-versatile lazy-tongs. In summary, One assured the bewildered that 'Mr Home is a very clever ventriloquist, a superior player on the mouth harmonicon; that he possesses an accordion, probably self-acting, a magic lantern, a lazy-tongs, much assurance, an accomplice or two . . . [and] a large circle of accommodating dupes.'

These, then, were the secrets that One was in, and the curious public must have read them with fascination – and a degree of disappointment. After all, while a lazy-tongs might have been used providing it had been dark enough, there remained the problem of why nobody had seen it when the light was better. There had been several séances at which the light had been good, where sitters had checked above and beneath the table, and it would have taken only one discovery of this suspicious device to expose Daniel as a fraud. Furthermore, it was difficult to reconcile the detailed descriptions of spirit hands with the end of a lazy-tongs. The use of a mouth organ to produce the music, on the other hand, must have seemed like an ingenious solution. It was certainly small enough to be easily concealed in the pocket, then removed when it was sufficiently dark. But the self-playing accordion was rather less convincing, since there is no evidence that Daniel ever possessed an accordion, and several witnesses stated that they had provided their own instrument. As for the use of a magic lantern: that was probably the weakest theory of all. It would need to be smuggled in and out of the séance, it would need to be lit (and remain lit in the dark) without anyone noticing, and even if it might explain a horizontal floating action, Daniel's earlier levitations had been vertical, as levitations should be.

Certainly, if Daniel was concerned about his secrets being revealed, he showed no sign of it. He seems to have derived a great deal of amusement from the article, which (he claimed) was playfully destroyed by the spirits at a séance shortly afterwards.[3] For the moment, however, the public had been informed that he might use a lazy-tongs, a self-playing accordion and a mouth organ, and if that were true, Daniel would have to be extremely careful in future séances. And if the magic lantern theory did not convince everyone, they did not have to wait long for another theory for his levitation. It seems that there was someone else who felt that she was in the secret, and unlike One, she had actually attended one of Daniel's séances.

Her name was Mrs Lynn Linton, a writer and one of the few women journalists of the period. She was also a good friend of Mrs Milner Gibson, and so had attended one of the séances at her home. Mrs Linton was, by her own admission, 'yearning to believe . . . to be forced by irrefragable proofs to accept one undoubted authority, which would have ended for ever certain gnawing pains'.[4] It was also well known that she had suffered huge grief when her adopted child, Eliza, had died as an infant. It must have therefore been traumatic when, according to a witness at the séance, a small spirit hand appeared, 'and then the baby (Mrs L's adopted child) showing its head, and finally spirit hands held up the little child so that all nine of us saw her shoulders and waist'.[5] Daniel had confirmed that this was Eliza, and most of those present had been moved to sympathy.

Mrs Linton, however, was not impressed. She had always called her daughter 'Lizzie', never used her formal name, and as far as she was concerned, this was clear proof of fraud on Daniel's part, one that 'saved me from all after dangers of credulity'. She saw many more strange happenings in the séance room, such as a chaise-longue being moved along the floor, and she witnessed what the author of the *Cornhill* article had described: Daniel's levitation to the ceiling, from where his voice was heard by those present, and upon which he scratched a mark with his nail to show he had really levitated. But Mrs Linton was not convinced, and thought she knew how it was done, and her theory had nothing to do with a lazy-tongs or a magic lantern.

'The room was almost pitch black,' she recalled, so '[t]here was nothing to have prevented Mr Home from drawing the chaise longue to him by means of a string round the front of his two legs, moving it by his own feet and muscles; standing on the centre-piece of the ottoman, and, with a knife tied to the end of a stick, scratching a cross on the ceiling. The rest was easy to ventriloquism and certain to credulity.'[6] This was not what the other witnesses thought had happened, of course, for they claimed that, despite the darkness, they had seen what had taken place. Nevertheless, it was an interesting theory, and certainly of interest to Charles Dickens, who knew Mrs Linton quite well.

Dickens was well acquainted with many of those who attended Daniel's séances, but he always refused to go himself. He was an enthusiastic amateur conjuror, but he was convinced that Daniel was nothing more than a trickster, and the periodicals he published suggested as much at every opportunity. Yet he never took the opportunity to see Daniel for himself. Mrs Trollope had tried to encourage him to attend one of Daniel's séances, but he had declined on the grounds that he was busy that night.[7] And when she asked again, less than a week later, he had replied that he 'would rather not'.[8] It was said that his friends even attempted to lure him to an innocent dinner where Daniel might be present, but one way or another he always managed to avoid it.[9] This strange reluctance led Mrs Browning to conclude that Dickens was afraid of what he might encounter, and pointed to the irony that he was 'so fond of ghost-stories, as long as they are impossible!'

Yet Dickens was in no doubt that Daniel was a fraud. 'Mr Home,' he told Mrs Linton, 'I take the liberty of regarding as an impostor.' The conditions in which the séances took place were, in his opinion, 'preposterously wanting in the commonest securities against deceit'. Furthermore, 'the people lie so very hard, both concerning what did take place and what impression it made at the time on the inquirer'. He was not accusing Mrs

Milner Gibson of lying, for she was 'an impulsive, compassionate, affectionate woman. But as to the strength of her head . . .'. Thus Dickens dismissed the conditions as uncritical and the witnesses as unreliable, but when Mrs Milner Gibson invited him once more to a séance, he again declined. And when Mrs Linton suggested he might be a more reliable witness, he quickly pointed out that 'personal enquiry on my part . . . is out of the question'.[10]

Mrs Linton had been present, however, and had her suspicions, and for Dickens that was clearly preferable to going along himself. So she wrote an article for his journal, *All the Year Round*, in which she criticized witnesses who claimed they had seen 'a medium' float upwards in a dark room, and make a mark on the ceiling. 'Not so,' she declared, 'the people present are only witnesses of the fact that the medium asserts this, and that he marks the ceiling; they are not witnesses [to] how he got up so high to make his mark. With ottomans, chairs, and darkness, he may have been able to climb, unperceived, so near, as to mark the ceiling.'[11] This may have been a more plausible explanation than the magic lantern theory, but alas it too was only a theory. After all, neither Mrs Linton nor Dickens had seen Daniel climb on top of the furniture. By her own admission, it had been too dark; and by his own reluctance, he had been elsewhere. But theories were all that sceptical Victorian readers had to go on, since the 'One in the secret' had not been in the room. And so the public were left with the theory of a woman who had been in the room, but had been in the dark, which was no doubt precisely how many Victorian readers continued to feel.

Despite these emerging explanations, the problem for the absent sceptic was that they had to choose between two rather strange scenarios. On one hand, respectable and intelligent witnesses publicly declared that they had seen Daniel levitatè. On the other, one respectable and intelligent witness suggested that they had all been deceived by a medium who had simply climbed on top of the furniture. Mrs Linton's theory might seem unlikely, and it may have been provoked by what she felt was an attempt to deceive her on a subject about which she was peculiarly sensitive. But for those who suspected Daniel was a fraud, it was certainly preferable to the idea that he had levitated. Indeed, when compared to the idea of levitation, even the magic lantern theory may have sounded rather plausible. The question, for the more open-minded, was whether intelligent witnesses could be deceived by such simple tactics, and whether their memories of what had been dimly perceived in the darkness were exaggerations of what had really happened.

As an amateur conjuror, Dickens knew that anyone could be deceived. And as he had already pointed out, séance conditions were open to trickery and witnesses were often keen to believe (and, therefore, prone to exaggeration). Daniel had been validated by educated and intelligent men, such as Howitt and Samuel Carter Hall, but was it not possible that such men could be deceived? It was true that they had been unable to detect trickery, but did that mean that no trickery had taken place? And though the secrets behind Daniel's levitation had not been revealed, was it not the job of a competent conjuror to deceive an audience without being detected, without his (often simple) secrets being revealed? The only way of distinguishing between a genuine medium and a clever cheat was for competent witnesses to assess the conditions and decide whether trickery had taken place. Mrs Linton's theory was a possible explanation, but it was based on the assumption that Daniel's many other witnesses were incompetent. Scientists might point out the problems of observation, but to mistake a man climbing on furniture for levitation, and to be sufficiently convinced to make a public declaration, required a degree of gullibility that few would have thought possible. If Daniel's secret was so absurdly simple, surely it would have been spotted, unless it was as dark as Mrs Linton claimed. But if that was the case, how could the witnesses have come to exaggerate so greatly? Could sane and otherwise sensible people really be so gullible, so desperate to believe?

Daniel knew only too well that his success depended upon the word of others that fraud was impossible. His mission remained on track only as long as competent witnesses dismissed the possibility of fraud. And so the question of gullibility and wishful thinking was a serious problem, for if his witnesses were thought foolish or desperate to believe, their word might not be taken so seriously. And this, he was about to realize, did not only apply to him, for there were many other mediums performing extraordinary feats, and spiritualists were often impressed with them. The success of Daniel's mission was therefore intertwined with the careers of his rivals, and with the credibility of the witnesses who declared that these mediums were also genuine. And the problem for Daniel was that these mediums included men like Charles Foster.

Foster was an American medium whose speciality was spirit clairvoyance. Names of deceased individuals were written on slips of paper, which were rolled into pellets so that Foster could not read them. Nevertheless, between Foster and the spirits, the names would be spelt out by spirit raps. He impressed a journalist from *The Times* who was unable to imagine how he might have been deceived, and wrote a remarkably open-minded article on this new star of spiritualism.[12] Howitt sat with Foster, and introduced controls to eliminate even the suspicion of legerdemain. 'I conjecture that nothing in the shape of evidence can be made more complete,' Howitt declared, 'not even, if an angel stood visibly before us, and provided the truth of these facts with a trumpet'.[13] Samuel Carter Hall wrote of his 'entire conviction as to the truth of Mr Foster's mediumship', and assured fellow spiritualists that it 'would have been so utterly impossible for him to have fraudulently done that which he did do, as to convert a diamond ring into an inkstand', adding 'that the persons present were such as must have detected fraud in any one who dared to practise it'.[14]

This was all impressive enough, until Foster was detected in fraud a few weeks later. The exposure was so convincing that the *Spiritual Magazine* determined to 'no longer soil our pages with his name or mediumship'. His secret had been simple enough, to switch the pellets for blanks and to read the names when nobody was looking (perhaps while they were checking under the table for evidence of trickery). What was more sophisticated was the conclusion of spiritualists, who agreed that he was a fraud, yet maintained that he was real. 'We believe Mr Foster to be a medium . . . of remarkable powers,' the *Spiritual Magazine* persisted, 'but we know him also to deceive and to cheat.' This seemingly contradictory position was based upon experience that it was 'lamentably common that real mediums will occasionally "help the Spirits".'[15] The most influential spiritualist journal of the period was admitting that it was lamentably common for genuine mediums to cheat. From a spiritualist point of view, mediums were not in control of the phenomena, and if under pressure to produce them, it was not so surprising that they occasionally resorted to fraud. There were, of course, a few problems with this argument.

First, it was hardly convincing to anyone who did not already believe in the phenomena, for if a medium was caught cheating on one occasion, it suggested he did so all the time. And second, it placed the entire responsibility upon the witnesses to detect fraud, since the only difference between genuine and fraudulent phenomena was that either fraud was detected on a particular occasion or it was not. But at least Foster had been caught by spiritualists, not by the *Times* journalist, and so the former could claim expertise and accuse the latter of gullibility, thus maintaining that they were the ones most competent to determine authenticity. So when a medium called Colchester arrived, Coleman announced with authority that Colchester was as genuine as Foster had been (at least on the occasions that he had not cheated). As far as Coleman was concerned, 'sceptics may save themselves the trouble of speculating on whether or not I may have been deceived by a sleight-of-hand trick. There was no trick in this case. It was broad daylight, and no possibility of deception.'[16]

Colchester was caught cheating almost immediately. The *Spiritual Magazine*, however, repeated the line they had taken with Foster. 'We do not agree that Mr Colchester is not a medium, for we know him to be one . . . but this system of mixing fact and fraud, is enough to put him out of the pale of those, whose manifestations we choose to record in the Spiritual Magazine.'[17] And so he too was expelled from their pages, though nobody ever admitted to having been deceived themselves. When they had seen him, they had not detected fraud, and so he had obviously been genuine on that occasion. And slowly but surely, these genuine though fraudulent mediums began to be spoken of again, and the *Spiritual Magazine* once again brought them within the pale and soiled their pages with them.[18]

Perhaps Howitt, Hall and Coleman were right: perhaps they were too astute to be fooled, though almost everybody else believed otherwise. And that included Daniel, for he was not at all impressed with Foster or Colchester, and he was perfectly aware that many spiritualists were taken in by vulgar cheats. And though many would say that he was no better, and that his feats were no less vulgar, there was still no evidence that he had actually cheated. There had been theories about the raps, the movement of tables, and even about his levitation, but nobody really knew if those were his secrets. After all, some of the tables had been large and heavy, and had moved in spite of others' efforts to prevent them. That did not sound like ideo-motor action, or the result of surreptitious use of the feet. And then there were the spirit hands that, according to some witnesses, melted in the grasp, and ENDED AT THE WRIST. They had been seen by many witnesses, and nobody yet had explained them. As far as actual evidence of trickery was concerned, there was only Dr Barthez, who claimed that Daniel had been caught, and that he used his feet to ring bells and tug at dresses. But then Barthez had not been present at the time, and even if it were true, his letter had not been published yet.

For the moment, at least, Daniel's mystery, and therefore his mission, remained intact. There were, after all, countless witnesses who dismissed the very idea of fraud; educated and intelligent men who denied that they could have been deceived. The problem for Daniel was that these included the likes of Howitt, Hall and Coleman, and if they were gullible enough to be taken in by mediums such as Foster, then their assurances that Daniel did not cheat would not carry much authority. For his mission to succeed, he needed his own feats to be distinguished from the trickery of others, and if his regular witnesses were incapable of doing this, then more competent witnesses were needed. He therefore sought the word of a more credible and critical observer.

Fortunately, there was one man who was the ideal witness. No scientist was more credible, no man more critical, and none more observant than Michael Faraday. It was said that his word was worth more than 'the testimony of large numbers of persons not so well practised in observing'. If anyone could convince the infidel that Daniel's abilities were genuine, Faraday was that man. He had already publicly dismissed séance phenomena, and had even said of spiritualists 'that many dogs have the power of coming to much more logical conclusions'.[19] But if he could only witness Daniel for himself, and be unable to explain what he saw, then the question of incompetent observation would have to be discarded. That, it seems, was the view of Sir James Emerson Tennant, Permanent Secretary of the Board of Trade. Not only had he attended Daniel's séances, but he was a man whom Faraday respected, and so he invited the scientist to a séance with Daniel, to observe the facts for himself. It was an invitation that Daniel welcomed – perhaps it was even a challenge he relished – but it seems that Faraday was not particularly keen to meet the challenge.

Faraday was certainly hostile to spiritualism, but his hostility was not only that of a scientist: he was a fundamentalist Christian, who believed that the Bible was literally true, and that spiritualism was blasphemous.[20] So when he was invited to a séance, Faraday did not want to attend, but nor did he want to appear narrow-minded. So he replied in language that hopefully would avoid both. He demanded to know whether Daniel wished him to investigate the phenomena, and whether he would 'be glad if their delusive character were established and exposed, and would he gladly help me expose it, or would he be annoyed and personally offended?' And even 'if the effects are miracles', Faraday continued, 'does he admit the utterly contemptible character of them?' He specifically instructed Tennant to 'show this letter to Mr Home'.[21]

To his relief, Faraday received a response that stated his conditions were unacceptable, and that, Daniel's supporters felt, was precisely what he was after. But it was not so easy for Faraday to escape, for he had never said these points were actual preconditions, and he must have been aware that, as such, they were unreasonable. And so, no doubt following some intense negotiations, Faraday reluctantly agreed to attend a séance. 'The time was fixed,' recalled Daniel, 'and Mr Faraday was expected.' Yet still he did not arrive, as he had found another excuse, and

Daniel was informed 'that Mr Faraday refused to come without having a programme'.[22] He 'was to have joined the party', recorded their hostess for the evening, 'however, he requested to have a programme, which he said was due to him as a scientific man . . . It being impossible to give a programme, he declined to join the séance.'[23] Once again, Faraday's terminology was either unfortunate or deliberate. Stage conjurors provided their audiences with a programme of the illusions they would see, but spiritualists always maintained that séance phenomena were unpredictable. To a scientist, it was a reasonable request to know in advance what one was supposed to be testing, but to a spiritualist it was obviously impossible, and the choice of words somewhat offensive. It was enough to prevent what would have been a most interesting encounter, and the result was that the expert observer saw nothing whatsoever. One can only wonder whether Faraday would have been convinced by Daniel's utterly contemptible miracles, or whether he would have established and exposed their delusive character. Either way, it would have been a worthwhile experiment, but then blasphemy is a risky business, even for a scientist.

As for Daniel, it may have been a temporary setback but his chance to be tested by scientists would come in time. In any case, his own priorities were, for the moment, more personal. Marriage to Sacha had brought not only social status but also emotional stability. His sensitive and insecure nature found solace in her frank and amiable manner, and the couple, it seems, were entirely content. Of their relationship, a friend observed, 'the measure of their happiness was completed by that calm domestic bliss, which is the pure source of earthly enjoyment . . . They could not but be happy.'[24] Happiness, however, is nothing if it is not temporary, and in 1861 Sacha contracted her husband's condition of tuberculosis. For several months she deteriorated until it became clear that she was dying. When she became bed-ridden,

Daniel dedicated his time to caring for her and, in the process, turned down certain requests for séances. It was at times like this that it became clear to him that many who sought his company were far from close friends, for when he declined requests, it 'gave great offence, both to Spiritualists and inquiring sceptics'. On one occasion a spiritualist complained so badly that afterwards Daniel wrote to apologize, explaining that it was due to his wife's declining health. The annoyed party replied, in somewhat brutal terms: 'I can only hope the good angels will in future do their best to arrange matters between séances and sick-beds'.[25]

After eighteen months of suffering, Sacha died on 3 July 1862. They had moved to France while she had been well enough to travel, and the last rites were administered by the Bishop of Perigueux, 'who wept like a child', and who remarked that, 'though he had been present at many a death-bed for Heaven, he had never seen one equal to hers'. The calmness with which a devout spiritualist encountered death must have been surprising, even for a man of God. It was said that 'disbelievers in Spiritualism looking on this gifted young woman, saw with wonder not only how calmly, but how joyously the Christian Spiritualist could face death'.[26] In her final days, she is said to have been in physical pain, yet in complete spiritual peace, accompanied by 'a Veiled Spirit', who slowly raised its veil as she approached her final breath. According to one report, though it was later denied by Daniel, he saw 'his wife changed visibly into an angel as she died'.[27] For all the controversy that Daniel attracted, his wife seems to have been universally loved. When they heard of her death, Sir Edward Bulwer-Lytton was 'pained', and Thomas Colley Grattan MP was said to have had 'tears in his eyes'. Daniel received countless letters of consolation and comfort both from fashionable acquaintances and from intimate friends, but the loss of another woman he loved was not without consequences. Though he never spoke of it himself, it was later reported that he had had a nervous breakdown.[28]

When he recovered, he learned that his wife's beautiful death was to be followed by a rather more ugly disagreement. Sacha's inheritance, which was substantial, was being retained in Russia, while her relatives disputed Daniel's legal right to the fortune. He travelled to Russia in an attempt to clear up matters, but returned without a ruble. There was, it seemed, going to be a very lengthy legal battle before he would receive what he felt was rightfully his. Meanwhile, he was once again financially vulnerable – threatened by 'pecuniary difficulties' – and as long as he refused to accept money for séances, he would have to find an alternative form of income. His choices limited and his health imperfect, he decided upon a controversial method of spreading his word more widely. Though he had not yet reached his thirtieth birthday, he set about writing the story of his life so far. *Incidents in my Life* was published in 1863, with an introduction and concluding chapter written, anonymously, by Robert Chambers.[29]

Incidents in my Life was an extraordinary book, even though the most extraordinary incidents in his life were yet to happen. It described very little of his early life, and was not at all detailed on his personal relationships. Most of the celebrities he had met, and who had witnessed such remarkable events, were simply not named. The events themselves were certainly described in full, with detailed accounts of what witnesses had seen, but few of the witnesses were referred to except by initials. This, Daniel said, was to protect their reputations from the animosity of the sceptical, from those who would have dismissed them as fools or madmen. But one man's name was certainly included, for Daniel had no interest in protecting him. Many pages were devoted to the controversy with Sir David Brewster, who had refused to admit publicly that he had been baffled by Daniel's feats, and had invented some conjectures to cover his embarrassment. Since then, Daniel had suffered many an insult, but now he had a chance to express his own opinion. He denounced Brewster as 'not only dishonest, but childish', and dismissed him as a 'wind-bag'. And then, as if that were not enough, he went on to accuse the great scientist of trying to claim credit for the inventions of other scientists, through anonymous articles (written by Brewster himself) in the *North British Review*. It was, therefore, a controversial book, in part for its anonymous sensational narratives of spirit hands and floating furniture, and in part for its denunciation of Brewster's own anonymous sensational narratives. Unlike for so many first-time authors, receiving notice was no great obstacle, for the reaction to the book was both rapid and hostile. 'I had no reason to complain of the neglect of the press,' Daniel recalled, 'for several journals fell foul of me with commendable speed.'

9

An international incident

'This impudent and foolish book,' wrote the *Athenaeum*; 'There is not a statement in the book so presented as to warrant a sensible man in paying attention to it.'[1] Home is 'a weak, credulous, half-educated, fanatical person', declared the *Saturday Review*, 'who has lived from his earliest years in a whole atmosphere of mirage and dreaming.' Meanwhile, the *Critic* criticized his 'unparalleled impudence', while the reviewer for the *Cornhill Magazine*, which had previously allowed its readers to withhold their belief from its own account of Daniel's séances, 'refused to believe a word of it'.[2] The book was even reviewed by Dickens, who described it as 'odious', and suggested that Daniel had been caught cheating 'somewhere in Italy'.[3] Dickens then privately boasted to Wilkie Collins that he had risked the libel laws in order to charge Daniel 'with one of his swindles in Florence', though the details of the swindle were not revealed. As for *Incidents in my Life*, it was, in Dickens's humble opinion, 'the book of a scoundrel without shame'.[4]

One might expect that the *North British Review*, a well-known and very respectable Edinburgh-based journal, would look more favourably on a boy from Currie and Portobello. But there had been criticisms of anonymous articles in that journal, and this anonymous reviewer was in no mood for favours. Having 'waded through the quagmire of Mr Home's autobiography . . . [he had] succeeded in extracting from the rubbish of the book an intelligible notice of the manifestations, prophecies and miracles . . . [It was sufficient] to establish their Godless and anti-Christian character', and such blasphemy caused 'every species of offence'. The review then focused, at considerable length, on the Brewster case, defending the great scientist from 'truthless and calumnious statements . . . [and from] the most reckless and unblushing falsehoods'. In remarkable detail, the anonymous reviewer described how Brewster had been misrepresented, and concluded that he had been entirely correct in assuming Daniel to be a simple conjuror. It was only a shame that Brewster had not been present at some of the more extravagant demonstrations described in the book, for the anonymous reviewer wondered what the great scientist would have made of them.[5]

The man who wrote these words was later revealed to be Brewster himself.[6] He went on to threaten a libel action, which worried the publishers so much that they withdrew the book. However, not every reviewer was quite as supportive of Brewster as he was himself, for when the *Spectator* reviewed *Incidents*, though it was certainly no friend of spiritualism, the critic had to admit that 'on the face of published correspondence, the hero of science does not acquit himself as we could wish or expect'.[7] And in the end Brewster did not bring a libel action, a new publisher was found, and a new edition appeared with the allegations quite intact. Brewster would continue to denounce spiritualism until shortly before his death in 1868, and it was only then that his private letters to his sister would be published, and spiritualists would be able to prove at last that the inventor of the kaleidoscope had indeed invented his conjectures about Daniel.

Shortly after Brewster's death, a séance was reported in which a spirit message appeared. The spirit announced that 'I am not convinced even now, but can see that I have much to learn – DAVID BREWSTER'.[8]

No doubt Daniel enjoyed his revenge, but it made little difference in the long run. The majority of the press had denounced him as a delusional charlatan, and his feats as the product of fantasy and trickery. And most of the public would have thought that this was a fairly accurate description. There were others, however, who were not so glib, and felt that the mystery surrounding Daniel's feats could not be ignored so easily. If he was a fraud, then his secrets must be fathomable and his actions capable of being detected. But if his methods could not be explained and he could not be caught, then however unlikely it might seem, perhaps his feats might be real. That, for some people, was the only honest scientific position. When the *Cornhill* reviewer refused to believe a word of the book, for example, he admitted that this was not a scientific position, it was simply preferable to believing the facts. The *Quarterly Review* also confessed that the 'internal evidence against his statements [i.e. the inherent likelihood of their not being true] has to be weighed against a very respectable amount of external evidence in their favour'.[9] And the *Morning Herald* went so far as to state that 'these manifestations appear to us to be in the highest degree improbable. But here we are met with evidence that, improbable or not, they have taken place . . . and may be found useful in revealing some of the yet hidden laws of creation.' The problem was put plainly by the *Literary Times*, which declared that if it was 'a true and honest book, it is one of the most important works ever presented to the world. But should the opposite be the case, then Mr Home is the greatest impostor that ever deluded mankind.'[10]

This, of course, was not how Daniel saw himself. He might be an impostor, perhaps the greatest in history, but he always maintained that his mission was of the most profound significance. He would regularly be denounced as the most despicable of charlatans, but as far as he was concerned, his critics were missing the importance of the mystery he represented. Instead, unable to explain the details of his trickery, they denounced him because of their suspicions, and accused him of fraud on the basis of rumour. Time and again, unsubstantiated gossip and erroneous claims were published as fact. A rumour that he had been caught cheating by a well-known gentleman was published in *The Times*, even though the gentleman in question had said nothing of the sort.[11] Elsewhere, it was claimed that Daniel had failed to produce any phenomena in front of conjurors, though that turned out to be a misunderstanding based on an allegation about Charles Foster.[12]

When Daniel went to France again that year, it was amid further rumours that 'he had been publicly detected and that his character there was so bad and so notorious, that he dare not shew his face again in that country for fear of imprisonment'. In fact, he was received at the Tuileries and promptly invited to a grand ball, even though the press assured the public 'that he would be no longer be received in any good society. All this and more we have heard a hundred times repeated.'[13] The allegations became so common that people who had never even met Daniel made public declarations bordering on the libellous. One Captain Noble got carried away, and wrote to the press declaring: 'Home is as rank an impostor, I verily believe, as ever lived.' A few weeks later, Noble was forced into a humiliating public apology, 'in large type'.[14]

Such was the aftermath of Daniel's autobiography, and perhaps it was all too much for a soul as sensitive as he. His writing seemed not only stranger than fiction, but much more controversial, and the claims he made provoked hostility from most of the public and press. It was the price he had to pay for the life that he had chosen, but at least he had discovered a role that he could play, one that suited his sensitive nature. Yet the sensitivity that worked so well in the séance room could not have coped easily with such unfair allegations, even if he were a charlatan. The vast majority of his witnesses, including those devout sceptics in Amsterdam, had watched intently for signs of fraud yet failed to discover any. He might have been a fraud, but there was no evidence yet that he had been caught cheating.

Meanwhile, Daniel persisted in seeing himself on a spiritual quest, and he continued to refuse money for séances. This was no small sacrifice, for the controversy surrounding the book was not sufficient to sell large numbers of copies, and his financial situation remained unstable. He was, therefore, once again in the position of considering how to make a living, and sought an independent means of income, one that might be less controversial, and more suitable for a man of a sensitive disposition. And so, to the dismay of friends, and to the surprise of almost everyone else, he decided to become a sculptor.

His friends tried to prevent this, and warned him that such a career was 'most unsuited to him'. But though he was not well off, Daniel was well connected. He was acquainted with Joseph Durham, who was known for his bust of Queen Victoria, though not for his bust of Sacha Home, which he had made as she was dying. Through Durham, Daniel met the American sculptor William Wetmore Story, who found a studio in which the aspiring artist might work. Daniel accepted the offer with the enthusiasm of a man with limited options. He spent several weeks among the artist colony in Rome, and attempted to prove, once again, that the sceptics were wrong. The most articulate of sceptics, however, was not convinced, for when Robert Browning heard the news, he predicted disaster. 'It is Story's own business,' Browning sneered, but if 'he chooses to take this dungball into his hand for a minute, . . . he will get more and more smeared'.[15]

Such articulate scepticism initially seemed overdone, for Daniel appears to have had some success at his new endeavour; indeed, it was said by some that he had 'great talent', that he was 'making rapid progress', and that he would be 'shortly commencing the practise of his new profession in Paris, where he intends establishing a studio'.[16] But whatever Daniel's artistic talents, his hopes that he might enjoy a less controversial occupation were soon to be dashed. It was not that his sculptures upset anybody, but simply that opinion would always be shaped by his well-known nocturnal activities. And in Rome such activities were much more problematic than in Paris or London. It was, therefore, not long before he found himself at the centre of an argument that quickly mushroomed into a major diplomatic row. '[T]he excitement that this news created,' recalled C. R. Weld, former assistant secretary to the Royal Society, 'you would have thought that Garibaldi or Mazzini had suddenly been discovered fomenting a revolution.'[17]

According to *The Times*, Daniel 'had been ordered to leave Rome in three days . . . which has occasioned great sensation'. The correspondent explained how Daniel had appealed to the British consul, who had gone to see the Governor of Rome, and had 'complained that any British subject should be interfered with in consequence of his opinions . . . and demanded that the obnoxious order should be rescinded'. The Governor had responded by speaking 'of the prohibition by the Government of all the practices of the black art, [but had] finally assented to Mr Home remaining, on condition . . . that he would desist from all communications with the spiritual world during his stay in Rome . . . Less fortunate than Mr Home has been a Dominican priest, who has been deprived of his curacy for reading Mr Home's book.'[18]

Daniel concentrated on sculpting, and held no séances, but it was still not enough to satisfy the Governor. Not so long ago he had been a guest of the Pope, but now his very presence in Rome was deemed undesirable. He could not guarantee that the spirits would not communicate with him, and so it was impossible for him to remain. According to the Governor, 'he is a sorcerer, and cannot be permitted in Rome; and he must go'. When spiritualists in Britain heard of this, they did their best to save face. The *Spiritual Magazine* reported that Daniel's friends 'rallied round him, and with expressions of detestation of the Government proceeded with him to the railway station by which he left for Naples . . . His quitting was quite an ovation.' In Naples he was 'received with great distinction . . . and has been elected an honorary member of the highest club there, and feted by the residents, both English and native'.[19] Before he left Naples he held a séance with Prince Humbert, later the King of Italy, and on the way home he stopped in Paris, where he held a séance with the French Empress.

Spiritualists were outraged at his expulsion from Rome, and complained publicly that 'perhaps excepting Spain, there is no country, excepting that governed by the infallible and holy father, where such a lunatic act could be perpetrated. What a laugh the holy father's patron, Napoleon, and Mr Home will have over the old gentleman when next they meet!' In a fit of anti-Catholic feeling, never too far from the surface of British Victorian attitudes, they denounced '[t]he scandalous frauds, and immoralities, impostures, cruelties, child snatchings, and bigotry of this poor priest-ridden place', and declared that '[i]f the Pope were other than a lunatic, he would have made Mr Home a cardinal, and have retained him to have sittings twice a week at the Vatican, that by means of his manifestations, the belief in the possibility of Romish miracles, might have some chance of being a little re-established.'[20]

This offended Catholic spiritualists, who complained to the editor about such outrageous comments. The *Spiritual Magazine* promptly noted that 'we have been seriously reprobated by several of our Roman Catholic friends . . . [and] we are sorry to give offence.' Nevertheless, it had to be admitted that the Pope's actions had been 'an abuse of his temporal power', indeed it had been an 'act of stupidity', and it did seem that nothing had 'any power in moderating the bigotry, and the savage fanaticism of the [Pope]'. And with that apology out of the way, it went on to repeat the view that virtually all Catholic miracles were 'a gross imposture', and that the only way to give them 'an air of plausibility' would be 'if the Pope could have Mr Home raised in the air at a solemn gathering in the Great Square of St. Peter's'.[21]

It seemed to be a strange hierarchy of incredulity in which those who believed in the most extraordinary miracles could so easily dismiss those associated with the Catholic Church; while at the same time Daniel could be expelled from Rome, not because he was a fraud but because his powers were deemed satanic. It was, however, little more than an acceptance of cultural norms: people believe what they are brought up to believe, at least until they are met with evidence to the contrary. Spiritualists endlessly declared the open-mindedness that had allowed them to be converted by the evidence, and castigated those who continued to hold to a position of scepticism without having seen the facts. Yet they could just as easily denounce Catholic miracles as blatant fraud, despite believing such miracles were possible, and without investigating the claims they denounced.

For Daniel, the situation was of a more personal nature. Since leaving, he had heard from the Greek Consul in Rome that further rumours were spreading. 'Some have given out that you were a secret agent of England,' he was told, 'others of the Emperor of the French, and some of Russia, but others have asserted you were the familiar spy of the ex-King of Naples . . .

you were held to mix in society as an unavowed diplomatist, a dangerous man, having intimate understanding with so many courts; and you became properly suspected by the governments.' Such slurs on his character were hardly new, but this had become an international incident, one with personal and possibly political consequences. And perhaps more importantly, it had cost him money, for he had already invested in the studio and sculpting materials. So Daniel took it upon himself to write to the Prime Minister, Lord Palmerston, complaining that he had 'been put to great expense as well as inconvenience by this expulsion . . . [and seeking] the best means of obtaining redress'. It was rather optimistic: the complaint was referred to the Foreign Secretary, Earl Russell, who instructed Mr Layard, the Foreign Office minister, to inform Daniel that he was 'not prepared to make any representation to the Roman government on the subject'.[22]

Daniel was not without political contacts, having met and entertained political figures of every persuasion. Despite having married a god-daughter of the Tsar, he was acquainted with Alexander Herzen, the father of Russian socialism, who had written to him about the emancipation of the serfs. He had, we know, befriended Robert Owen, the father of British socialism, as well as countless members of the British aristocracy; and though one former Lord Chancellor, Lord Brougham, had remained very quiet, another former Lord Chancellor, Lord Lyndhurst, had been more impressed. Daniel had conducted séances for Whigs and Tories, radicals and conservatives, proponents as well as opponents of Free Trade, trade unions and universal suffrage. The leading advocate for repeal of the Corn Laws, John Bright, had seen Daniel's feats on several occasions, not without having to negotiate a busy diary, and though he was not a spiritualist, he was unable to think of any other explanation for what he had seen. '[I]f it be true,' Bright told an American consul, 'it is the strongest tangible proof we have of immortality.'[23]

Daniel was also, of course, a close friend of the wife of the President of the Board of Trade, himself an equally fervent Free Trader, but Milner Gibson refused to be involved in his wife's activities. He had been embarrassed in the House once already, and had no intention of allowing himself to be humiliated again. And so, in the end, Daniel's case was put by John Arthur Roebuck, the obstinate but eloquent Member for Sheffield. Roebuck was no spiritualist, indeed Benjamin Coleman felt that 'had he been presiding as a Master in Lunacy at an investigation into my mental condition, he would not have hesitated to pronounce me incapable of the management of my own affairs'.[24] He was, however, an experienced political fighter: he was an original founder of the Anti-Corn Law League, and when the Tolpuddle Martyrs were convicted for being members of a trade union, it had been Roebuck who led the campaign for their release. But though he had been a thorn in the side of every government since he had entered the House in 1832, it was now 1864, and his radical views had faded. 'The hopes of my youth have been destroyed,' he wrote that year, 'and I am left to reconstruct my political philosophy,' and he went on to denounce trade unions, and later to oppose Gladstone on policies he had himself once supported.[25] It was, then, with a degree of apathy, though not without a spark of wit, that Roebuck rose in the House of Commons to address the question of Daniel's expulsion from Rome.

According to the *Morning Star*, 'Mr Roebuck rose to ask the Under-Secretary of State for Foreign Affairs whether any steps had been taken to obtain from the Papal government redress for the injuries done to Mr Home by that Government.' He 'had no feeling for Mr Home's profession, further than having contempt for the whole thing, [but] whatever might be the wonderful and mysterious power of Mr Home, he ought to be protected as a British citizen'. 'England must protect her subjects,' he declared in an appeal to national pride, yet 'when Earl Russell was asked what he would do, he said, "I will do nothing." This provoked 'Much laughter, caused by Mr Roebuck imitating the voice and manner of the noble lord.' And he ended by demanding that the Prime Minster protect Daniel 'against the tyranny of the Roman Government'. On behalf of the government, the minister, Mr Layard, replied that they could not interfere, for 'The Roman authorities feared that these spirits would communicate with Mr Home whether he wished it or not, and they objected to their making Rome their dwelling-place.' This, too, provoked laughter, much to the annoyance of Roman Catholic MPs; but not so much laughter as when Roebuck acknowledged, to Milner Gibson's utter horror, the feelings of the President of the Board of Trade, whom he thought to be a spiritualist.[26] Oddly, when Milner Gibson later resigned, the new appointee to the position of President of the Board of Trade was John Bright.[27]

Robert Browning must have followed events with a mixture of intrigue and disgust. He had never got over his initial hostility, and had continued to spread rumours that Daniel was a fraud.[28] It was said by Browning's friends that the mere mention of Daniel's name caused 'foamings at the mouth', and provoked 'stamping on the floor in a frenzy of rage'.[29] Only the previous year, he had gone 'to a party at Lady Salisbury's and came right upon him – though I could not believe my eyes'. A moment later Daniel vanished, and Browning boasted: 'I can't help flattering myself that the announcement of my name did him no good.'[30] Daniel remained a unique topic of disagreement in the Browning household, so much so that when he was writing his will, Browning confessed real concern that his wife might make 'a present of [the money] to Mr Hume, the day after receiving it'. He 'could think of no sillier, or to him, more objectionable thing for Mrs Browning to do with her money'.[31] As it turned out, it was Elizabeth who died first, and when Browning got over his loss, he realized he was at least now free to say what he thought about Daniel. He was about to launch his fiercest, and most public, attack, using his most effective ammunition. To make matters worse, a quite different confrontation was emerging from across the Atlantic. Two men from New York were due to arrive, and the novel miracles they performed were to threaten Daniel's reputation. From both sides, Daniel's mission was under threat, and more secrets of the séance were about to be exposed, including that of the mysterious spirit hands.

10

Mr Sludge and the Davenport brothers

Ira and William Davenport hailed from Buffalo, New York. They had, we are told, 'an exuberant flow of humour and vivacity, both from habit and constitution, and [were] much inclined to conviviality and social amusements'. As teenagers they toured small-town America demonstrating spirit manifestations to paying audiences, engaged by a man called Luke P. Rand. In Oswego, New York, they were convicted, along with their manager, for 'having a public exhibition without a license', and faced with the choice of a fine or a month's imprisonment, chose to accept the hospitality of the local jail. It was there, they solemnly affirmed before God in a sworn affidavit, that their manager was instructed by a mysterious voice in the cell to 'walk quickly out and onto the attic window yonder, and let thyself down by a rope, and flee from this place'. The 'angelic command', we are told, 'was strictly obeyed'.

Their managers did not always stick around, but the boys were accompanied regularly by William Fay, a childhood friend from Buffalo. It was said of Fay that while playing marbles as a boy he had been 'suddenly seen to rise from the ground and float into the branches of a tree'. If this were true, the *Spiritual Magazine*

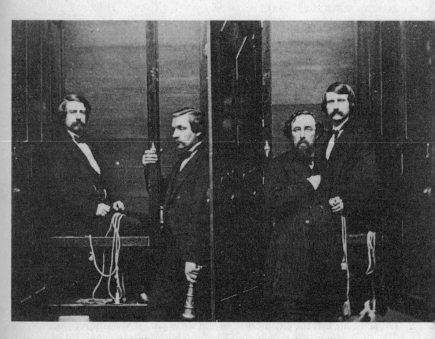

Ira and William Davenport sitting in their spirit cabinet
and looking relatively trustworthy compared to the two
men who are about to tie them up. (*Mary Evans*)

noted, it was 'a very promising beginning'. However, it was admitted by spiritualists that 'If there be any conjuring or imposture, he is clearly one of the party, and must be watched equally with them.' Such suspicions were justified, but Benjamin Coleman appeared to have none when he visited the Davenports' apartments in the hope of conversing with a spirit. 'The brothers consented,' Coleman reported innocently, 'but Mr Fay begged me to excuse him, as he had an engagement elsewhere.' The lights were put out, a voice was soon heard, and the Davenports confirmed that it was the voice of a spirit. Whether the voice sounded like Fay, Coleman does not tell us. However, he does report that when he asked a question of the spirit, he was immediately interrupted by one of the Davenports. He also admits that he could hear the 'spirit' moving beside him in the dark. Despite these clues, Coleman's conclusion was that, while he was 'keenly alive . . . to the possibility of imposture . . . The manifestations witnessed in the presence of the Davenports . . . are not produced by the active agency or co-operation of either of these young men or of any confederates.'[1]

Later, the brothers and Fay were joined by Rev. J. B. Ferguson of Nashville, Tennessee. Ferguson had left Nashville after it was taken by Union forces during the Civil War, and he became the front man for the Davenports' performances, at which point he was suspected of being a confederate. Nevertheless, to most who met him, he seemed entirely sincere in his spiritualist beliefs, and such apparent sincerity convinced many that the Davenports deserved serious attention. That said, when they arrived in Britain, they were taken under the wing of Mr Palmer, a manager of public entertainments, who had as it happens, been a former manager of John Henry Anderson.

But for all the suspicious circumstances surrounding the Davenports and Fay, their performances bewildered almost all who witnessed them. The centrepiece of the demonstration was a 'spirit cabinet', a large wardrobe with doors that partially covered the front, and in which the brothers would sit. Inside the cabinet were musical instruments, such as a tambourine, trumpet, bell and guitar, along with two chairs to which the brothers would be tied securely with rope. The lights would be extinguished and, moments later, the instruments would be heard playing, and would fly into the air through the space at the front of the cabinet, where 'spirit hands' would also appear. When the lights went up and the doors were opened, the boys would be seen still tied securely to the chairs. They did not explicitly claim any extraordinary powers, leaving witnesses to draw their own conclusions, but as the sessions were accompanied by a sincere talk on spiritualism by Rev. Ferguson, spiritualists soon concluded that this was the work of the spirits.[2]

It was not only spiritualists who found these events mysterious: the boys' rise to fame in Britain was largely the result of convincing Dion Boucicault. Boucicault was a well-known playwright whose stage productions had recently achieved sensational success thanks to pioneering special effects. Using ingenious technical methods, he recreated live on stage a burning building, a cave filled with lapping water, and the collapse of a rope bridge over a crevasse. Could such an expert on staged illusions be deceived by trickery? He witnessed the Davenports and Fay in his own home on Regent Street, and in the presence of such notables as Viscount Bury MP, Sir Charles Wyke, Ambassador to Mexico, and Captain Inglefield, the Arctic investigator. Six guitars and two tambourines, along with a new piece of rope, were bought for the occasion, though the instruments that were actually used included two bells, a violin and a brass trumpet. After the brothers had been tied securely, and the doors closed, a 'Babel of sounds arose from the cabinet', and spirit hands appeared at the opening. The Arctic investigator took hold of the hands, and 'stated to the touch they were apparently human hands', and when the Ambassador to Mexico went into the cabinet, 'several hands touched his face and pulled his hair'. And when Viscount Bury had a peek inside the cabinet, he saw a hand 'descend upon him, and he started back, remarking that a hand had struck him'. A whole series of similarly strange effects followed in that eminent company, which, when they later signed a public declaration that they had found it all inexplicable, included the surprisingly conspicuous name of Robert Chambers.

The press was naturally quick to investigate, with mixed results. A *Times* journalist, the same one who had been so impressed with Charles Foster, gained a rather stronger impression when 'he received a blow on the face from a floating guitar, which drew enough blood to necessitate the employment of towel and sponge'. Later, when the gentlemen of the press attended, they arrived in greater numbers. There was, from the start, 'uproar and excitement, and quarrelling with the arrangements' over who should do what, after which 'Laughter, jeers, and jokes became the order of the day.' The *Daily News* reporter moved 'for fear of the trumpet being thrown upon his head', and missed the appearance of the spirit hands, much to his frustration and the amusement of others present. In the process of checking the cabinet, one reporter pushed his hand through the opening, and immediately 'a shout was raised of "There's a hand!" amidst roars of laughter'. Throughout the proceedings, 'talking and laughing and smart and even obscene jokes were repeated' and, as a result, 'They saw little and heard nothing but themselves and some execrable music.'[3]

Others took the decision to attend a more civilized séance, and saw things that were significantly more impressive, allowing the Davenport brothers to retain an air of mystery. The Davenports were, for Edwin Arnold (later Sir Edwin Arnold) of the *Telegraph,* either 'the embodiment of a mutual and colossal self-deceit, or the silent heralds of a social revolution which must shake the world'. It was, however, a mystery that might be solved, for there were those whose expertise provided them with greater insight into how such feats could be performed. 'The "wizards" have only to perform exactly the same things,' Arnold concluded, 'and the public will agree with their view of what at present is *not* easily explained.'[4]

And of all these wizards, only one was a Great Wizard, at least according to his own publicity. Following his second disastrous fire, which had resulted from his scandalous and unruly masked ball, John Henry Anderson had been busy. He had found temporary venues and gone out of his way to create an exotic atmosphere for his audiences, boasting that his theatre was 'Nightly ventilated by the improved form of the Great Hindustani Punkah, scented with Franjipani, and Diffusing Odoriferous Coolness throughout the House'. But even that was not enough and, still deep in debt, he decided to look further afield for new audiences. He sailed from Liverpool with his enormous show and, three months later, arrived in Australia. For the next year and a half his 'success was immense', though his plans to hold another masked ball 'created excitement amongst tradesmen and anxiety amongst goodly folk'.[5] He then set off on a second American tour and, en route, was dubbed 'The Clever White Man' by the King of Hawaii. His tour had begun successfully, but his planned visit to Virginia was scuppered by the Civil War, when secessionists ripped down his posters as a way of pointing out that a Wizard of the North was not welcome in the South. Struggling to recoup his losses, he left his wife and son in America, and would never see them again. When he returned to Britain in 1863 he was still in debt; but when he heard about the Davenport brothers, he recognized them as new enemies to be fought, and the inspiration for a new routine that might draw the crowds.

John Henry was now almost fifty years old, but his battle against spiritualism had never ended. He continued to sell his booklet, which with every new edition, explained how thousands had been driven insane by this blasphemous faith. He sneered at a book written via spirit communication, which claimed to have been (in an unfortunate wording) 'written without the necessity of thought on the part of the writer'. And though he had never attempted to explain the phenomena of Daniel Dunglas Home, he felt confident that the Davenports' activities were capable of explanation. Their secret, in fact, was rather obvious, and had been considered by virtually everyone. All that the boys did was perfectly possible if they were able to escape from the ropes, and then quickly re-tie themselves. Suspicions had been raised when certain observers noticed that, after the phenomena occurred, one of the brothers was seen 'breathing irregularly and coughing. He was unmistakably panting, the trunk was bedewed with perspiration, and the heart was beating violently.'[6] It had also been pointed out that Indian jugglers performed a similar feat of escapology, in which they were tied up inside a sack and thrown into a river. Helpful critics suggested that the Davenports should be treated likewise, with one of their supporters inside the sack to ensure that no trickery took place. But people were only guessing, and what they wanted was a conjuror who could duplicate everything the Davenports did and thus prove that it was indeed trickery. And so the Great Wizard determined that he would do this, or rather that somebody else would, for at his age such antics were out of the question.

He therefore enlisted the help of his daughters, of whom he had several, though not as many as he claimed, for some of the young ladies travelling with him, though described as his daughters, were actually his mistresses. Lizzie Anderson, however, was of true Anderson stock, and it was she who played the part of the medium, and prepared to have herself tied up with rope.

The anticipation of such a performance was enough to attract a keen and eclectic audience to St James's Hall in London. According to the *Standard*, among those who attended, 'There were authors, journalists, architects, soldiers, sailors, doctors, lawyers, men of science, and most unmistakably "rowdies", and all in a state of most demonstrative eagerness.'[7] And being a true Anderson, Lizzie delivered a truly Andersonesque exposure. There were, confessed a sympathetic reviewer, some 'awkward mishaps [that] marred the exhibition, and to a great extent nullified its utility'. So many people were trying to check things that everyone got in each other's way, 'much to the discontent (not inaudibly expressed) of all parties'. And after witnessing the demonstration, the *Standard* confessed: 'the original demonstrations [of the Davenports] remain as inexplicable as ever.' There were further performances, but the bound young Lizzie continued to struggle, and the press had to conclude that she did not 'go any considerable length towards unravelling the mystery surrounding the Davenport Brothers. We must wait till Miss Anderson has had a very great deal more practice.'[8]

Other conjurors practised more thoroughly, however, and it was not too long before the Davenport spirit cabinet act was being performed even better than the original. The most successful exponent was John Nevil Maskelyne, who personally witnessed the Davenport act and declared that he would do the same without the help of the spirits. It was the start of a highly successful career in conjuring for Maskelyne, and reflected the beginning of the end for the Davenports. They continued to tour, but they met with hostile audiences in many towns and cities, and occasionally provoked riots that ended in their cabinet being smashed to pieces.[9]

And yet, throughout all of this, those who had believed in them refused to change their minds. Whenever the brothers were accused of cheating, spiritualists simply pointed out that it was well known that genuine mediums occasionally cheated, and that sometimes mediums 'help the spirits'. Nevertheless, it seemed that when a knot was tied that was secure, the brothers were unable to help the spirits any more than the spirits were able to help them. As for the duplications by conjurors, the *Spiritual Magazine* admitted that 'the conjuror was able to untie the rope . . . and again that he was able to re-tie himself', but maintained that 'the two things are totally dissimilar'.[10] They seemed quite similar, however, to Coleman, that paragon of scepticism, who went to see Maskelyne perform his spirit cabinet at Crystal Palace, and was so convinced that this was what the Davenports were doing that he came to the only possible conclusion: Maskelyne was himself a genuine medium.[11]

It was the sort of conclusion that could prove dangerous. Edward Sothern, the well-known comic actor with a love of practical jokes, publicly claimed that he and his friends had held a private séance and produced 'all the manifestations of floating about the room and so on, familiar to those who have concerned themselves with the ridiculous exhibitions of Mr Home and the Davenports'. Coleman, on hearing of this, concluded that, if Sothern had indeed done what he claimed, he must also be a medium. Sothern replied with playful glee: 'We outdid everything attempted or accomplished by Home . . . but I have not the slightest hesitation in saying we did *not* do them by spirit agencies. I look upon every spiritualist as either an impostor or an idiot.' Coleman, considering himself neither of these, continued to insist that Sothern was as genuine a medium as the Davenports (which was, of course, precisely the point that Sothern was making). But the actor's sarcastic denials were enough to provoke the stockbroker to wreak revenge. Coleman subsequently published an article in which he claimed that Sothern, while touring America, had mesmerized and raped a young actress, and had wrecked his marriage in the process. A few weeks later he was at the Old Bailey, charged with criminal libel by Sothern, who was accompanied by his wife. The sentence Coleman received, a fifty pound fine, was denounced as 'absurdly inadequate' by the press, who suspected the judge of being a spiritualist.

Some of the conclusions reached by spiritualists were also, in the opinion of many, absurdly inadequate. According to the *Spiritual Magazine*, the genuineness of the Davenport manifestations depended upon the brothers being unable to release themselves from the ropes. The very same journal, however, reported their ability to release themselves instantly from knots, but on that occasion concluded that it was the work of the spirits.[12] Later, when a sitter in Brighton saw the figure of Ira Davenport moving around the room, the spiritualist interpretation was not that he had released himself, but that this was evidence of a 'spirit double'. And later still, when the boys were in Michigan, and a spirit hand was smeared with ink during a séance, and the lights went up to reveal that Ira's hand was covered in ink, it was suggested that the ink had been transferred from the 'double' to the medium by the spirits.[13] And if the boys were literally caught red-handed, it was all attributed to bad spirits who 'made the boys do what they were unconscious of doing themselves'.[14] Despite all the duplications and exposures, the *Spiritual Magazine* never questioned the brothers' authenticity, not even when it reported that 'these gentlemen are again in prison in America for showing their manifestations without a conjurors license . . . It seems strange that such a thing could happen.'[15] And later still, when a new biography of the Davenports avoided mentioning Fay, 'so as to make it appear that he was not of the party', the *Magazine* noted somewhat innocently that this was odd, since Fay 'was certainly as remarkable a medium as either of the Brothers'.[16]

Such are the lengths to which the mind will go, once it has

established an initial premise. But spiritualists were hardly unique in this respect. For it was not so different from the desperate attempts by critics to dismiss all séance phenomena without ever having seen any. Or from when the discovery of fossils, which showed that the earth was much older than the Bible suggested, inspired the theory that God had placed fossils on earth in order to test our faith. Nor was it so different from attempts by Christians to come to terms with Darwinian theory. But spiritualist beliefs were different in that they were much more controversial to begin with, and so the spiritualists' defence of the Davenports was bound to be dismissed by the majority as utter nonsense. And with people such as Coleman as Daniel's regular witnesses, how much less impressive did that make their testimony regarding him? Many others, including Chambers, insisted that Daniel could not possibly have cheated, but when Chambers said the same of the Davenports, it made many wonder whether he was a reliable witness, or the victim of, to use his own words, 'the liability besetting us all to deceive ourselves into a belief which gratifies the faculty of wonder'.

Comparisons between Daniel and the Davenports were understandable, but unfair. He was no stage performer, had never sold tickets, and no conjuror had managed to duplicate his feats. There were theories and there had been accusations, but his record remained second to none, and, since he never worked within a cabinet, the spirit hands that he produced could not be his own. After all, witnesses regularly reported that his own hands were in sight. Daniel was a superior medium, and had convinced many sceptics that he was no vulgar conjuror. Ironically, one key difference was that, unlike a conjuror who performed his tricks on cue, many of Daniel's séances passed without anything happening at all. This, he claimed, was because he was not in control, only a medium through which the spirits worked. It was also, one might suggest, a useful 'out' if conditions became difficult. Nevertheless, the fact that his séances were sometimes a failure was enough to convince some that he was not a conjuror, while the fact the Davenports performed to order meant that 'their pretensions are open to far more suspicion than those of Mr Home'.[17] And while no other medium questioned Daniel's abilities, he (much to Coleman's frustration) denounced the Davenports as a pair of 'colossal humbugs'.[18]

But despite Daniel's attempts to distinguish himself from other mediums, many in Britain felt they were all the same. Daniel, the Davenports, Hayden and Foster had all come from America to ply their trade, and the British refused to be found so gullible. They had heard of the American tendency to mislead the English, and of the hoaxes and exaggerations that came out of that country.[19] They had heard the humbug of P. T. Barnum, and of the scams that deceived innocent British people into investing in fictitious American railroad companies. The fact that such scams often involved British con men, and that the humbug of John Henry Anderson was actually admired by P. T. Barnum, did not lessen their xenophobia. And so the mediums from America were dismissed as 'Yankee conjurors', and Daniel, though Scottish, was called an American, which no doubt made him all the more suspect.[20]

Even those who did not suspect Americans, or at least did not suspect Daniel of being one, regarded Daniel with enormous suspicion: as well as being associated with blatantly fraudulent mediums, he was targeted individually on a regular basis. He was, after all, the most famous medium, and so the most obvious of targets. But he had also made a number of enemies who personally detested him, and none more so than Robert Browning, who had accused Daniel of being a fraud, and relieved himself by threatening to throw him down a flight of stairs. He had called him a dungball, and foamed at the mouth, and stamped in a frenzy at the mention of his name. But he had eventually calmed down, and if the name came up, he was now in the habit of merely referring to him as 'vermin'.[21] Browning's more relaxed attitude was the result of his having once again relieved himself.

He had published a poem that he had managed to keep secret from his wife, starting on it more than four years before, in the winter of 1859-60, and never allowing her to see it.[22] Now that she was dead, and could not be hurt, the work was ready for public release. It was a long poem, a very long poem, and it was about a spirit medium. The medium was a cowardly fraud called Mr Sludge, but everyone knew it to be based upon Daniel, a fact confirmed by Browning himself after Tennyson complained that the poem was too long.[23]

'Mr Sludge, "The Medium"' takes the form of a drunken confession. With each line, the reader learns of the ruthless deceit of Mr Sludge, and his utter contempt for the gullible victims he has swindled out of money. There was even the occasional clue as to how he fooled them:

> 'To turn, shove, tilt a table, crack your joints,
> Manage your feet, dispose your hands aright,
> Work wires that twitch the curtains, play the glove
> At end o' your slipper, – then put out the lights' [445–8]

> '. . . I cheated when I could,
> Rapped with my toe-joints, set sham hands to work,
> Wrote down names weak in sympathetic ink,
> Rubbed odic lights with ends of phospher match,
> And all the rest . . .' [800–5]

These lines were Browning's attempt to explain Daniel's feats, and some were rather novel. There was nothing new about tables being turned and tilted, or even shoved; and the theory that raps were caused by cracking joints had been around since the start of Daniel's mission. As for the use of wires to twitch curtains, or the writing of names in sympathetic ink, these had no association with any feat that Daniel had performed. However, the 'odic lights with ends of phosphor match' was Browning's theory for the spirit lights that witnesses had occasionally reported. And he also thought he knew how to explain the spirit hands: a spirit hand was no more than a 'glove at end o' your slipper'. It was only a guess, but it might at least explain why the spirit hand 'ENDED AT THE WRIST'.

If Browning had solved the mystery, Daniel showed no sign of being concerned. Indeed, he was reluctant to believe that the poem was even about him. 'There is nothing whatever to connect his portrait of Sludge with myself,' he insisted, 'and no one even slightly acquainted with me could discover one point of resemblance.'[24] He found it difficult to identify with the cringing, cowardly character of Mr Sludge, for he felt that they had so little in common. For example, in the poem, Sludge's confession had been induced by 'an over-dose of champagne' and 'continual potations of egg-nog', yet it was well known that Daniel himself was a man of temperance. On reflection, however, that made him suspicious that Browning 'did intend his portrait of Mr Sludge to represent me, for he once remarked of me that I was in the habit of being brought home drunk by the police every night'. No doubt he finally grasped the fact that he was the intended target of Browning's pen, but the very thought that he might not have realized this would no doubt have frustrated Browning even more. The poet continued to make derogatory remarks about Daniel over the following years, accusing him of various kinds of fraud, but it would be many years before he would be given a final chance to expose him.

From Daniel's point of view, Browning's poem may have

damaged his image, but it did not ruin his mission. For while Browning was a figure of considerable note, there were others no less eminent who begged to differ. In fact, it was at this time that Daniel attracted the attention of that most influential of Victorian thinkers, John Ruskin. Ruskin has been called the greatest of Victorians, his interests covering science and religion, philosophy and poetry, politics and art. He had also taken an interest in spiritualism, but after sitting with one medium he found himself 'very unfavourably impressed'. When he heard that Daniel was different from other mediums he requested a sitting, with the result that his attitude was transformed into one of enthusiastic conviction. Ruskin was eager for further séances, and when he discovered that Daniel had left the country he was sorely disappointed. '[Y]ou never told me you were going away,' he wrote to him, 'come to see me the moment you come back.'

Daniel was in New England and, not for the first time, had more practical concerns than the opinions of writers. His 'means were very small at this time', and his attempts to gain a certain amount of financial independence had not been too successful. His book had caused considerable animosity, including a ferocious review by Dickens, and his hopes for an artistic career had been thwarted by his expulsion from Rome by the Vatican. Still, he refused to accept money for séances, and continued to hope for an alternative source of income that might release him from his dependence upon his patrons. On his travels he met the American poet Sarah Helen Whitman, who attended a séance she said she would never forget. Perhaps she saw the spirit of her deceased husband, Edgar Allan Poe, but she certainly hoped to meet Daniel again, and though an admirer of Browning, she subsequently dismissed 'Mr Sludge' as a 'blot on the scutcheon'. Perhaps this was what inspired Daniel's new career, for it was here that he began to give public readings of poetry.

Many a reader might have chosen a poem of Browning's, but

Daniel did not. Instead, he chose Henry Howard Brownell's *Bay Fight*, which described the defeat of the Confederates at Mobile Bay, at which Brownell himself had been present. Daniel's reading was deemed 'masterly and daringly original', and his ability to conjure up the battle scenes was such that, in New York, 'a young Southerner present was maddened out of all self-control, and sprang at the reader like a wild beast'. An equally extreme, though quite different, impression was made upon a journalist who reported that Daniel read 'Beautifully, wonderfully. His pathos is exquisite, his humour perfect . . . He is grace itself; his manner is thoroughly refined, his voice rich and of large compass, his facial expression unequalled. Home is a marvel.' And if that were not enough, his hands and feet were 'beautiful', his head was 'excellently shaped', and he had, as so many seemed to appreciate, 'fine teeth'.[25] Even in such an apparently harmless profession, Daniel could charm as easily as he could provoke. But even to less admiring observers, Daniel seemed to have a gift for reading, for Brownell himself met him, and thanked him, and was subsequently converted to spiritualism by him.

Public readings offered limited financial reward, and when this became increasingly apparent, Daniel returned to Russia in the hope of claiming Sacha's inheritance. There he was installed, on command of the Tsar, in one of the Imperial palaces. Unconcerned about the potential consequences, he held innumerable royal séances: Count Alexis Tolstoy travelled from Siberia to see him, and the Tsar even agreed to be godfather to Daniel's son. It was a promising welcome, but he was quickly reminded that his influence was less significant than these social gestures suggested. Though Daniel had all the necessary legal documents, Count Koucheleff, who had previously been such a generous host, continued to refuse to hand over any money. It had been three years since Sacha's death, but it would be several more before Daniel would legally obtain her inheritance. 'During that time,' he wrote to one of his many other patrons, 'I shall be very poor, as indeed I am at this moment.' And so he travelled back to England, the necessary costs having been found somewhere.

When Daniel returned, he discovered that Ruskin was still desperate to see him. But Daniel, it seems, was no longer so impressed with celebrity. He had learned that famous acquaintances could be fickle, just as powerful enemies could be cruel. The wealthy and renowned might desire his company – or more likely seek an opportunity to witness his feats – but they did not provide him with the means to do without them. Ruskin was a great man, but Daniel had met great men before; perhaps his only chance to assert his own position was to turn down the appeals of such great men. When Daniel had passed through London on the way to Russia, Ruskin had announced to Daniel's host that he was coming 'on Monday to take possession of Mr Home . . . please tell him this, and hold him fast on Monday morning till I come'. Yet once again Ruskin was too late, for Daniel had already left. Now that Daniel was back in London, Ruskin wrote once more to say, 'I hope I may soon see you. Please say that I may.' Almost a year later, Ruskin was continuing to plead for another séance, though it seems that his wish was never granted.

Daniel had a difficult winter, during which time his 'ill-health was aggravated by anxiety about the future . . . and struggles of poverty'. His portrait was painted by William Pickersgill, and Landseer sent him a drawing of his dog. But this was of little comfort to a man with consumption, and finances that were in similar decline. He was, however, looked after by his friends in both respects. While he stayed with Dr Gully to recuperate, his seven-year-old son Gregoire was taken away to be cared for by spiritualist friends. Gregoire had already had an unconventional upbringing, one not so different from that of his father: he had been taken from his homeland at an early age, had lost his mother shortly afterwards, and would often rely upon the hospitality of friends rather than family. Daniel must have been aware of his own parental shortcomings, and this would have made it all the more important to improve his situation. Yet though his health improved temporarily, at his own insistence hospitality rather than a salary remained the reward for his séances. He therefore returned to the problem of earning an independent living. And, once again, his choice of career was considered entirely inappropriate.

Rumours emerged that Daniel was to appear on stage, playing the lead role in a new West End production of *Hamlet*. Even for Daniel this was remarkably ambitious, but not everyone reacted with scepticism. Lady Loftus Otway, who had unlimited confidence in Daniel, bought him a pair of foils for the occasion, and begged him to reserve her a ticket on opening night. But it seems that few others were confident it would work. Friends warned him that he lacked the necessary experience, and pointed out that 'no man ever played Hamlet for his debut'. And the stage, after all, was an 'arduous calling' for someone in his state of health. Others, less concerned for his wellbeing, went out of their way to intervene. Dickens, who had some influence over the manager of the theatre, did what he could to ruin Daniel's plans. When the performance finally went ahead without Daniel, Dickens boasted that he 'had the honour of stopping him short'. Daniel was subsequently given the opportunity to play less challenging roles, but despite being announced in playbills, he did not appear on stage. And though Dickens did not claim responsibility for this, he expressed deep satisfaction. 'I believe the public to have found out the scoundrel,' he wrote, 'in which lively and sustaining hope this leaves me at present.'[26]

Daniel remained hopeful of a stage career, but with such

powerful enemies he decided upon a safer approach. He had considered the possibility of further public readings of poetry in America, but had not thought 'he had the courage to give readings in England'. It was here, after all, that he seemed to provoke the most unpredictable reactions. Yet his choices were always limited, and his celebrity here was as great an attraction as anywhere else. And so he decided to renew his career in public reading, but his British tour was to begin with a talk upon a subject that would attract a sympathetic audience. He would give a lecture on spiritualism at Willis's Rooms, a Georgian assembly rooms off St James's Street, to which Charlotte Brontë had gone to hear Thackeray lecture only fifteen years earlier. What Daniel did not expect was that he would attract an equally celebrated visitor, but one who was not sympathetic in the slightest. For among the largely friendly crowd would be a face he had not seen before. The name was familiar, but they had never met, and now they were to meet in a most public arena. Daniel was about to come face to face with the Great Wizard of the North, and the encounter was not going to be pleasant.

The Wizard and the widow

John Henry's career had been remarkable. He had performed for royalty all over the world, from Queen Victoria to the Tsar to the King of Hawaii: and though he borrowed freely from fellow conjurors, he remains, so far as one can ever be sure, the first magician to pull a rabbit out of a hat. He had a reputation for enjoying a regular tipple, and engaging in an occasional fight, and there had been those ongoing rumours about his relationship with his so-called daughters. Yet he had achieved fame and success around the world, and he remained, as Harry Houdini later acknowledged, the greatest of conjuror showmen.

But in 1866 he was in serious trouble. The attempts to perform the spirit cabinet had drawn lukewarm reviews, and his 'final farewell appearance' in London had been so unprofitable – he admitted to losing eleven hundred pounds – that it had genuinely proved to be his final farewell appearance in London. Although it was later said that he returned to Australia, and embarked on a tour of India en route, this seems to have been just another exaggeration. He declared himself bankrupt in 1865, having lost £26,526, a figure so large one is forced to remember that it was provided by the greatest of conjuror showmen. From then on he seems to have been reduced to touring the English provinces and his native Scotland, with mixed success.

It was then, at this lowest point in his career, that he heard Daniel was to give a lecture on spiritualism at Willis's Rooms. And so, with nothing to lose, he decided to attend. It was an appropriate meeting place for two unusual individuals, for Willis's Rooms was also the venue of a wedding breakfast celebrating the (fake) marriage of the Aztec Lilliputians, at which the 'bride' wore a low-cut satin dress and 'a lace veil, which caused her a great deal of trouble'.[1] And the encounter between the Wizards of the North was no less troublesome, if hardly as affectionate. For the world's most famous medium stood on stage and argued for the genuineness of his miracles, while the most public enemy of spiritualism sat in the audience, in uncharacteristic silence, until he could remain silent no longer.

When Daniel rose to speak, a reporter from Dickens's *All the Year Round* provided readers with a truly diabolical image. His eyes were said to be 'pale grey with a redness round the rims that comes and goes', his hands were described as 'long, white and bony', and his teeth, which had so far received unanimous praise, were denounced as 'large, glittering and sharp'. When Daniel began speaking he might have recognized his enemy in the audience, for soon he attacked John Henry's most cherished argument. 'It has been argued that insanity is a natural result of the belief [in spiritualism],' he declared. He had therefore investigated this claim while in Connecticut, and found it to be bogus. 'The state statistics gave as inmates of the Hartford Insane Retreat, thirty-seven from being spiritualists,' he pointed out, yet when he had 'asked the superintendent how many patients were there who had [actually] been rendered insane by spiritualism. Without a moment's hesitation he replied, "*Not one.*"'

How John Henry must have flinched at this attempt to refute the statistics he had so often cited, though never produced. But how would Daniel avoid the various explanations that had been provided for his phenomena? As for the attempts to explain the phenomena, Daniel continued, there had been conjectures, but none deserving serious attention. It had been said, for example, 'that I had a great number of cats to sleep with me, and by this means became so charged with electricity, that the rappings were heard in my presence'. Another theory had been 'that I held my feet a long time in ice water, and then sat by the Emperor [of France], putting my feet in his hands, and so he thought he had touched a corpse-like hand'. And the desperate guesswork continued now, for it was 'currently reported that my feet are like monkey's feet, and that I can do as I please with them. Some of my friends have even asked to see my feet without shoes or stockings, that they might contradict this.' Such explanations, like those of the Great Wizard, were 'fantastic, far-fetched, and inadequate'.

All of this seems to have been too much for John Henry, who had so publicly advertised both the fraudulent nature and dangers to the mind of spiritualism. And it did not help that John Henry had turned up 'in a condition', we are told, 'which made it painfully evident to all present, that he was not fit to address a public meeting'. Throughout the lecture, he had left the room, 'resorting to a fountain of inspiration from which he constantly returned, with a flush on his countenance'. But now he had had enough, and he stood up and began to walk threateningly towards Daniel, yelling 'Swindler! Humbug!', and pulling off his overcoat as if he intended to fight with him. According to Dickens's publication, 'the conjuror had no intention of challenging Mr Home to fisticuffs. He had merely taken off his great-coat to give fuller play to his lungs in a mediated effort of oratory.' But Daniel seems to have felt the threat was rather more physical, and promptly jumped off the platform.[2] The ushers were called, and John Henry was removed from the building as quickly and quietly as possible, which was not before Daniel, by his own admission, 'had listened to a *tirade* of abuse'.[3] After he had gone, though not until then, Daniel remarked with relaxed eloquence that John Henry 'had evidently visited the buffet once too often', and went on to finish his lecture by concluding that his phenomena were intended 'to draw us closer to God'.[4]

As John Henry negotiated his way home, he no doubt thought of several more impressive things he might have said. This, his only opportunity to tell Daniel what he thought of his blasphemous and dangerous creed, might have been more effective with more foresight – or fewer visits to the buffet. Instead, it had been a brief and bizarre encounter, and one that seemed to sum up John Henry's current predicament. And from this time on, though he never claimed there was a connection, John Henry reported that members of his family 'died one after the other'. He never performed in London again, nor did he tour abroad. A few years later he died in Darlington, and his medical certificate gave the cause of death as 'the general decay of nature'.[5] His place as the pre-eminent British conjuror and debunker of the supernatural would be taken by Maskelyne, who had duplicated the Davenport routine so much more efficiently. From Daniel's point of view, the threat posed by the Wizard, even if largely a physical one, was now over. But whether Maskelyne would do any better in solving Daniel's secrets still remained to be seen.

Daniel was physically weak, and his public readings had not earned him enough to sort out his finances. In an attempt to get round his refusal to hold séances for money, his friends decided to form the Spiritual Athenaeum, an institution intended to be 'a rallying point for Spiritualists and their friends', and to offer Daniel the paid position of Resident Secretary. This he accepted, along with lodgings at the Athenaeum's new premises on Sloane Street. The arrangement led to a significant improvement in his financial situation, though not in the way his friends had intended. For though it brought him an enormous amount of money, with came the greatest scandal of Daniel's colourful life, one that would convince many that he was indeed a fraud.

The scandal came in the person of Mrs Jane Lyon, a remarkable woman who provoked remarks that were seldom charitable. She was the illegitimate daughter of a cheesemonger, and had married the wealthy, but weak, Charles Lyon. He had died a few years before, leaving his widow a fortune worth a hundred and forty thousand pounds. Mrs Lyon was in her sixties, short, stout, and childless. She had had little formal education, and was regarded by some as a vulgar woman. And so, though her wealth gave her access to fine places, her manner prevented her from meeting fashionable people. She was an enthusiastic spiritualist, however, and had naturally heard of Daniel, who was well connected but in financial difficulty. Such was the potential for disaster that began to be realised on 2 October, 1866, when Mrs Lyon walked into the Spiritual Athenaeum at 22 Sloane Street.[6]

Of their first encounter Daniel recalled that she claimed to be a more wonderful medium than he, and that she was less interested in spiritualism than in his knowing 'them high folks'. On being shown evidence that he was an acquaintance of aristocracy, she declared: 'Well, you are a celebrity and it is only a pity you should be so poor.' She had expected him to be 'proud and stuck-up from knowing so many great folks, but I like you very much and I hope you will like me'. Two days later she was back to question him about his connections, and, presumably satisfied, she promptly proposed to adopt him as her son. As she later explained, she had few friends and she disliked her family. She liked to chat to Mrs Pryor, 'who sold mixed sweets', and she was fond of her sister-in-law, Mrs Clutterbuck, but then she was old and sickly and had plenty of money already.[7] And so she offered to settle upon Daniel 'a very handsome fortune', and suggested that they take a house, and travel abroad together so that they might meet 'great folks'. According to Daniel, 'she threw her arms about me and kissed me', an act he thought 'rather violent, but her age and the conversation we had just had, seemed to justify her conduct'. Later, however, on 7 October, when he promised that he would love her like a mother, she replied: 'The less of that kind of love the better,' and declared instead that she would love Daniel's son 'with a mother's love'. The deal was closed by her kissing him, and handing him a cheque for fifty pounds.[8]

This was Daniel's account, to which he added that he tried to return the cheque the next day, but that she refused to take it, and so he cashed it at the bank. On the question of adoption and the level of settlement, Mrs Lyon consulted Daniel's friend Samuel Carter Hall. Three days later Daniel received a letter from her, stating that she wished to make him an 'entirely Free Gift' of twenty-four thousand pounds, and the day after that they went together to the Bank of England where the transaction was completed. Smaller sums of cash also followed, which, Daniel tells us, he accepted to avoid causing offence, and later Mrs Lyon changed her will to make him her sole beneficiary. This was arranged through the solicitor William Wilkinson, a spiritualist and a good friend of Daniel. In December, Daniel changed his name by deed poll to Daniel Home Lyon, and received another present of sixty thousand pounds. Around this time, Mrs Lyon 'was absurdly affectionate', so much so that at a dinner party, 'even the servants made remarks on her conduct'. In January 1867 she placed another thirty thousand pounds in a trust for Daniel, which was once again arranged by his friend William Wilkinson.

Things began to go wrong soon enough. According to Daniel, Mrs Lyon took possession of his jewellery box, and had Sacha's clothes altered so that she could wear them herself. She boasted of Daniel's fashionable connections and complained if he was addressed as Home, for now his name was Lyon. Daniel's friends noted her harsh treatment of him, and the servile condition to which he had been reduced; one even told him that he would not have stood that for thirty thousand pounds a year. But whatever he may have suffered in private, the public soon heard a quite different story, when Mrs Lyon filed a Chancery suit against Daniel for the return of all her money, and accused him of having swindled her. She served a writ against him to prevent him leaving the country, and a warrant for his arrest was issued. On 18 June 1867 Daniel was taken into custody and held in Whitecross Street Prison.

Daniel's sudden wealth had naturally aroused many people's suspicion, and the charge by Mrs Lyon simply confirmed what some already thought. She claimed that the huge monetary gifts she had given to Daniel had not been her idea. On the contrary, she had been instructed to do so by the spirit of her dead husband, during séances in which Daniel had been the medium. This was music to the ears of Robert Browning, and news of it came from a seemingly reliable source: Dr Liddell, Dean of Christchurch, father of Lewis Carroll's Alice, and a nephew by marriage of Mrs Lyon. According to Browning, he 'told me all of the rascality of Hume, and how his own incredible stupidity as well as greediness wrought his downfall . . . the sheriff's officer arrested him at a snug evening party – threw him into prison'. He had been up to no good, as had 'his respectable associates, S. C. Hall and Wilkinson, who have both got pretty pickings out of the plunder'. And if all this were not enough, Browning had been told by Mrs Lyon's lawyer that 'Hume wanted in the first place to marry Mrs Lyon . . . There's a misfortune for Miss Hayes, Mrs Milner Gibson and such like vermin!'[9]

While Browning had no difficulty believing all this, he had no evidence of his own. He would have loved to prove that Daniel was a cheat, but he had to rely on the testimony of others. And so he continued to accuse him in private, for his chance to expose him publicly had not yet arrived. Meanwhile, Daniel's friends and followers dismissed the allegation. His innocence or guilt in the matter would be determined by the larger question of whether his abilities were genuine or fraudulent. Those who regarded him as a fraud had already decided that he deceived others in order to benefit (in kind, if not in cash); those he had convinced of his spiritual sensitivity were hardly likely to believe such a story. But now his innocence or guilt was to be determined in the High Court, presided over by Vice-Chancellor Sir George Giffard, and before an eager public and an inquisitive press. And as the *Spectator* pointed out: 'The case which is being tried is to some extent a test of the reality of spiritual manifestations.'

The trial of Lyon versus Home took place in the spring of 1868. On the last day of March, American spiritualists had celebrated the twentieth anniversary of the birth of Modern Spiritualism. The trial began in London the following day, on the morning of 1 April, which some would have said was appropriate. The public wasted no time in forming a lively queue outside the court, as the case, according to *The Times*, 'excited public attention to an extent quite unprecedented in the annals of the proceedings of the High Court of Chancery'.[10] And those who were fortunate enough to gain a seat in court were rewarded with scandal, intrigue and humour.

According to Mrs Lyon's sworn affidavit, she had been told by the spirit of her dead husband to regard Daniel as a son, and that he should be made financially independent. The message had been communicated through raps that occurred in Daniel's presence on the 6 October. Subsequent messages instructed her to make the various large payments to him, and when she had altered her will to make Daniel the sole beneficiary, she had done so 'under the full conviction and belief that it was dictated by my late husband and that I was complying with his wishes'. It was only later, when her 'eyes had been opened', that she realized she had been 'altogether imposed upon and made the dupe of the said Defendant', that these instructions from 'the spirit of my said late husband were not in reality so given, but that they without exception emanated entirely from the said Defendant'. He had 'worked upon my belief in his supposed power until he acquired almost unlimited control over my mind'.[11]

In support of her allegation Mrs Lyon produced manuscript books containing records, written in Daniel's own handwriting, of alleged conversations between Mrs Lyon and her husband's spirit. In these she had been told by the spirit of Mr Lyon, and in Daniel's handwriting, that Daniel was 'the best medium on earth', that she should not seek the advice of any other medium, and that it was desirable to 'get control of her mind'.[12] Much of her story was corroborated by one Mrs Fellowes, the wife of her late husband's nephew, and by another Mrs Fellowes, the wife of her late husband's other nephew. Both Mrs Felloweses confirmed that Mrs Lyon had said 'she had only obeyed her husband's commands as communicated by his spirit through the mediumship of the defendant', and that 'she was the victim of the grossest imposition'. Along the way, Mrs Tom Fellowes explained to the court, much to their amusement, that 'Mr Home [once] told Mrs Lyon that a groan she had heard proceeded from a spirit that was hoarse.'[13] Further circumstantial evidence was provided by Mrs Sims and Mrs Pepper, both of whom had resided with Mrs Lyon, and had got the same impression from what they had heard while listening outside the door. No evidence was provided by Mrs Pryor, who sold mixed sweets, or by Mrs Clutterbuck.[14]

When Daniel appeared in the witness box, the *Telegraph*

described him as 'of rather fair complexion, light hair and moustache. He has a somewhat effeminate appearance.' No mention, on this occasion, was made of his teeth. In response to the allegations, Daniel denied any spiritual communications had taken place prior to her proposal of adoption, which had been the seventh of October, not the sixth as she claimed. It was true that there had been a rapped message from the spirit of her late husband on that day, but only after Mrs Lyon had decided on the adoption, and, anyway, the raps had been nothing to do with him. The gifts he had received had nothing to do with spiritualism; indeed spiritualism had barely been mentioned. He produced several letters from Mrs Lyon that expressed affection, concern for his finances, and the occasional instruction to eat properly. One letter in particular, signed by Mrs Lyon, stated her intention of giving Daniel 'an entirely free gift', with no reference to spiritualism. He claimed that at least one of the Mrs Felloweses had tried to come between Mrs Lyon and himself, that she had made derogatory comments behind Mrs Lyon's back, and that Mrs Lyon had admitted she was 'bad-minded' and only after her money. Several witnesses for the defence testified that Mrs Lyon had explicitly denied that her generosity had anything to do with spirit communications; and Eliza Clegnow, a servant girl, testified that she had heard Mrs Lyon say she would get her money back by claiming she had been influenced by the spirit of her late husband.

Under cross-examination Mrs Lyon showed little consistency, other than in her inability to remember what she had said or written. Nevertheless, she was adamant that there had been spirit messages from her husband before her decision to adopt. The 'Witness grew very excited about this point', recorded *The Times*, 'and burst into a long, rambling statement, which was with difficulty checked.' That she had been under Daniel's influence was challenged by the exhibition of a memorandum book, in which she described Daniel as 'a greedy, fawning, sneaking, lieing [sic] hypocrite'. And when the servant girl, Eliza Clegnow, was mentioned, the 'witness flew out with denunciations of her as a saucy, dirty, dangerous story-telling slut'.[15] Meanwhile, Daniel insisted that he had been warned not to get on the wrong side of Mrs Lyon, and that she once boasted that when her mother had been on her deathbed, and had asked to see her, she had said 'that she might die like a dog by the way side and I would not move a finger to save her'. This, Daniel explained, had caused his mouth to fill with blood.[16]

The accusations flew back and forth, and the press dutifully reported them all, though the *Spectator* felt that 'The suggestions made by both sides as to a contemplation of marriage are too disgusting to be dwelt upon.' Other sections of the press felt that such details were in the public interest. And so the public well beyond the courtroom heard how both plaintiff and defendant accused each other of wanting to marry, and how each claimed they themselves had been repulsed by the idea. According to Mrs Lyon, Daniel had said he 'was anxious to marry an elderly lady . . . that he intended to make to me proposals of marriage, but I told him that the subject was distasteful to me and I silenced him upon it at once'. According to Daniel, he had gradually become aware that she 'contemplated the possibility of warm relations between us', and it was his rejection of her advances that had caused her to become bitter. When she had suggested marriage, he had replied: 'That can never be while God gives me reason.'

The motivation for her gifts to Daniel, and her reason for changing her mind, were central to the case, so there was much discussion about who was fond of whom, when and to what extent. On the occasion of the mortgage deeds being read out, Daniel recalled, she had 'put her left arm round my neck and fondled my cheek . . . I was mortified.'[17] 'Certainly my arm was not round Dan's neck,' Mrs Lyon replied, 'but I remember his arm was round my waist, and his other hand was on my head, smoothing my hair.' She denied that she had ever loved him – 'I disliked him, . . . I was not attached to him . . . I never loved him.' When then asked why she had signed her letters so affectionately, she replied: 'I am sure I don't know . . . very extraordinary.' She adamantly denied ever having kissed him, then admitted she had on two occasions, but only because he had asked. 'The tone in which Mrs Lyon mimicked Home's entreaties that she would kiss him', reported the *Police News*, 'seemed to cause great amusement.'[18]

The public, not surprisingly, took sides in the argument, and Daniel's arrival and departure at court were accompanied by a combination of cheers and hisses, in which the hisses predominated. At the end of the fourth day, as he was returning to his lodgings on Jermyn Street, he came across a group of men on the opposite side of the street. According to Daniel, one of them ran towards him, carrying a knife, and attempted to stab him, but he held up his arm and managed to block the thrust. Thus he survived the second attempt on his life to which there were no other witnesses, though once again there was physical evidence, as the following day Daniel appeared in court with a wound on the back of his hand.

But all such evidence was irrelevant to the case, for it was Daniel's abilities as a medium that would carry more weight in the question of his innocence or guilt. And fortunately for Daniel, others came forward to testify both to his character and to his extraordinary abilities. Dr Gully pointed out that Daniel had always refused money for séances, and Robert Chambers finally went public in a declaration of support of the medium's 'irreproachable character'. But of greater worth was a letter read out by an electrician called J. Hawkins Simpson, who had 'carefully tested varied phenomena due to Mr Home's mediumship'. And more significant yet was the testimony of Cromwell Varley, the Atlantic telegraph engineer, who claimed he too had 'examined and tested [the phenomena] with Home and others, under conditions of my own choice, under a bright light, and have made the most jealous and searching scrutiny'. In the middle of a most controversial and potentially damaging court case, Daniel was receiving public support from scientifically trained observers, men who had tested his abilities and found them to be genuine. It was a significant and unexpected development, and one that was to worry many scientists when they read their newspapers the following day. But it did not, at the time, worry the prosecuting counsel, who simply requested that Daniel produce a spirit rap. 'There was instantly a dead silence in the court to hear it,' the press reported, and when Daniel replied that he could not do so, there was 'an expression in court as of disappointment, particularly on the part of the ladies, who had eagerly leaned forward'.

The verdict was delivered on 22 May, the morning of which saw 'an ugly rush for seating accommodation', though not until 'a considerable number of young and fashionably dressed ladies were favoured by earlier admittance'. In his summing up, Giffard admitted that nobody could have read the evidence presented by Mrs Lyon, 'without coming to the conclusion that reliance cannot be placed on her testimony'. The court costs had actually been 'very seriously increased', not only by her unwarranted allegation towards Mr Wilkinson, but also by 'her innumerable misstatements in many important particulars – misstatements on oath so perversely untrue that they have embarrassed the Court to a great degree and quite discredited the plaintiff's testimony'. 'She said almost anything which occurred to her from time to time,' Giffard continued. 'In fact, it comes to this: she contradicts everything.'

Nevertheless, much as he mistrusted all that she had said, he did not believe that Daniel had been, as he claimed, under her influence. 'I disagree entirely,' the Vice-Chancellor declared, for Daniel's appearance, his history and the evidence in court, 'lead irresistibly to a widely different conclusion'. And if he had been in a position of influence over Mrs Lyon, had he been responsible for spirit communications that led to her paying him the sums of money? Daniel had denied this, of course, but Mrs Lyon's principal witnesses had testified that this was precisely what had happened. In the opinion of the Vice-Chancellor, 'much more occurred on Sunday 7 October, 1866 [when the agreement had been made] in the shape of manifestations and communications than the Defendant admits.' And even if he had not been responsible for these communications, 'if the Defendant had not been a medium he could not have gained this influence over the Plaintiff'. It remained the case, in the Vice-Chancellor's opinion, that spiritualism was 'mischievous nonsense, well calculated, on the one hand, to delude the vain, the weak, the foolish, and the superstitious; and, on the other, to assist the projects of the needy and of the adventurer'. In short, spiritualism was nonsense, and it had, one way or another, given Daniel undue influence over Mrs Lyon. He was therefore instructed to return the sixty thousand pounds she had given him, and she, who had so misled the court, was ordered to pay his costs and those of Wilkinson.

It was the sort of verdict from which both sides could claim victory, and so they did. Daniel's supporters consoled themselves with the fact that Mrs Lyon's honesty had been questioned, and that the decision had been based on the judge's dismissive views of spiritualism. His critics, on the other hand, could simply point out that he had lost. Sections of the press made regular jokes at Daniel's expense – 'Since he got into Chancery his spirits have quite left him' – while others were left to take it more seriously. After all, Daniel might have avoided being caught in the séance room, but now he had been publicly found guilty of fraud. His glorious mission seemed as close to ruin as it had ever been.

But if the Lyon versus Home case was severely damaging to Daniel's reputation, it did at least provide him with some real and lasting comfort. His initial imprisonment at Whitecross Street Prison had been made tolerable by the companionship of two young gentlemen, Lord Adare and Lord Lindsay, who stayed with him until he had been released on bail. These men were to remain Daniel's closest companions throughout the next bizarre episode in his life, and were about to tell the world of his most famous miracle. And the fact that scientific gentlemen had publicly testified in favour of both him and his feats had already provoked concern among scientists. 'In the public courts of England,' the physicist John Tyndall complained, 'men with heavy scientific appendages to their names had testified, on oath, their conviction that the phenomena reputed to manifest themselves in the presence, and through the agency of Mr Home are "not due to the operation of any of the known laws of nature". This solemn testimony had been circulated through the length and breadth of the land.'[19] And from Tyndall's point of view, things were about to get considerably worse. For despite Daniel's current humiliation, these initial declarations were to stimulate further scientific investigation that might yet declare his feats to be real.

12

Rising to Adare

During the trial Daniel had resigned as Resident Secretary of the Spiritual Athenaeum. Having thus lost both his salary and his accommodation, he moved in with Lord Adare. His new lodgings in Ashley House, Westminster, were perfectly comfortable, but his situation was not at all promising. After the trial his reputation was seriously tarnished, and his financial position was weaker than ever. A second marriage might certainly improve things, if it were to the right sort of lady, but given his current circumstances, this did not seem very likely. As for his first wife's inheritance, there were no signs of securing that in the near future. For things to change dramatically, it was going to take a miracle. Whether he considered this either metaphorically or literally, he was fortunate to be living with Lord Adare.

Viscount Adare was the only son of the third Earl of Dunraven. He was thin, wiry and monocled, with a passion for sports that he had indulged at Oxford through cricket and tennis, hunting and yachting. His father had become interested in spiritualism after being impressed by Sir David Brewster's first reaction to Daniel, on the steps of the Athenaeum Club, and Adare himself had attended séances with Daniel at the home of

Dr Gully. Now he was living with Daniel in Ashley House, a third-floor apartment on Ashley Place, just round the corner from where Westminster Cathedral stands today, and only a few blocks from Buckingham Palace. Here, the energetic sportsman became immersed in physical phenomena of a more spiritual nature, befriended by a most sensitive, delicate sufferer of consumption.

The two men were clearly very close, sharing a bedroom and a great deal of time together. When Adare was ill, which was surprisingly often, Daniel cared for him with affection and intimacy. According to Adare, on one occasion he 'sat down beside me and pressed me close to him'; on another 'he sat for some little time holding one of my hands in his and pressing the other against my heart'. When they prayed together he 'took my two hands, joined them within his . . . [and] something affected me so much that I burst out crying, and the tears ran down my cheeks'. But when Daniel 'passed his hand across my throat, [it] stopped the crying immediately; he then made passes over my head and down my side, took my hand and kissed it, kissed my forehead and said, "Good night".' At other times when Adare was ill, Daniel 'warmed his hands at the fire, and commenced shampooing me over my chest, stomach, legs and feet', and under spirit guidance 'made me unbutton my waistcoat, and began sounding my chest as doctors do; he then rubbed and patted over my chest, loins and legs, occasionally turning around as if to seek advice from someone'.[1]

It was a little strange, perhaps, that the adventurous athlete became the sensitive patient, and the men's physical intimacy, though not necessarily anything more than what Adare recorded, expressed a bond that went beyond that of mere roommates. The séances that the men shared were equally strange, even by the standards of previous ones. They both knew the famous American actress Adah Isaacs Mencken, and when she died,

Daniel predicted that she would visit them in spirit. Later, he announced that she had appeared, and Adare saw a 'luminous cloud-like body floating in the air'. When Daniel told him she had taken possession of him, Adare saw that 'she was speaking through him. He walked slowly over to my bed, knelt down beside it, took both my hands in his, and began speaking. I shall never forget the awfully thrilling way in which she spoke.' Another time, Daniel predicted the appearance of spirit lights, and then told Adare he could see spirit lights, 'and then I began to see the lights'. It would be suggested later that Daniel's influence over Adare was remarkable.[2]

While the two men were close, they were not alone, for they shared a friend in Lord Lindsay. The Master of Lindsay was the only son of the twenty-fifth Earl of Crawford, who, like Adare's father, had been convinced for many years of Daniel's abilities. Lindsay had been educated at Eton and Cambridge, and was a bibliophile with a particular interest in astronomy. A decade after this, in fact, he would be President of the Royal Astronomical Society and a Fellow of the Royal Society. By then he would have resigned his commission from the Grenadier Guards in order to represent Wigan as a Member of Parliament, and he would later become a trustee of the British Museum. Such credentials would later be held up as important, though in 1868, he was but a twenty-one-year-old graduate and a Guard stationed at the Tower of London. Daniel told him dreadful tales of the 'strange and horrible influences' there, describing 'several spirits at the Tower in most graphic language'. And when he told him he would 'have a curious manifestation at the Tower, quite alone', Lindsay later reported that 'he had had strong manifestations that evening when alone'.[3]

On the evening of Sunday 13 December 1868, the three men were at Ashley House, along with a fourth companion, Captain Charles Wynne. It was not the first time they had all been together, and it was not the only time they saw strange things in Daniel's presence. On one occasion, Lindsay and Wynne had seen 'tongues or jets of flame proceeding from Home's head'. On another, Lindsay had seen 'an indistinct form resembling a bird', though this had been invisible to Adare and Wynne. When Lindsay had 'perceived [a] figure in the chair, and said he was leaning his arm on [Wynne's] shoulder', Wynne 'said he could feel that there was someone there, but he saw nothing'. Between them, the men reported an incredible variety of bizarre visions, even if they did not always share them at the same time. But it was on the evening of December 13 that they witnessed what became Daniel's most famous feat.

That evening, according to Adare, Daniel 'got up and walked about the room. He was both elongated and raised in the air . . . He then said to us, "Do not be afraid, and on no account leave your places"; and he then went into the passage. Lindsay suddenly said, "Oh good heavens! I know what he is going to do; it is too fearful".' Adare asked what he was going to do. 'I cannot tell you,' Lindsay replied, 'it is too horrible!' But then a spirit told Lindsay that he must inform Adare, and so he explained that Daniel was 'going out of the window in the other room, and coming in at this window'. They then heard Daniel go next door, and heard the window open, and moments later, 'Home appeared standing upright outside our window.' Daniel then opened the window and walked in, 'sat down and laughed'. What, asked Wynne, was so funny? He was merely thinking, he explained, 'that if a policeman had been passing, and had looked up and seen a man turning round and round along the wall in the air he would have been much astonished'.

Adare was then told to go and shut the window in the next room, but when he went to do so he noticed that it was open by less than a foot. He asked Daniel how he had managed to squeeze through, and Daniel took him next door to show him. He told him to stand a little distance off, and 'he then went through the open space, head first, quite rapidly, his body being nearly horizontal and apparently rigid. He came in again feet foremost.' Adare recalled that he could not see how he was being supported, that 'He did not appear to grasp, or rest upon, the balustrade, but rather to be swung out and in.' And the windows he had passed between, Adare pointed out, that he had horizontally left and returned through, were on the third floor. Later, Lindsay himself confirmed: 'I saw the levitations . . . when Home floated out of the window . . . he went out of the window in a horizontal position, and I saw him outside the other window (that is, the next room), floating in the air. It was 85 feet from the ground.'

This was the testimony of two fine and noble gentlemen, and such respectable individuals were surely to be trusted. The first account appeared shortly afterwards, in 1869, in a book entitled *Experiences in Spiritualism with Mr D. D. Home*. The book was written and printed (for private circulation) by Adare and his father, and described nearly eighty séances witnessed by them over many months. There were many strange experiences, but the one event that attracted most attention was this levitation from the third floor. It was not the first time Daniel had reportedly levitated, but it was, even for his most ardent admirers, 'the most striking'. At least he could not be accused of using a magic lantern or climbing on top of furniture. In the aftermath of the trial, when his reputation had been seriously damaged, such a miracle might give him more positive publicity and remind the world that his glorious mission should be taken more seriously. The problem, from Daniel's point of view, was that he had for the moment, a rather restricted audience. Only sixty or so copies of the book had been printed for interested friends and family. And then, as soon as these had been distributed, the Earl of Dunraven regretted his decision and attempted to recover the copies. The reason for his sudden change of heart was, perhaps, that the Catholic Church, to which he belonged, informed him in no uncertain terms of its hostility to spiritualism. The result was that he destroyed all the copies of the book that he could, and barely a handful survived. Daniel might have floated out of a third floor window but, no doubt to his frustration, hardly anybody knew this.

Fortunately, there would be another opportunity for the world to hear of this most wondrous feat, for that same year an extraordinary decision was made. Daniel's trial had attracted the public testimony of men of scientific attainment, each describing how they had investigated Daniel's feats, and how they had concluded that they were real. It had prompted something of a debate, not least within the various debating societies that met and argued around the capital. The London Dialectical Society was a distinguished group that became particularly intrigued by the question and, unlike its fellow debating societies, determined to find the answer. A committee was established to begin an investigation into the 'Phenomena alleged to be Spiritual Manifestations', consisting of thirty-three individuals, and including eminent scientists and sceptics. There was the naturalist Alfred Russel Wallace, who had come up with the theory of natural selection, but had given Darwin the chance to publish first. Wallace was a scientist of enormous repute, yet he had been investigating spiritualism for years and had already published a book that declared such phenomena were genuine. Then there was Charles Bradlaugh, the radical reformer whose republican atheist views were to keep him out of the House of Commons for years. G. H. Lewes, the biologist who had humiliated Mrs Hayden, and T. H. Huxley, who had spread so effectively the word of Darwin, were also invited to join the committee, but both declined, 'having better things to do'. Even if spiritualist phenomena were true, Huxley sneered, they merely 'furnish an additional argument against suicide. Better live a crossing-sweeper than die and be made to talk twaddle by a "medium" hired at a guinea a séance.'[4]

For eighteen months the committee obtained oral and written evidence from witnesses, and carried out experimental séances, including four with Daniel. Present at these was Bradlaugh, who would have made a most impressive convert, but alas he was not so receptive as Lords Adare and Lindsay. The results of these séances were 'feeble and inconclusive', and he thought the movements and sounds that he saw and heard were 'of too slight a character to entitle one to come to any conclusion, except that it might have been easily produced without extraordinary means'.[5] But the oral and written evidence was considerably more impressive, obtained as it was from more sympathetic witnesses. Adare did not give evidence – perhaps he felt he had said enough already – but Lindsay was certainly there, and more than made up for the absence of his friend.

'I have frequently seen Home', Lindsay told the committee, 'go to the fire and take out red-hot coals, and carry them about in his hands, [and] put them inside his shirt.' Lindsay had confirmed the heat of the coals when he 'touched a coal with the middle finger of my right hand, and got a blister as large as a sixpence'. On another occasion, he continued, 'I saw Mr Home, in a trance, elongated eleven inches. I measured him standing up against the wall . . . I can swear that he was not off the ground or standing on tip-toe, as I had full view of his feet.' At one point, he 'was elongated horizontally on the ground; Lord Adare was present. Home seemed to grow at both ends, and pushed myself and Adare away.' He had, indeed, seen the most remarkable events, but perhaps too many and too remarkable. He had seen Daniel's eyes 'glowing with light', and he had seen, 'on my knee, a flame of fire about nine inches high'. He had once seen 'a crystal ball, placed on Mr Home's head, emit flashes of coloured light . . . After this it changed, and we all saw a view of the sea.' And, as if that were not enough, 'I saw a grand pianoforte raised in the air about four inches.' But seeing strange things was nothing new to Lord Lindsay. 'I used to see the spectre of a black dog,' he admitted. 'It seemed to glide along: I never saw it walking. I often went up to it and pushed my stick through it'.[6]

It was amid such wondrous tales of visions that Lindsay confirmed he had seen Daniel float out of one window and in through another. He got the address wrong, and he disagreed with Adare upon whether there was a balcony outside the window, and upon the width of the ledge, and later upon whether there was even a ledge. He agreed with Adare that it had been the third floor (though Adare later recalled it had been the first floor), and that it had been '85 feet from the ground' (he later said it had been seventy-five feet, which would still have made Ashley House taller than Buckingham Palace). Nevertheless, he was in no doubt of what he had seen, even if it had been in the dark, though he differed with Adare over how dark it had been: 'I have seen the levitations, but not in a brilliant light,' he admitted, stressing a moment later that 'I once saw Home in *full light* standing in the air seventeen inches from the ground.'[7]

Fortunately for Daniel, many other witnesses testified to having seen his extraordinary feats, and with greater consistency. Cromwell Varley told how he had investigated Daniel thoroughly, from a position of scepticism and fully aware of the vulnerability of the senses, and had been entirely satisfied. Robert Chambers was less helpful, merely writing a letter that avoided any statement of belief, though he did sign it. But Benjamin Coleman was present, and described how an accordion had floated into his hand and played 'Angels Ever Bright and

Fair'; how he had seen '*when Mr Home was absent* . . . a long dinner table rise up, supported only by its two end legs'; and how a wreath had floated from Daniel's head towards him. 'I took it,' Coleman recounted, 'placed it on my own head, and retained possession of it for many weeks afterward.' Daniel told the committee that he went to the theatre in order to stop dwelling upon the phenomena, and that he always felt sick after elongations. He also answered the various, and sometimes bizarre, questions of the committee. It was true, he replied, that there were male spirits and female spirits, and that they had 'passions and affections', but they did not have children. He had never, he insisted, seen a spirit dog; he had seen birds, but not fish; and he had seen an apparition of a flower, and one of a bottle, but never one of a potato.[8]

Less impressive mediums were also discussed, dividing some of the witnesses in their opinions. One witness had paid 'several half crowns' to the medium Mrs Marshall, without discovering any information. He had, however, seen 'a sort of cataleptic seizure of those present, which principally affected the ladies. They foamed at the mouth and shook each other. They began to talk nonsense.'[9] On another occasion, Mrs Marshall had contacted the lost missionary explorer, Dr Livingstone. The spirit, Dr Livingstone presumably, had explained that 'savages boiled his body and ate it'. When Livingstone was subsequently discovered alive in Africa, a spiritualist concluded that the spirit had simply lied. The chairman asked how he could distinguish between a lying spirit and a fraudulent medium. 'You cannot distinguish,' the spiritualist replied, 'but in that case it was the spirit that was lying.'[10]

All this took time, and when it was over there was much debate about what it all meant, which further delayed publication of the report. When it finally appeared, it became clear that the sub-committees had come to radically different conclusions. One group announced 'that motion may be produced in solid bodies without material contact, by some hitherto unrecognised force'; another admitted they had seen nothing worth recording; while members of the sub-committee investigating Daniel disagreed among themselves. And the overall conclusion after months of investigation was that 'the subject is worthy of more serious attention and careful investigation than it has hitherto received'.[11] It was a conclusion with which many would subsequently agree, some because they felt further serious enquiry was necessary, and some because they felt there had been no serious enquiry yet.

In the opinion of the *Morning Post*, the Dialectical Society report was 'entirely worthless', the *Pall Mall Gazette* called it 'contemptuous', and others dismissed it as 'a piece of absurdity'. '[T]he Report', declared *The Times*, 'turned out to be nothing more than a farrago of impotent conclusions, garnished by a mass of the most monstrous rubbish it has ever been our misfortune to sit in judgment upon.' As for the more playful *Sporting Times*, it denounced spiritualists as 'contemptibly stupid – insane I should say . . . Most of the Spiritualists with whom I am acquainted are vegetarians, teetotallers, anti-smokers, anti-vaccinators, and I know not what also. Perhaps this fact may help to explain their otherwise inexplicable folly.' The more scientifically minded *Athenaeum* drew upon the language of psychology. Daniel's friend Mr Jencken, who had presented a paper on the laws that regulate spiritualist phenomena, was diagnosed as 'an extremely absurd person', while his paper was dismissed as 'a really painful exhibition of mental disease'. 'The book will not fail to be talked about,' the journal admitted, 'but the talk, whatever else it may be, will not be complimentary.' As for Daniel, despite all the weird and wonderful accounts that had been given about him, it was his alleged levitation that was focused upon. Lindsay was dismissed by the journal as 'the subject of one of those optical illusions that often afflict people of feeble digestive powers and irregular habits'.[12] Other sections of the press admitted that they were baffled, but no more so than when they read of levitating Indian fakirs, and they wondered whether there was a point to it all.

Yet there remained those who felt it was their job to supply a more serious explanation for such extraordinary testimony. The psychologist W. B. Carpenter made reference to expectant attention, unconscious cerebration, trickery, self-deception and misinterpretation of observed facts. But for the most part, he gently dismissed Lindsay's account of the levitation as unreliable due to the inconsistency of his narrative, the fact that it had happened in the dark, and Lindsay's unreserved belief in the medium. It was, for Carpenter, simply further proof that reports are dictated by the subjective belief of the observer. '[B]elievers will affirm that they saw Mr Home float out of one window and in at the other,' he declared, 'whilst a single honest sceptic declares that Mr Home was sitting in his chair all the time.'[13] This striking difference in testimony between believers and 'a single honest sceptic' was, for him, sufficient proof that it had been a hallucination. It was also sufficient proof for a colleague, Dr Hammond, who concluded that 'It is scarcely necessary to pursue the matter any further.'

Spiritualists wondered who this 'single honest sceptic' was who had declared that Daniel had been sitting in his chair all the time. Hammond had assumed it must have been Captain Wynne, who had been the only other witness present at the Ashley House levitation, and who had never confirmed what Adare and Lindsay had seen. But when Wynne read of this, he immediately wrote to a spiritualist journal to confirm that he had indeed been a witness, and then wrote to Daniel to swear to his 'having gone out of the window and in at the other' (though he recalled that it had been eighty feet above ground).[14] Nevertheless, when

Carpenter next wrote about belief as the explanation for the imaginings of spiritualists, the first example he provided was Lindsay's account of 'Mr Home sailing in the air (by moonlight) out of one window and in at another'.[15] It was all too much for Alfred Russel Wallace, who demanded that Carpenter name his 'honest sceptic', and if he could not, then he should acknowledge that his own beliefs had led him to imagine things.[16]

The problem with the levitation at Ashley House was, once again, a problem of testimony. Three men of unimpeachable integrity had agreed upon the basics, but had disagreed upon much of the detail. It could be argued, and indeed it was, that the height of the levitation was hardly the point, any more than the date or the location. But it could also be argued that the details were crucial, since every discrepancy devalued the testimony; and if witnesses could not remember how dark it was, or how far apart the balconies were, or whether there was even a balcony, then how could one be sure Daniel had not simply stepped between the windows? For over a century the Ashley House levitation would be argued over by sceptics and believers: it would be denounced by Houdini, defended by Sir Arthur Conan Doyle, and debated by every generation since it happened – assuming it happened at all.

But in the immediate aftermath of the report, the bizarre nature of the testimony had to be weighed against the apparent reliability of the witnesses. And while many of the witnesses might easily be regarded as dubious, similarly extraordinary events were being confirmed by Cromwell Varley and Alfred Russel Wallace. 'The fact that some men, respectable in intellect and conversant with science, have testified their faith in the reality of the phenomena,' announced the *Telegraph*, 'makes it worth our while to investigate the matter with keener eyes than if the believers were all impulsive and unscientific observers.' Even *The Times* eventually agreed that 'if it proves nothing else it proves that it is high time competent hands undertook the unravelling of this Gordian knot'. With this in mind, *The Times* journalist actually attended some séances with Daniel, though he failed to unravel the knot any further. And so he complained that 'our scientific men have signally failed to do their duty by the public, which looks to them for its facts'.[17]

The publication of the report showed that, in the opinion of many, this was a scientific question, and one that had not yet been answered. Daniel's feats might be simple tricks, embellished by exaggeration and wishful thinking, but it was difficult for scientists to dismiss it all as nonsense when people such as Wallace and Varley were so adamant. 'I wish you to understand', Varley wrote to the physicist J. J. Thomson, 'that it is not a question of *belief* in the marvellous on our part, it is a case of *actual knowledge* that these phenomena *do* occur.' The question of belief would always be relevant, and the theories of Carpenter would continue to assert that it was a matter of expectant attention, hallucination and, occasionally, straightforward trickery on the part of the medium. And perhaps such theories might explain what was going on, but further investigation was clearly necessary, and by someone with solid scientific credentials.

There was one man who had already come to this conclusion, and by the time the Dialectical Society report was published, he had already begun experiments to discover what was really going on. His reputation as a scientist was impeccable, and he had set out with no prior agenda in mind. In the *Quarterly Journal of Science*, which he edited at the time, he declared that he had seen and heard enough to convince him that proper investigation was required. And so he announced, in 1870, that it was 'the duty of scientific men, who have learnt exact modes of working, to examine phenomena which attract the attention of the public'. With this he began a series of experiments involving Daniel, to test his abilities in a more scientific manner than had ever been the case before. This would be Daniel's greatest challenge, but if successful it would provide him with a unique scientific endorsement, and would change for ever how people spoke about the mysterious feats that he performed.

13

The first psychic

While the Dialectical Society had been debating, Daniel had been forced to consider more practical matters: he was still in debt, and no closer to obtaining Sacha's fortune. And though he had a son to support, he refused to sell the valuable jewels he had been given by royalty, despite being advised to by a friend. He was not homeless, nor was he hungry, for there was never a shortage of hosts and patrons who would help when needed. But his stubbornness demanded financial independence, and he continued to give public readings, despite his unpleasant encounter at Willis's Rooms. After all, his gift for reading poetry had been recognized in America, when his delivery of *Bay Fight* had brought the battle scene to such life that not only had a Southerner attacked him, but a friend had later remarked: 'I don't see how he could help flying at you.' Daniel did not relish the idea of giving readings in Britain, but times were tough and options were limited. So he toured the country, giving readings appropriate for an English audience, reciting Hamilton Aide and Tennyson. Aide had already attended one of his séances, and now Tennyson expressed a wish to sit with Daniel. Despite the fact that he had heard many stories from

Browning, Tennyson was 'much more inclined to believe than disbelieve'.[1] Daniel read in Liverpool, Glasgow and Edinburgh, was praised for his 'pathetic yet forcible rendering', and before long the press were describing him 'as one of our best readers [who] caused a marked sensation amongst the audience – many of whom were melted to tears'.

It was not an easy way of making a living, for there was no shortage of music hall acts who were equally eager for billing. Daniel's pathetic and forcible renderings had to compete with singers, dancers, comics and conjurors. In Edinburgh, he wrote that 'the agent here was very unwilling to engage me, and told me that readings "did not take" . . . that [the last reader] was a dead failure, and that [another] had been hissed off the platform'. In the end, he was engaged 'for a merely nominal sum', topping the bill above 'Miss Dunsmore, the favourite Scottish vocalist' and 'Mr J F Cook (of the Royal English Opera Company)'.[2] In such impressive company, he stepped on stage 'knowing that others had been hissed off', and with such disturbing thoughts in mind, 'went on with fear and trembling'. His readings won over the crowd, however, and he received 'round after round of applause, and such an encore. My every piece was encored.' Such was his boast as he wondered 'what the papers will say tomorrow'. Much to his disappointment, the *Scotsman* not only failed to review him, but claimed he had 'been engaged at great expense'.[3] The *Edinburgh Courant*, on the other hand, confirmed that he was 'loudly applauded', but noted that it was in part because 'Mr Home took occasion to explain that he was not, as was generally supposed, an American, but that his birthplace was within six miles of Edinburgh.'[4]

He could claim links with many parts of the world, and as the world changed, so did his employment prospects. In France, one of his former patrons, Napoleon III, was politically weak, unpopular at home and increasingly isolated internationally. He had even been denounced as the Anti-Christ by one concerned Christian from Philadelphia, partly because of his involvement in spiritualism, and partly because of his involvement in Mexico, but mainly because his life and reign had been predicted so clearly in the Book of Daniel. The proof of this, as provided by the concerned Philadelphian Christian, included the little-known fact that the name Louis-Napoleon (Napoleon III's previous title), when translated into Latin and Greek, and converted into numerals (with certain amendments), added up to 666.[5] There were, however, rather more serious concerns for the French Emperor in Europe. He had supported the expansion of Prussia under Bismarck, as long as it had weakened Austrian power, but Bismarck was now expanding too far for his liking, and so Napoleon declared war on Prussia. It was a dangerous gamble, and one that he lost. The Franco-Prussian war led to the end of the Second Empire and the emergence of the Second Reich, as France lost its last monarch and Germany gained its first. After the war, Napoleon left for retirement in England, and King William of Prussia accepted the crown of a new united Germany in the palace of Versailles.

The war correspondent of the *Daily Telegraph* wrote from Versailles: 'Among our party was Mr Daniel Home, the celebrated Spiritualist, whom the King promptly recognized, and addressed very kindly.' Daniel, who had conducted so many controversial séances for Napoleon III, had also impressed King William, who spoke to him, 'reminding him of the wonders that he (Mr Home) had been the means of imparting to him, and inquiring about "the spirits" in by no means a sceptical tone'. On the contrary, the King 'had told many of his friends of the wonderful manifestations he had seen in Mr Home's presence: [but] his friends did not believe him'.[6] The *Telegraph*'s war correspondent was none other than Lord Adare.

Adare had recently married – an event Daniel seems not to

have been enthusiastic about – and, following publication of his controversial book, he had taken a job that took him out of the country. At the same time, Daniel tried yet another line of work for which he seemed entirely unsuited: he became war correspondent for the *San Francisco Chronicle*, and the two men had set off to cover the Franco-Prussian war. They were at the front of the Battle of Sedan, and witnessed the destruction and human suffering of the siege of Paris. Daniel managed to rescue a wounded German officer – who subsequently thanked him for saving his life – but suffered great stress from being surrounded by so much pain and starvation. On one occasion he befriended a German sergeant who was talking to some French children. The soldier spoke no French, but, being the father of eight, believed the children could understand him. Daniel was moved, and gave a cigar to the soldier; later that same day he found the man dead, with the unsmoked cigar in his pocket.

As the tragedy of war took its toll on him, the sensitive medium left France to recuperate in Russia, and prepared for his next personal battle. It would not be a matter of life and death, not even in the sense that spiritualists might regard their creed. It would be a matter of science, truth and understanding. At least that is how it might be interpreted, though nothing so contentious could ever be so simple. It was now the spring of 1871, and he returned to London, to face the scientist who would test him as no one else had done, and Daniel's particular place in history would finally be decided.

William Crookes had been elected a Fellow of the Royal Society on his first application, at the age of 31. He was, among other things, the editor of *Chemical News*, chemistry being his particular area of expertise, but his primary claim to fame was that he had discovered the element thallium, using his own pioneering method of observation known as spectroscopy. His scientific colleagues had accepted his findings and his place in the history of science had been guaranteed. Now he was about to begin a new series of observations and experiments, with a view to discovering something considerably more controversial than thallium, and with which his scientific colleagues would have much more difficulty – and his place in the history of science was about to be modified.

It did not take long before his plans were made public, and not in the way he had intended. 'Mr Crookes, editor of the Chemical News', announced the *Athenaeum* in its 'Science Gossip' column, 'is engaged in an investigation on spiritualism, but, it is said, with far from satisfactory results.'[7] This was frustrating for Crookes, who complained that they might have waited until he was ready to announce what he had found. But now that the news was out, he felt he should explain his reasons for such a controversial endeavour. At first, he had believed that the phenomena of the séance room were the product of 'superstition, or at least, an unexplained trick'. But through informal observation, he had become convinced that 'certain phenomena . . . occur under circumstances in which they cannot be explained by any physical law at present known'. This, he declared, was 'a fact of which I am as certain as I am of the most elementary fact in chemistry'. He dismissed the view of Michael Faraday that a scientist should set out with a clear idea of what was possible and impossible in nature, for until science knew everything, it did not know what was possible or impossible.[8] The job of the scientist was to investigate through careful experimentation, not to reject phenomena as impossible without proper enquiry. And while there had been countless extraordinary reports from séances, there had not yet been proper scientific enquiry. Indeed, where he did agree with Faraday was that many dogs were capable of coming to more logical conclusions than spiritualists. The conditions of the séance room were open to fraud, and the observations of spiritualists were suspect, and all this amateur talk of animal magnetism and electricity was meaningless. '[T]he real workers of science', Crookes warned his colleagues, 'must be extremely careful not to allow the reins to get into unfit and incompetent hands.'

Science, he argued, could deal both with fraud and inadequate observation by providing properly controlled conditions and appropriate instruments of measurement. And a scientific man did not require the extravagance of human levitation, he merely asked that a power 'which will toss a heavy body up to the ceiling, shall also cause his delicately-poised balance to move under test conditions'. In the testing of the existence of any new force it was quality, rather than quantity, that mattered. 'The Spiritualist tells of heavy articles of furniture moving,' he pointed out. 'But the man of science . . . is justified in doubting the accuracy of the former observations if the same force is powerless to move the index of his instrument one poor degree.' It was in this attitude of open-minded scepticism, and with complete faith in the objectivity of experimental measurement, that Crookes announced his intention to examine the phenomena, 'in order to confirm their genuineness, or to explain, if possible, the delusions of the honest and to expose the tricks of the deceivers'. Whatever happened, scientific methods would 'drive the worthless residuum of spiritualism hence into the unknown limbo of magic and necromancy'.[9] All he needed were some phenomena to test and a subject capable of being tested, and there the choice was simple enough.

Nobody else had shown such willingness as Daniel to be tested, or been so successful when under scrutiny. He had been introduced to Crookes by the wonderfully adventurous Lady Burton, widow of that equally wonderful and adventurous

Oriental traveller and scholar Sir Richard Burton. And two of the many phenomena reported in Daniel's presence were particularly suitable for scientific experiment: the alteration of the weight of objects; and the playing of instruments, normally an accordion, without human contact. Both could be tested in controlled conditions that eliminated the possibility of fraud, and neither could easily be dismissed as hallucination in the way that, for example, spirit hands might be. And so Crookes went about setting up a laboratory in his London home, and constructing foolproof test procedures that would rule out the possibility of lazy-tongs, self-playing accordions, magic lanterns and such things. And if these experiments led to positive results, they would confirm the reality of Daniel's feats. When all was ready, he invited Daniel to be tested at his domestic laboratory at 22, Mornington Road.

When Daniel arrived, Crookes was not alone. With him were two men who would verify what was to happen, for Crookes did not want to be accused of inaccuracy, or lack of proper observation, or perhaps of having been mesmerized by Daniel. The force he was investigating was so controversial that sceptical scientists would suggest any alternative explanation rather than accept its existence. So in attendance was, firstly, William Huggins, a gentleman astronomer who had pioneered observation of celestial bodies. Huggins had demonstrated that stars were made of the same elements found on the sun and earth; he had examined the emission of gas from novas and of light from comets, and had attempted to measure the speed of stars. This evening, however, the acute observer of otherworldly phenomena was to observe events closer to home.

Alongside Huggins was Edward Cox, a Serjeant-at-Law and former MP who had a keen interest in the phenomena being tested. Cox had attended many séances, and was considered by some a balanced observer. He had denounced certain mediums as frauds, upsetting many spiritualists in the process, but he had no doubts that some of the extraordinary phenomena he had witnessed were genuine, and he had the utmost faith in Daniel. So Huggins and Cox, along with the discoverer of thallium and a laboratory assistant, set about testing the world's greatest spirit medium, to determine finally whether he was genuine or fraudulent.

The somewhat strange apparatus for the first experiment was set up on one side of the room. There was a table and chair, and beneath the table a steel cylindrical cage. Inside the cage was a brand-new accordion that Crookes had bought himself, and which Daniel had neither handled nor seen before. Daniel sat down, placed his hand within the cage, and held the accordion, keys downwards, with thumb and middle finger at the other end. From this position, with his every movement being watched by witnesses on either side, he was expected to have the accordion play.

'Very soon,' Crookes reported, 'the accordion was seen by those on each side to be waving about in a somewhat curious manner; then sounds came from it, and finally several notes were played in succession.' Crookes's assistant went under the table, and saw that Daniel's hand 'was quite still', yet 'the accordion was expanding and contracting'. It then began 'oscillating and going round and round the cage, and playing at the same time'. As the observers confirmed Daniel's hands and feet had not moved, 'a simple air was played'. Daniel then took the accordion out of the cage 'and placed it in the hand of the person next to him. The instrument then continued to play, no person touching it and no hand being near it.' Moments later, they 'saw the accordion distinctly floating about inside the cage with no visible support'.

Next they moved over to the other side of the room, to the scene of the second experiment. There was another table, and attached to its edge was the end of a thirty-six-inch mahogany board. The board extended horizontally from the table, its far end being supported by a spring balance that hung from above. Daniel placed his fingertips on the near end of the board, which was resting on a support at the end of the table. In this position, rather like having a see-saw with the fulcrum at one end, no amount of pushing down at this end could move the other end. Nevertheless, his task was to affect the weight of the board, which would be measured by the spring balance at the other end. Crookes and Huggins stood on either side, 'watching for any effect which might be produced. . . . Almost immediately, the pointer of the balance was seen to descend. After a few seconds it rose again. This movement was repeated several times . . . The [far] end of the board was observed to oscillate slowly up and down during the experiment.' Daniel then placed two small objects, a card matchbook and a small hand-bell, between his fingers and the board, to show that he was not exerting any

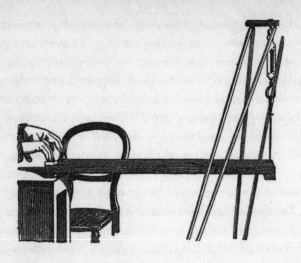

downward pressure. 'The very slow oscillation of the spring balance became more marked,' Crookes reported, and Huggins saw it gradually descend to an additional downward pull of three-and-a-half pounds. To check that Daniel could not have done this by pushing, Crookes stood on top of the end of the board, but even when he 'jerked up and down', he could not move the index more than two pounds. Daniel had been sitting in an easy chair, 'his feet as well as his hands closely guarded by all in the room'.

In July Crookes made the announcement. It appeared in the *Quarterly Journal of Science*, of which he was also the editor.[10] It might have been published elsewhere had his fellow scientists allowed it, and it might not have appeared at all had Crookes not been the editor. It went as follows: 'These experiments appear conclusively to establish the existence of a new force, in some unknown manner connected with the human organisation, which for convenience may be called the Psychic Force.'

The term was certainly convenient: Cox had already suggested it. 'I venture to suggest', he had written to Crookes the previous month, 'that the force be termed *Psychic Force*; [and] the persons in whom it is manifested in extraordinary power, *Psychics*.' Crookes, it seems, agreed on the term, to avoid lengthy or confusing words. 'I have ventured to give the name of Psychic', he explained, 'to avoid periphrasis.' He also avoided explaining what the term 'psychic' meant, other than to say it was as good as any other. As for 'the correlation existing between that and the other forces of nature', he admitted, 'it would be wrong to hazard the most vague hypothesis'. Nevertheless, the term was born, and Crookes acknowledged that it was only with Daniel's co-operation that he was 'enabled to affirm so conclusively the existence of this Force'. Daniel had been the subject of the experiments that had given to the world a psychic force; it was in him that this force was strongest, and it was only in him that this force had been experimentally verified. So it was that Daniel Dunglas Home became the world's first psychic. There only remained the question of whether anyone might disagree.

Crookes's announcement, the press reported, 'set all London on fire, and the Spiritualists rabid with excitement'.[11] Their excitement was hardly surprising: the extraordinary events they had so often witnessed, that had been regularly dismissed as imposture and delusion, had been tested by a renowned scientist and confirmed as genuine. Perhaps, finally, all those accusations of gullibility and incompetent observation, all those condescending looks and hints at mental illness, would now give way to a more open-minded enquiry. But however excited spiritualists were, they were not entirely happy, for they did not agree with Crookes. It was important that a man with his credentials had both investigated the phenomena and publicly stated what he had found, and he deserved the greatest respect for having the courage to do so. But he had explained the phenomena in terms of a Psychic Force, and that was hardly spiritualism. If anything, it was precisely the opposite. Crookes had avoided saying anything about how this force might operate; he had refused to theorize on any cause, but he had been clear that this was a natural, not a supernatural, force. And Cox was equally clear on this, that 'assertors of a Psychic Force . . . hold it to be a purely physical phenomena, and wholly within the domain of science'.

It was, of course, the physical domain with which science dealt; it did not have the vocabulary to speak of spirits, unless to dismiss them entirely. And spiritualists had no problem with a psychic force, if that is what scientists wished to call it; this force was simply a means through which the spirits interacted with this world. For spiritualists, spirits were the cause behind the psychic effect, and not to mention them was to miss the point entirely. They might at last have had their phenomena validated by science, but they had lost the spirits in the process. Their main consolation was that the argument had shifted, the facts had been established – and established by science. Now it was a matter of arguing that only a spiritual theory could explain the facts.

However, scientific facts were not that simple, even without spirits; science was not merely the observation of facts but the construction of theory to explain such facts. And until one could provide an acceptable theory, a plausible explanation for how such facts occurred, it could not be considered proper scientific knowledge. And when the facts reported were so controversial, when they flew in the face of existing ideas of how the world worked, not to mention the day-to-day experience of most people, they were never going to gain immediate acceptance. They were, after all, only facts as reported by observers, and the problem of testimony was well known, as was the vulnerability of the senses. So when scientists reacted to Crookes, it was in much the same way that they had reacted to non-scientists, which was not at all what Crookes had expected.

It was not that they did not take him seriously: on the contrary. Professor Balfour Stewart, a renowned physicist, responded in the journal *Nature*, at that time a new but already influential scientific journal. He admitted that Crookes's experimental results posed a problem: a problem of testimony, 'one of extreme difficulty'. What does one do with testimony, Stewart asked, assuming the witness is not trying to deceive us, and that he has not been deceived himself? Even then, the experience reported might be subjective rather than objective, one that might be caused by an electro-biologist or mesmerist. Though we know such altered states can be induced, we do not know 'under what conditions one man is capable of influencing another, or whether a man or body of men may not be capable of influencing themselves'. And the fact that séance phenomena have never, as far as he knew, been witnessed 'in broad daylight before a large unbiased audience, would lead us to suspect that they may be subjective rather than objective, occurring in the imaginations of those present'. And much as Crookes's experiments 'deserve the greatest respect', and even though he used precise measuring apparatus rather than simply relying upon his own observation, 'what avails the most perfect instrument as long as we suspect the operator to be under a mental influence?' In short, Crookes might be a scientist, and he might have used scientific instruments, but even scientists can be hypnotized, and he might only have thought he saw the instruments move.

It was one thing to dismiss visitors to a séance as the victims of hallucination, but to suggest that a scientist's experiments might have been imagined was enough to start a whole new argument. The theory that Daniel might mesmerize his audiences was hardly new, and the fact that every expert in mesmerism who had witnessed him had ruled this out had already made it, at best, a partial explanation. But to apply the same argument to a scientific experiment was to undermine the authority of scientific observation. Crookes was a chemist, Huggins an astronomer: they were 'men accustomed to weigh the evidence of their senses with the utmost caution', a reader of *Nature* pointed out. 'When such men testify that some mysterious force acted upon a lever,' the critic continued, 'we should be as ready to believe them as if Dr Huggins announced a new planet or Mr Crookes a new metal; their testimony is as valuable in the one case as in the other.' But this was not how others saw it, and the testimony of Crookes continued to be questioned, until he was forced to respond.

When first embarking on the project, he pointed out, various periodicals had expressed their faith in his ability to discover the truth, but now that the facts were not as they had hoped, 'so much the worse for the facts'. Some people 'have fallen into the error of regarding me as an advocate for certain *opinions*', he complained, and 'Having evolved men of straw from their own imagination, they proceed vigorously to slay them under the impression that they are annihilating me.' Not only had some suggested he had been mesmerized, but others 'have gone so far as to question my veracity'. This was 'an argument I cannot condescend to answer', he complained, 'accustomed as I am to hav[ing] my word believed.' He was a scientist, in the business of observing and reporting facts, and 'All who know me . . . will, I hope, take it for granted that the facts I lay before them are correct.' They might complain that such facts are impossible, but whether possible or not they were true, he insisted, and if Faraday had taken the time to test Mr Home, he would have observed the same facts. To reject new facts was an unscientific attitude, one that 'has been opposed to all great discoveries'.[12] Thus, he defended his new scientific facts against the unscientific conservatism of his critics, and waited to see what suggestions they might come up with next.

'Is Mr D. D. Home a were-wolf?' asked E. B. Tylor in an unexpected development. Tylor was one of the first anthropologists, and was responding to the idea that reports of humans transforming into werewolves might be explained by a mesmeric experience induced by the 'were-wolf'. The idea had been proposed by Alfred Russel Wallace, and was a criticism of Tylor's own theory that werewolf beliefs were simply the product of superstition and insanity. Tylor's response was to attack Wallace's belief in the equally strange phenomena of spiritualism, and suggest that mediums such as Daniel had 'the power of acting on the minds of sensitive spectators, so as to make them believe they see what he pleases'. This argument did nothing to influence Wallace, who pointed out that he himself was an experienced mesmerizer, that what happened at Mr Home's séances was quite different, and that not only had the most experienced mesmerists ruled this out, but many had actually become spiritualists. This did not convince everyone either, but at least the theory that Daniel was a werewolf was not discussed in *Nature* again.[13]

As for the theory that psychic phenomena were purely subjective, Crookes was confident he could deal with that line of criticism. He had thought his scientific credentials would be sufficient to establish the facts, and had not expected to be told that he had simply imagined it all. Nevertheless, he was sure his scientific critics could not continue along these lines. As he pointed out in the clearest possible terms, the very idea that any new scientific discovery might be explained as a hallucination of the experimenter would, he declared, 'entirely stop the whole progress of research in any branch of science'.[14] He encouraged his colleagues to carry out similar experiments, and as others obtained similar results, he felt confident his new discovery would be verified. '[I]t cannot be many years before the subject will be brought before the scientific world in a way that will enforce attention,' he wrote to a sceptical colleague, confessing that he was driven 'by the desire of being the first scientific experimenter who has ventured to take such a course'.[15] And as he contemplated his place in the history of science, he continued to refine his experiments so as to remove all possible criticisms.

There had been vague suggestions that somehow Daniel had pushed on the board in such a way as to affect the spring balance, and so Crookes designed a new set-up in which Daniel made no contact with the board whatsoever. A container of water was placed upon the board, and Daniel was required simply to place his hand into the water. In such a position, he could not possibly push down upon the board, yet the psychic force could operate through the water. In response to other critics, Crookes also used an instrument that recorded a trace of any changes in the weight of the board. Once again he obtained positive results, and in an obvious jibe at Balfour Stewart, he pointed out that even if Daniel had 'biologised' the experimenters, 'it will hardly be contended that Mr Home biologised the recording instruments'.[16]

Convinced of the importance of his findings, Crookes submitted a paper to the Royal Society. The man chiefly responsible for considering its worth was Sir George Gabriel Stokes, a mathematician and physicist, Lucasian professor of mathematics at Cambridge, and secretary of the Royal Society. Crookes knew and had worked with Professor Stokes. Only a few years earlier, in fact, Crookes had received a grant from the Royal Society to carry out research into spectroscopy, and had collaborated with Stokes. Things had gone so well that Crookes later admitted: 'If what I owe to Stokes is deducted from my work there will be precious little left I can claim for my own!'[17]

But that was spectroscopy, and this was a Psychic Force, and when it came to a Psychic Force, neither Stokes nor the Society was in the mood for similar assistance. The existence of such a force was a challenge to the existing laws of physics, and the argument that a competent scientist might imagine his results was an insult to competent scientists. There was, however, an alternative argument, one that could reconcile Crookes's results with the laws of physics, and could protect the reputation and authority of competent scientists. The argument was simple: Crookes's results were wrong because Crookes was incompetent. And so, whether they really believed this or not, certain senior members of the scientific establishment began to attack Crookes's reputation.

It began in a reasonable enough manner, with Stokes replying to Crookes's papers to claim that he had found some possible error in his experiments. Stokes did not wish to meet Daniel, nor did he wish to see the effects, though he would like to see the apparatus, but he did not have time. In any case, he was not convinced that, in the first experiment, Daniel could not have pushed down on the board, and the second experiment was no more convincing. When Daniel had placed his hand in the water, this would have caused a displacement of the water in the container, which in turn would have increased the weight of the container by the weight of the displaced water. If the container was not exactly above the fulcrum of the board, this would have caused a very slight see-saw effect, which would have been registered on the spring balance as a change in weight at the end of the board. This, of course, was basic physics, and Crookes was quick to reply. Daniel had dipped only the tips of his fingers into the water, while he himself had immersed his hand in the container yet failed to register any change in weight, so this could not possibly account for the result. In any case, he had moved the bowl exactly above the fulcrum, so no additional weight at that point could alter the spring balance at the end of the board. And when Stokes casually suggested that some minor tremors might have been caused by 'a passing train or omnibus', Crookes pointed out that he had not obtained 'mere tremors . . . but a steady vertical pull of from 4 to 8 lbs'. Stokes did not continue the debate, however, and Crookes was left wondering what he and the Royal Society thought about his work.

Three weeks later, much to his surprise, Crookes read in the news that the Royal Society was quite open to 'the existence of a force in nature as yet unknown', providing there was 'scientific evidence adequate to establish its probability'. However, the article continued, the experiments of Crookes showed 'an entire want of scientific precision', and his paper 'was not regarded as one deserving the attention of the Royal Society'. Crookes promptly wrote to the newspaper, demanding to know the basis for this unwarranted allegation, only to discover that it was 'not founded on mere rumour. The words we used contained an exact copy of the words [used] . . . by one of the secretaries [of the Royal Society], Professor Stokes.' Why Stokes had published this rejection so publicly in the press, in such insulting language and without a formal response, Crookes found himself 'unable to explain'.

He was not defeated, however, and sent off another paper to the British Association for the Advancement of Science, and this time he received a formal response. The referee had not had sufficient time to read the paper, so was obliged to 'be hasty'. In short, he was not convinced, and 'I don't see much use discussing the thing in the sections, crowded as we are already.' If others wanted to volunteer to investigate the subject further, 'I don't see any objection to appointing such a committee. . . . I have heard too much of the tricks of Spiritualists to make me willing to give my time to such a committee myself.' The official report by the British Association on Crookes's paper was signed by Sir George Gabriel Stokes.[18]

Crookes's article was reprinted in *English Mechanic*, provoking further reaction. The chemist John Spiller, who had attended some séances, though not the tests on which Crookes's paper was based, had witnessed Daniel's accordion effect, and claimed he had discovered the method. He had said nothing at the time, and had actually agreed with Crookes on what had occurred at the séance; but now he had realized the secret. Alas, all he would divulge was that it had something to do with a 'monster locket attached to Mr Home's watch-chain'. Whatever this was supposed to mean, Spiller also claimed that Crookes's fellow experimenters had been threatened with legal action unless they signed his account of the experiments. This was a claim Crookes found 'intrinsically absurd', given that this was supposed to have happened at the home of Edward Cox, a lawyer. When it came to Spiller's ambiguous theory about how the accordion effect might have been faked, Crookes was more threatening. 'I advise Mr Spiller to keep silent about this "monster" locket in future,' he warned, 'or, like a second Frankenstein, he will find he has conjured up a monster from his own inward consciousness which will devour his reputation.' This seems to have worked, as Spiller promptly withdrew his allegation.[19]

Meanwhile, across the Atlantic, more specific criticisms were made of Crookes's experiments, though not based on any deeper understanding. A 'leading American scientific engineer' by the name of Sellers wrote to the *Journal of the Franklin Institute* to say he had suspicions about the board used by Crookes. According to a book he owned, a mahogany board of the dimensions described should have weighed more than thirteen pounds, not six pounds as Crookes had stated. He wondered, therefore, where this board had come from, and who had made it? Perhaps Daniel had supplied it, which would make the experimental results look rather suspicious.

Crookes explained, with his patience at a limit, that he had weighed the board himself, and could guarantee that, whatever Mr Sellers' book told him, the board he used weighed six pounds. And as he had owned it for about sixteen years, he had to confess, with a hint of sarcasm, 'I am sorry I cannot inform Mr Sellers who made my mahogany board.' But as for whether he had used a board supplied by Daniel, 'is it seriously expected that I should answer such a question . . . Will not my critics give me credit for the possession of some amount of common sense?'[20]

His critics had only begun, however, and a devastating attack soon appeared in the *Quarterly Review*, a serious high-brow journal.[21] The article, 'Spiritualism and its recent Converts', was anonymous, but the author was obvious from the importance he placed upon the work of W. B. Carpenter. The phenomena of spiritualism could all be explained by expectant attention, unconscious cerebration and ideo-motor action, the anonymous author pointed out, as Carpenter had already shown. This was considered a satisfactory explanation by 'the highly intelligent class, to whom it was immediately addressed', and 'by the ablest of our physiologists and psychologists'. It was not appreciated by those predisposed to believe, who lacked 'scientific culture', were deficient in 'practical good sense' and, as Carpenter has already remarked, 'are no more to be argued with than are insane patients'. As for the larger physical phenomena, they were probably all conjuring tricks. Scientific enquiry was desirable, but spiritualism had already been investigated by eminent scientists, such as Faraday and Carpenter, and they had shown it to be nonsense. Now along had come Crookes, claiming he had discovered something that they could not.

Carpenter then proceeded with his anonymous criticisms. Crookes 'knew nothing whatever' of the investigations of other scientists, 'was entirely ignorant of the previous history of the subject, and was not even acquainted with the mode in which Professor Faraday had demonstrated the real nature of Table-turning'. His co-experimenter, Huggins, 'is one of a class of scientific amateurs', a specialist in his field but suffering from 'a want of that broad basis of *general* scientific culture'. He might possess certain 'powers of observation', but he had no training in 'the strict modes of experimental enquiry', and 'his simple trustingness' made him particularly open to deception. This was intended to be 'as little offensive as possible to Dr. Huggins', who was, after all, Vice-President of the Royal Society, though he was casually reminded that this was a 'distinguished office he at present holds by favour of the President'.

Fortunately for Carpenter, 'dealing with Mr Crookes is much less difficult'. The discoverer of thallium had 'made creditable use of his very limited opportunities', and he had been 'rewarded by the Fellowship of the Royal Society', but 'this distinction was conferred on him with considerable hesitation'. His abilities were 'purely technical', he was 'a specialist of specialists, being totally destitute of any knowledge of Chemical Philosophy', and was 'utterly untrustworthy [in] any inquiry which requires more than technical knowledge'. As for the third of the party, Edward Cox, he was briefly dismissed as 'one of the most gullible of the gullible, [depending upon] what appeals to his organ of Wonder'.

So much for the experimenters – but what of the experiments? The board experiment was simply invalid, since there had been no measurement of 'the *actual downward pressure* of Mr Home's fingers' on the board. This would have been 'the very first step in the inquiry if Professor Faraday had been conducting it'. However, Mr Home probably 'managed to impart a rhythmical motion to the board', by pushing on it 'while the attention of the witnesses was kept fixed upon the index, three feet off'. This was nothing more than the misdirection of the conjuror. As for the experiment using a bowl of water, this 'was really produced by the tremor occasioned in Mr Crookes's house by the passage of a railway-train'. And this was 'not an invention of our own', Carpenter anonymously assured his readers, 'but a fact communicated to us by a highly intelligent witness, who was admitted to one of Mr Crookes's séances'. As for the accordion effect, it was under a table, inside a cage, the notes were vague and the witnesses unreliable. In any case, 'the performance on this instrument *with one hand* is a juggling trick often exhibited at country fairs'. And before he finished, Carpenter took a swipe at Cromwell Varley, who was also little more than a technician, and whose 'scientific attainments are so cheaply estimated . . . he had never been admitted to the Royal Society'.

It was not Carpenter's first denunciation of spiritualism and spiritualists, but this time he had gone too far. According to the *Birmingham Morning News*, the 'leading scientific men of the metropolis; whatever they think of the particular investigations of Mr Crookes, they are unanimous in expressing their denunciations of this article in the Quarterly'. Even the title was inaccurate, the paper pointed out, speaking of recent converts to spiritualism. Thus, 'Mr Crookes is a spiritualist because he explicitly denies the fundamental tenet of Spiritualism, and Dr Huggins is a spiritualist because he says nothing whatever about it.'[22]

From Crookes's point of view it was a string of misrepresentations and outright falsehoods. For one thing, he pointed out, Varley was actually a Fellow of the Royal Society. As for himself, Carpenter's accusation that he was ignorant of Faraday's experiments was 'utterly false'. He had been shown Faraday's device by Faraday himself, and had used it ever since. Carpenter would have realised this, but when he met Crookes, he had refused to listen to him. According to Crookes, Carpenter had insisted he could explain everything by unconscious cerebration and unconscious muscular action, and had proceeded to do so with 'a stream of unconscious egotism'. To refute the charge that he was a 'specialist of specialists', Crookes provided a long list of achievements in a variety of areas. And as for his fellowship being awarded with 'considerable hesitation' – he had been invited and accepted upon his first application, an event somewhat rare for a man who was only thirty-one at the time.[23] The Royal Society itself admitted that this allegation was unfortunate, and the admission was published in the *Telegraph*, though not until May of the following year.

Meanwhile, Carpenter gave lectures in which he informed the public that Crookes's experiments were 'good for nothing'. He pointed out, as Stokes had done, that when Daniel's hand was dipped in the water, this would have caused an increase in the weight, and if the container had not been over the fulcrum, this would have affected the spring balance. He even demonstrated this by placing a glass of water on a scale and dipping his finger into the water to show the increase in weight. When Crookes again complained about this misrepresentation, that he had dealt with this by placing the container exactly over the fulcrum, Carpenter replied that his understanding of the experiment was 'on the authority' of Professor Stokes. When Crookes then wrote to Stokes, he in turn claimed that he could not remember exactly what he had told Carpenter, but that the latter might have confused the details with an earlier conversation. Carpenter assured Crookes that if he had misrepresented his experiments, he would correct this. If he ever did, it was not as publicly as he had misrepresented them.[24]

The details, of course, were lost on the majority of the public, who could hardly be expected to keep up with all the accusations and refutations. For many, it was simply a matter of how plausible they found the idea of a Psychic Force, or even of spiritual intervention, and then a question of whose expertise they trusted. Newspapers were not so quick to dismiss Crookes's scientific credentials, and neither were their readers. When a letter to *The Times* claimed that 'No really scientific man believes in Spiritualism', the letter-writer was reminded that Crookes, Varley and Wallace were clearly 'scientific men'.[25] And when, during the British Association conference of 1871, Professor Allen Thomson denounced all spiritualistic phenomena, the local paper responded immediately. An editorial stated that the paper was by no means an advocate of spiritualism, but it regarded Thomson's remark as unscientific, since equally qualified scientists had investigated and testified to the reality of some phenomena.[26] A similar position was taken by London's *Evening Standard*, which dismissed Carpenter's criticisms of séance phenomena as weak. He had selected 'a few of the most extravagant and imperfectly attested stories about spiritual phenomena, and dismissed them with little sarcasms that involved no argument whatever . . . We do not want to side with the spiritualists,' the *Standard* continued, 'but it would be an affectation at the present day to say what a year or two back we might have been entitled to say – that no evidence is before the world in support of their views that demands respectful consideration.'[27]

And so the world considered this new evidence, and the implications of what it all meant. As scientists, the press and the public differed on the topic, everybody who was anybody, and many who were not, had to decide what to make of Daniel Dunglas Home. Harriet Beecher Stowe was deeply impressed, and wrote to George Eliot to find out what she thought. 'I desire on all subjects to keep an open mind,' Eliot replied, but 'He is an object of moral disgust to me, and nothing of late reported by Mr Crookes, Lord Lindsay and the rest carries conviction to my mind that Mr Hume is not simply an impostor.'[28] Charles Darwin, on the other hand, was deeply troubled. 'If you had called here after I had read the article,' he confessed to Lady Derby, 'you would have found a much perplexed man. I cannot disbelieve Mr Crookes's statement, nor can I believe in his result.'[29] Francis Galton, then General Secretary of the British Association, decided it was worth seeing for himself. He was so impressed with what he saw that he wrote to Darwin. 'The playing of the accordion, held by its base by one hand under the table', he told Darwin, 'was extra-ordinary.' He suspected Crookes was 'thoroughly scientific', and that further investigation was 'well worth going into'. Providing that Home would 'put himself at our disposal', he asked Darwin, 'will you go in for it, and allow me to join? . . . if I could *ensure a dozen séances*, at which only our two selves and Home were together'.

Darwin was certainly interested, and wrote an encouraging letter to Crookes, and a 'very kind' letter to Daniel, but he was, for the moment, extremely ill. 'I regret it,' he told Galton, 'but I dare not accept Mr Home's extremely liberal offer.' He was 'too weak to go out', at least for the present, but he suggested the use of new experimental apparatus, and begged Galton, 'Do not give up yourself.' Galton persisted, and sent 'a letter of overtures to Home' along with Darwin's suggestions, 'but got no reply'. Three days later, he wrote back to Darwin that 'The spiritualists have given me up, I fear. I can't get another invitation to a séance.' A week later, he wrote again: 'I wonder if I have offended Home by my last letter to him – he has never replied.' Five months passed without a response, as Crookes assured Galton 'that Home's presence was very important, for the experiments were far more successful when he was the medium than when anyone else was'. Finally, Darwin was informed that Daniel had left the country. 'He is now in Russia,' Galton patiently explained, 'and will not return until May. So I wait.'[30]

And so he waited, and so did Darwin, but Daniel never replied. It was said that he fled to avoid their scrutiny, that perhaps he realized he would finally be found out. He had already been tested and declared to be genuine, so why take a chance with the most influential scientist of the century? Perhaps this was true, but Daniel had another reason for leaving: his personal life had once again predominated over his glorious mission. As Crookes was defending his scientific reputation, and attempting to convince his colleagues of this new force, the first psychic was still in financial difficulty. He had therefore returned to Russia in the hope of finally gaining possession of his late wife's inheritance. The trip was not entirely enjoyable, for in Moscow he was accosted by Count Leo Tolstoy, who said to him: 'I am surprised and disgusted', then left without further explanation.[31] The journey proved successful, however, and his finances were at last made secure. They were then improved further by a second marriage, again to a member of the Russian nobility. Julie de Gloumeline was the daughter of an Imperial Councillor, and sister-in-law of Professor Boutlerow, Professor of Chemistry at the University of St Petersburg. Boutlerow also tested Daniel, and obtained impressive results with his brother-in-law.

But further experiments with scientists, for one reason or another, were not something Daniel desired. Instead, in early 1872, he published the second volume of his autobiography, which described the evidence given at the Lyon versus Home trial in great detail, yet ended without mentioning the verdict. By April, he and his wife were living in Paris, where a daughter was born in the summer, and where she died in the autumn. She was buried in the cemetery at St Germain-en-

Laye, where Daniel himself would finally rest. And it seemed at this point that it might not be so long before he joined her. Following the death of the infant, his tubercular condition worsened, and he and his wife took to spending winter in Nice. He visited England in 1873, but didn't get in touch with Darwin or Galton. His declining health, and his improved finances, meant that he had neither the energy nor the need to prove himself again. Though he had never really been a professional medium, Daniel effectively retired, and was never to return to Britain.

Perhaps he felt that his mission was over, that he had done as much to convince the infidel as anybody could. Despite all the accusations and attempts to expose him, his feats remained a mystery. He might have been a charlatan with a mesmeric personality, but he had now been tested in experimental conditions, and many who felt that spiritualism was nonsense were beginning to wonder whether Daniel, at least, had genuine powers. Such was the authority of a scientific experiment. He had always relied upon the word of others that fraud was impossible, and now that Crookes had put his own reputation on the line, his critics were struggling to dismiss him as an unreliable observer. Perhaps significantly, it was Crookes who was now being accused and insulted. Daniel neither needed nor wanted further controversy.

Darwin never managed to attend a séance with Daniel, and his initial interest would soon turn to dismissiveness. This was not Daniel's fault, however, for the mediums who followed the first psychic would often cause such reactions. Though they seemed to be capable of even more remarkable feats than Daniel, they would run the risk of going too far, and would often do so with disastrous results. And so it gradually became apparent to spiritualists that the facts had yet to be established after all, as Crookes's reputation as a reliable observer was threatened by suspicions of incompetence. The situation would eventually reach the point where Daniel would be forced out of retirement to publish his final book. Its purpose would not be to convert the infidel but to denounce both mediums and spiritualists, to expose the former and embarrass the latter by revealing certain secrets that had never been revealed before. In the process, he would earn the gratitude of enemies and the hostility of friends, who would accuse him of worse than being a werewolf. But before all that, there was the matter of his being compared to Jesus.

14

The last word

Daniel's remaining years were spent in France, Italy and Russia, living as comfortably as his health and finances would allow. And as he enjoyed his retirement, and Victorian scientists struggled to respond to the idea of a Psychic Force, Christians considered the implications for the miracles of the Bible. They had been finding it difficult lately to argue that the ancient miracles were true, for all kinds of testimony were being questioned these days. It was being said that no scientific man believed in the creation story of Genesis, and of other biblical miracles it was stated that 'if Christianity rested on their veracity, it would surely come to ground'.[1] Yet miraculous phenomena seemed to be occurring in contemporary drawing rooms, and the growing body of evidence that suggested these miracles might actually be real was leading many Christians to wonder whether spiritualist faith rested on more solid foundations. 'There is no creed whatever that rests upon such strong evidence,' it was admitted, 'they have been submitted to scientific tests, and have never yet been disproved.'[2] So how could a Christian believe in the miracles of Jesus, yet reject the miracles of Daniel Home? 'For not only is the testimony offered by spiritualists immeasurably stronger,' one theologian pointed out, 'but it conforms far more closely to scientific conditions.'[3] After all, Jesus had never been tested by scientists, and whoever may have witnessed his miracles at the time, there existed only four official sources, written some time after the event.

The reasons for testimony being accepted or rejected, however, are never quite so simple. Spiritualists could rightly point out that floating in the air was no more implausible than walking on water, and that the witnesses in the former case were not only first-hand eye-witnesses, but that they had also been cross-examined by committee. These were scientific arguments, however, and the miracles of the Bible rested upon religious grounds. There had been a time when theologians argued that the miracles of Jesus were supported by reliable testimony, but that was no longer a tenable position. 'We in this generation', the Dean of Westminster admitted, 'do not believe in the Gospel because of the miracles, but in the miracles because of the Gospel.'[4] The miracles were true because the Bible was true, and that was not a matter of accurate testimony, but of the internal evidence of revelation. The Bible revealed the truth of God's word, and the miracles were simply a manifestation of His word. It was not an entirely new argument, but it was increasingly employed, and part of a growing distinction between scientific and religious evidence.[5] It was a distinction that had been embraced by scientific Christians, such as David Brewster and Michael Faraday, and one that allowed them to accept the word of Matthew, Mark, Luke and John, while dismissing the word of Daniel as blasphemous. But it made the question of testimony all the more confusing, and forced the Victorians to ask themselves whom they could trust, and on what basis.

For spiritualists it was rather simpler, since they regarded the floating of tables and mediums as having religious significance, and the communications from the other world as revealing the nature of God. But it would not be quite so simple for much longer, for the miracles of the séance room were changing too. As Daniel entered into retirement, other mediums rose to prominence, and the rivalries among them sparked a new and lasting crisis, one that would ensure that he never fully retired. The result was somewhat paradoxical, as it led to Daniel's word being questioned by spiritualists, yet accepted unquestioningly by sceptical scientists. And it came about through the clashing of various agendas. It was partly a question of jealousy, partly a question of judgement, and largely a matter of Agnes Guppy and the dubious miracles she performed.

Before she had married the elderly spiritualist Samuel Guppy, Agnes had impressed Alfred Russel Wallace with what became the signature piece of her mediumistic abilities: the materialization of all manner of objects upon the séance table. These spirit productions always took place in the dark, but when the lights went up, there would invariably be something surprising on the table. 'We were all thunderstruck', reported Wallace on one occasion, 'to see the table half covered with flowers . . . They consisted,' continued the great naturalist in admirable detail, 'of fifteen chrysanthemums, six variegated anemones, four tulips, five orange-berried solanums, six ferns of two sorts, [and] one *Auricula sinensis*.'[6] And it soon became clear that Mrs Guppy was a medium for all seasons. 'During the recent frost and snow, at the séances with Mrs Guppy', reported the *Spiritual Magazine*, 'the manifestations have consisted chiefly in the production of snow and ice.'[7] At other times, the table-top had seen the arrival of grapes, fruit, feathers, bread, and live eels and lobsters.

Wallace was baffled as to where such an extraordinary buffet might have come from, though some suspected that they were concealed within Mrs Guppy's ample petticoats. If this were true, it was merely a question of anticipating requests and having sufficient stocks to satisfy demand. Perhaps this might explain what happened on a later occasion, when 'several of the company expressed a wish for some article to be brought by the spirits, as a manifestation. Mr Clark asked for some spring onions — immediately we heard something falling . . . and on the light being struck spring onions were found on the table in considerable profusion . . . Mr Swinburn asked for an apple, and Mrs Fisher asked for an orange.' There was then, however, an adjournment, when 'Some rhubarb from the garden had been asked for'.[8]

Mrs Guppy's most famous arrival on the tabletop materialised after she teamed up with Frank Herne and Charles Williams. Herne and Williams were gradually establishing their own reputations as mediums, though Herne seems to have had the closer relationship with Mrs Guppy. One morning, for example, when Mr Guppy was walking into the breakfast room, he found his young wife there. 'Suddenly she screamed', her husband reported, 'and said that something had tumbled down. I at once entered the room, and there was Mr Herne on the settee, looking dazed, like a person half awake.' Mr Guppy had complete faith in his wife, however, and concluded that Herne 'had been brought there by some unseen power'.[9]

On the evening of Mrs Guppy's most famous feat, Herne and Williams were conducting a séance in their lodgings at Holborn. Seven innocent witnesses had been gathered, and the spirits were soon heard. The voices were, they were informed, those of John and Katie King, regular spirit visitors to the dark séances of Herne and Williams. According to an ear-witness account, Katie King had promised to transport an object on to the table, when somebody jokingly suggested that they make Mrs Guppy appear. John said, 'Katie, you can't do it.' Katie replied, 'I will, I tell you I will.' John said, 'I tell you, you can't.' She answered, 'I will.'

And so the spirit conversation went, until a witness protested: 'Good Gracious! I hope not; she is one of the biggest women in London.' But it was too late, for a moment later there was 'a great bump on the table, and one or two screams', and 'somebody called out, "Good God! there is something on my head." A match was instantly struck, and there was Mrs G, standing on the centre of the table.'[10] According to one witness, she was 'trembling all over'.[11] According to another, 'She was not by any means dressed for an excursion, as she was without shoes, and had a memorandum book in one hand and a pen in the other. The last word inscribed in the book was "onions", the ink of which was wet.'

The witnesses, who included a 'Manchester merchant of high standing' and a BA of Cambridge University, who described himself as 'a scientific man', escorted Mrs Guppy home, where her friend confirmed that she had been 'reading a newspaper in the intervals of conversation, and when she had raised her head from reading, Mrs Guppy could not be seen'.[12] It was enough to convince the Manchester merchant and the scientific man that imposture was a ridiculous idea. 'The possibility of her being concealed in the room', declared the merchant, 'is as absurd as the idea of her acting in collusion with [Herne and Williams].' And most of the public agreed that one was no more absurd than the other, but neither came close to the absurdity of the idea of a very large medium being instantly transported across London while she was writing the word 'onions'.

It was easy, therefore, for the press to mock. '[L]et Katie [King] bring the Queen of England, the Prince of Wales, the ex-Emperor of the French,' they challenged, 'or any person under lock and key in any of Her Majesty's prisons.'[13] Yet sarcasm was not enough for W. B. Carpenter, who felt that a scientific explanation should nevertheless be provided. And so, rather than simply suggest that Mrs Guppy had been hidden in the room, he attempted to explain her arrival as a 'subjective sensation', brought about by a state of 'expectant attention'.[14] Such are the responses of the rational mind to an event beyond the boggle threshold, an event so absurd that no explanation is felt necessary, though if an explanation is felt necessary, then even an absurd one will do.

For those who accepted the reality of spiritual intervention, there were few events that seemed inherently absurd. If the spirits could make a table float, an accordion play, a man levitate, there was nothing that much more surprising about invisibly transporting a vegetable or a Mrs Guppy. It was only to the sceptical public that such phenomena seemed so obviously ridiculous, but for those who believed in miracles, anything was possible. Believers in such strange miracles were in a minority, however, which meant that mediums had a limited audience. And while public mediums conducted daily séances for a standard fee, private mediums competed for the patronage of wealthy spiritualists.[15] And, if anything was possible, it was natural enough that mediums would compete by attempting to produce the most impressive phenomena they could. So it was that séance phenomena became more startling and wondrous, and spirits began to appear in fuller form. In America, the medium Kate Fox had moved on from raps and begun to materialize complete spirit forms, and British mediums, in an attempt to catch up, began to do the same. Mrs Guppy sat in a cabinet so that she was hidden from the sitters present, and produced the faces and limbs of spirits in what some denounced as a spirit 'Punch and Judy' show. Herne and Williams followed suit, and as the competition grew, the spirit forms became larger and more complete. But when a complete spirit form finally appeared it was not via Guppy, Herne or Williams, and that was when the rivalry among mediums really began.

It did not help matters that the new star medium was young and rather pretty. For in the battle to attract a gentleman sponsor, youthful, feminine good looks were not available to the likes of Herne and Williams, or for that matter Mrs Guppy. After all, there were many reasons for going to a séance: that so many mediums were women was certainly one attraction to gentlemen sitters, and it was fairly common for a female medium to end up marrying an older gentleman spiritualist. There were even those who were quick to criticize if the medium was not considered attractive enough. Sybil, for example, was 'a big, fleshy large-boned woman of an utterly uncertain age', complained one male sitter of his medium, and 'the pervading idea that you had when you looked at Sybil was that there was *too much of her*'.[16] Needless to say, this voyeur was much more impressed when Florence Cook arrived on the scene, for Florence was considered a great improvement on the likes of Sybil or Mrs Guppy. 'The time seems to have gone by for portly matrons to be wafted aerially from the Northern suburbs to the W.C.,' he reported in reference to Mrs Guppy's transportation from Highbury to Holborn, 'and we anxious investigators can scarcely complain of the change which brings us face to face with fair young maidens in their teens to the exclusion of the matrons and the spinsters.'[17] And it was the threat of exclusion by a fair young maiden that would provoke the portly matron.

After all, Florence Cook was not only young and attractive, but also talented. Herne and Williams had taken her under their wing while they had been developing their form of the spirit cabinet. This was not unlike the Davenport brothers' set-up, with the medium being tied up prior to any spirit materializations. Florence had also worked with Mr and Mrs Nelson Holmes, a mediumistic couple who, like Herne and Williams, spoke regularly to the spirits of John and Katie King.

After this, she went on to a successful solo career and, by the spring of 1873, had managed to produce the first full-form materialization of the spirit of Katie King. It happened, we are told, while Florence was sitting in a cupboard out of sight. According to an eye-witness report in the *Daily Telegraph*, 'though we had left [Florence] tied and sealed to her chair, and clad in an ordinary black dress somewhat voluminous as to the skirts, a tall female figure draped classically in white, with bare arms and feet, did enter'. A few moments later, she went back into the cupboard, and when the sitters later went in, they found Florence 'with her dress on as before, knots and seals secure, and her boots on!'[18]

Needless to say, there were those who suggested that Katie King was simply Florence, temporarily released from her bonds, and wearing a different dress. The fact that the first dress had been 'somewhat voluminous as to the skirts' even suggested where the white dress might have been concealed. But Victorian gentlemen sitters were reluctant to suspect such an unsavoury source of the phenomena. Here, after all, was an attractive medium, able to materialize a spirit not only in its fullest form, but also in the equally attractive form of Katie King. King appeared with increasing regularity, and began to walk round and talk to those present, to shake their hands, perhaps even offer a kiss on the cheek. The competition for a place at Florence's séances grew almost as rapidly as the envy of the portly matron.

Indeed, it was often said that Agnes Guppy was a jealous woman, and it was not long before fellow mediums realized that 'Mrs G is now engaged in an attempt to bedaub the character of Miss Cook.'[19] The truth of this became clear to all at a séance in December 1873. Present at that séance was one Mr Volckmann, a good friend of Mrs Guppy who later became her second husband. When Katie King appeared and walked round the room, she offered to shake Mr Volckmann's hand, but Volckmann instead grabbed her round the waist, and attempted to expose her as Florence Cook. A scuffle followed, in which Volckmann was removed from the room with sufficient force that he lost some whiskers, and Katie quickly retreated to the safety of the cabinet. After a delay of about five minutes, a delay that some would regard as significant, the cabinet was opened, and Florence was found securely tied in her original black dress.

Perhaps Florence got off lightly, for it was said that Mrs Guppy was so bitter at having lost her patrons to her rival, and so jealous of her 'doll face', that she had initially planned 'to throw vitriol on the face of the spirit, hoping thereby to destroy forever the handsome features of Miss Florrie Cook'.[20] The incident provoked a furious debate, as spiritualists argued about whether this proved the most wondrous of materializations to be a sham. Most condemned Volckmann for his outrageous behaviour, warning that such handling of a spirit might kill the medium, and insisting that the spirit was genuine, since no white dress had been found despite a search (though they failed to mention where they had looked).

But the event led to other exposures, one of which ended in a young lady medium being found 'in an attire which was confined to chemise, stocking and a pair of — !', at which point she claimed that an evil spirit 'had all but stripped her naked'. Another exposure occurred at the house of Edward Cox, with the young and equally attractive Mary Showers. Showers began to produce a spirit head, when Cox's daughter decided to take a closer look. According to Cox, 'in the struggle . . . the spirit headdress fell off. I was witness to it all and the extraordinary scene that followed – the voice crying out "You have killed my medium!" – . . . [which] was quite needless, for she was neither killed nor injured, beyond the vexation of discovery.'[21] Mr and

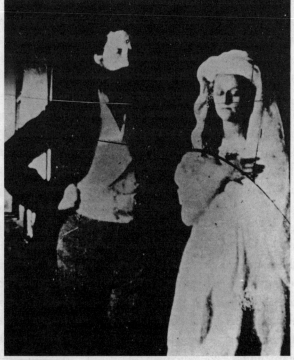

William Crookes poses with the spirit form of Katie King —
or is it Florence Cook the medium (top)? (*Mary Evans*)

Mrs Nelson Holmes were also exposed, when another supporter of Mrs Guppy struck a match at a moment when Mrs Holmes, the medium, was supposed to be tied up. Instead of being restrained securely in her place, she was seen 'dancing about the room', and on realizing she had been discovered, she muttered in the strange voice of her spirit guide: 'O de blackguard, de blackguard, to break de conditions by striking a light.'[22] The Holmeses returned to America, and there they managed to convince Robert Dale Owen of the genuineness of a full-form spirit, until their servant girl, Eliza, finally confessed that the spirit had simply been her in costume.

Spiritualists attempted to come to terms with these exposures: were they true exposures of fraud, or perhaps the result of evil spirits? And if they were fraudulent, did that mean all such materializations were untrue? As the controversy rolled along, William Crookes began some new experiments. He sat with the American medium Kate Fox, and with Herne and Williams, and was convinced that what he saw was genuine. And, in the aftermath of the Volckmann exposure, he began a series of experiments with Florence Cook, and, rather than concluding that she was a fraud, he became convinced that Katie King was a genuine spirit. He took King's arm, and complimented her on her beauty, even posed with her in photographs. The very idea that a scientist of note could behave in such a way with an alleged spirit led many people to wonder whether something else might be going on. Even spiritualists expressed concern that Crookes's interest in Florence was more than scientific, and later it was claimed that Florence confessed to having had an affair with the discoverer of thallium.

Following his experiments with Florence, Crookes decided to test Mary Showers, and failed to discover any signs of fraud with her. He also tested Annie Eva Fay, a stage performer whom even the most open-minded of investigators dismissed as an 'undoubted cheat'. Yet Crookes did not catch her cheating either. It was not until Showers confessed to Fay, and Fay then informed Crookes, that he realized he had been deceived. He then used Fay to get a written confession from Showers, and promised not to expose her publicly if she promised to give up her tricks. 'Do not therefore say anything about this,' he begged Daniel, when he informed him of the whole affair. It was, after all, rather embarrassing, and not simply because of the matter of fraud. Showers's mother, he told Daniel, 'found out I was meeting her daughter and fired up at it, putting the worst construction on it'. That, and the fact that one of Showers's accomplices had 'written very shameful things about me', was enough to convince Crookes that he was 'getting a reputation of a Don Juan'. He insisted that he was entirely innocent, even though notes he had sent to Showers suggested otherwise. But these were forgeries, Crookes insisted, for Showers's mother had intercepted his original notes, steamed open the envelopes and replaced his notes with ones of her own, written in his handwriting.[23] Whatever the truth of the matter, it was hardly surprising that eyebrows were raised and that there was gossip, for people are never quite sure what to believe in matters of testimony.

For Daniel, this was all very depressing. It made little difference to him whether Crookes had been enamoured with the young ladies, whether he had been merely flirtatious or even immoral. What was important was that the nature of séance phenomena was changing, and for the worse. The competition among mediums had led to such jealousies and rivalries that the attempts to produce more impressive manifestations had produced instead only suspicious results. That spiritualists seemed to accept unquestioningly even the most suspicious phenomena only encouraged mediums to push their luck, resulting in more and more exposures. Widespread gullibility made spiritualism seem less plausible to the public, and made the infidel almost impossible to convert. And, from a more selfish point of view, the way Crookes was investigating mediums such as Cook, Showers and Fay, and actually validating their phenomena, could only make his validation of Daniel look more suspicious. The only consolation was that much of this was kept as quiet as possible, with spiritualist journals reluctant to publish the exposures, and then only alongside the views of those who sided with the victim. An accusation was made, the medium denied being responsible, and evil spirits were judged to be the cause. And if the medium were suspected, it was already a well-known fact that genuine mediums occasionally 'helped the spirits'.

But the exposures of mediums continued. Annie Eva Fay, who had been tested both by Crookes and Cromwell Varley, was later found to be involved in trickery. Then Henry Slade arrived from America and had the spirits write messages on slates, and the *Spiritual Magazine* announced that 'Slade is taking the place so long vacated by D D Home', describing him as 'the most remarkable medium of modern times'.[24] But he too was apparently caught cheating, taken to court and found guilty, and quickly left the country in order to avoid imprisonment. Spiritualists argued that mediums such as Fay and Slade had also been tested in proper conditions, and so they were clearly genuine mediums who, as history had so often shown, occasionally resorted to trickery. This was as logical from their point of view as it was unconvincing from the point of view of sceptics. The scientists whose interest had been sparked by Crookes began to take the whole thing much less seriously. 'The Lord have mercy on us all,' Darwin declared, 'if we have to believe in such rubbish'.[25]

Amid all the exposures, some spiritualists began to lose faith, not so much in the reality of spirits as in the authenticity of mediums. As the new stars of mediumship rose to fame and, on occasion, were exposed to shame, spiritualists reacted accordingly. Some left the movement but many hailed the new mediums as the greatest ambassadors of spiritualism. After all, without the phenomena, spiritualism could hardly survive, and as Daniel was no longer available, lesser mediums received the plaudits. And this was not to his liking. For it was often said that he was 'jealous of any and all mediums'.[26] And perhaps it was jealousy on Daniel's part, or concern about the legacy of his mission, or perhaps both, that led him to write his final book. The primary purpose of this book would be to expose the trickery of fraudulent mediums. 'Of course,' he admitted in a private letter to a friend, 'there will be a storm.'

The storm slowly brewed as word spread of Daniel's intentions, dividing the opinions of spiritualists as sharply as it provoked the hostility of mediums. 'I was assailed, both openly and anonymously', Daniel observed, 'with slander, lying charges, foul personalities, [and] venomous abuse . . . [but] it was what I expected.' He was also assailed, both privately and politely, by expressions of support from concerned potential targets. Nelson Holmes attempted to get on side by claiming that he was in agreement with Daniel: he too felt that the frauds should be exposed, though naturally this did not include him and his wife. Instead, he suggested that Daniel focus on Mrs Guppy, complaining of the 'Guppy warfare on the Holmes', and claiming that she 'used her pretended mediumship for based purposes, and gave séances solely for assignation meetings, to better enable certain disreputable parties to further carry out their lewd propensities'.[27] Even Kate Fox wrote to Daniel, congratulating him on his courageous decision. 'I was contemplating doing it myself,' she claimed, so do get in touch if there was 'anything I can do to aid'. 'I have never said an unkind word about you,' she casually pointed out, 'for I have never had an unkind thought towards you, and I do not believe those who have said that you have spoken harshly of me.' And she ended by saying how much she liked Mrs Home, and suggesting that the two of them really must come for dinner.[28]

Over the following weeks and months, spiritualists and mediums alike waited to discover whom Daniel would choose to condemn, and to whom he might show mercy. And while some attempted to get on side, others chose more aggressive tactics, and the book was written amid the curses of theosophists and the growing threats of mediums. 'From what I hear on every side,' Daniel complained to a friend, 'there is to be a "war to the knife" carried on against me for my honesty in exposing as I do the many horrible abuses.' He had not yet decided to name guilty parties, but he warned that 'If this warfare is not kept within certain limits I will print a "key" . . . [and give] facts which I have in the present work withheld.'[29] His enemies, however, had already been provoked, and 'in certain quarters dark hints had been thrown out that Home would not live to complete his work'.[30]

It was in April 1876 that the news broke, to the relief of so many of Daniel's enemies. A French telegram was copied in newspapers throughout Europe and America, and the world was informed that Daniel was dead. *New York World* announced that 'Home, unquestionably the most widely famous "Spiritualist" and "medium" of our time, died suddenly on Saturday while travelling on a railway between St Petersburg and Berlin. It added, in a somewhat vulgar obituary, that 'If only the half of what has been told of Mr Home is true, to suppose him dead merely because he happened to leave his corpse in a first class compartment would be absurd.'[31] The news spread and the obituaries multiplied. They were read by Daniel's friends with deep regret, by his enemies with great relief, and by Daniel himself with some amusement. His corpse had never been found on the train: it was just another false report, probably originating in the mind of an optimistic enemy.

Typically, the truth spread rather more slowly than the lie, so much so that when Daniel met Alexandre Dumas in Nice a month later, 'he stared at me and said, "In the first place, you died a month or two ago; and in the next place you look positively younger".'[32] However, the truth was too slow in reaching the town of Elwood, New York, by then the home of Mrs Mary Cook, the aunt who had adopted Daniel as a boy, taken him to Connecticut and later thrown him out of her home. She had recently read the report of her nephew's death, but only a day or two later did the local paper explain that it was inaccurate, and by then it had announced the death of Mrs Cook herself. '[H]er departure', the obituary reported, 'was caused by the shock of hearing the false intelligence of Mr Home's sudden death. A paralytic seizure was the result, and the poor lady never rallied.'[33]

Daniel's book finally appeared, and it was entitled *Lights and Shadows of Spiritualism*, the shadows metaphor amounting to an undiluted attack on the weak-mindedness of spiritualists and the fraudulence of mediums. On spiritualists, Daniel declared, 'the very thought of communion with the dwellers in another world appears to intoxicate these unfortunates almost to madness. . . . [some] pin themselves to a particular delusion, with a fanatical tenacity which nothing can affect. Others flit tirelessly from mania to mania.' And with regard to mediums, he noted that some of the manifestations were so absurd that they demonstrated only the sheer gullibility of the unfortunates. There had been, for example, the 'spirit' of John Wilkes Booth who had told his American sitters: 'I, and Lincoln, often have a cosy chat up here [and we] agree that it was just as well I shot him.' And there had been supposed communications from Jesus' apostles, who claimed they had 'sold little pamphlets on the life and doings of Jesus to bring us money'; that they had never trusted Judas 'as he was always a very loose sort of character'; and that Pilate, when he had met with Jesus, had told him: 'None of your miracles here!!' Such communications, Daniel declared, 'would be ludicrous were they not so disgusting'. He denounced the miracles of Mormonism as 'delusions', those of theosophists as 'beneath contempt', and the teachings of certain American spiritualists as 'blasphemous'. But it was the fraudulent phenomena of so many of his rivals that drew Daniel's particular venom: he declared their manifestations so ludicrous that 'Only a few crack-brained and perverse-minded enthusiasts [could] promulgate such nauseous folly.'[34]

In particular, he noted, there were those full-form spirit materializations so fashionable these days. 'I have had the honour of speaking face to face with six or seven Mary Queen of Scots', he sneered, 'of all ages and appearances.' He had even observed the spirit of Oliver Cromwell wearing boots that did not fit him. And then there were the ubiquitous appearances of John and Katie King, who materialized so solidly that they had 'tea and cake' with the sitters, and who offered such spiritual advice as the need for 'regular baths' and a 'bottle of Guinness every day'.[35] And for those readers for whom sarcasm was insufficient, and who did not already find these 'Punch and Judy mediums' ridiculous, he pointed out the sheer number of spirits who had been grabbed, and found to be the medium, though he did not name the mediums themselves. After all, it was well-enough known who was associated with John and Katie King, and there was no need to name the guilty medium when he could simply name the guilty spirit, and make it quite clear that there was little difference between the two. And so, having implied the guilt of Herne and Williams, the Holmeses and Florence Cook, Daniel then proceeded to explain how easy it was to fake a spirit.

'Those who have never investigated this matter', he told the reader, 'would be astonished by the small space required for the articles necessary to materialize a spirit.' The gauze-like material used to drape over the medium could be easily concealed in the lining of pants, vest or coat, even behind a tie and under the collar. When spiritualists claimed they had searched the medium, such searches were never thorough enough, and, in any case, he knew of at least one medium who hid his materials in the cabinet prior to being searched. Needless to say, female mediums could hide far bulkier objects, as 'ladies' dresses offer such facilities for concealment'. The tying up of mediums was utterly pointless, since conjurors such as Maskelyne had demonstrated how easy it was to escape from the bonds, and even handcuffs were ineffective, as keys could be carried in the mouth.

Worst of all, it all occurred in darkness, in conditions that entirely prevented investigation, except by friends of the medium, who would never suspect fraud in the first place. And when a medium was actually caught, the spiritualist journals refused to publish the exposure, even when it was a spiritualist who had caught the medium by the hand, while the other hand was 'engaged in taking from his head and face a pair of false whiskers *a la John King*'. This particular victim had been a pupil of a well-known medium, who himself had been caught dressed up in a pair of 'spirit' pantaloons made from the *Daily Courier*, an exposure that had been publicly disseminated, with a degree of pride, in the *Daily Courier*. Such were the blatant methods used by unscrupulous mediums to convince gullible dupes. One American medium, who was reported to have 'gradually faded away into thin air before us until not a vestige was seen', had used nothing more than a thin fabric 'arranged to simulate a robe, and gathered at the top into something like the shape of a head'. This 'puppet-like construction' had been held outside the cabinet by the medium inside, made to nod, and then been gradually drawn into the cabinet. In dark conditions, and before an audience of unquestioning believers, these simple ruses could lead to the most impressive testimony, but in good light and in front of critical observers they would be rightly exposed.

Such criticisms would, Daniel knew, upset many spiritualists, not to mention anger the mediums, and 'Punch-puppets of "John Kings" will be made to squeak out indignant anathemas.' Nevertheless, if spiritualism was to survive, then fraud must be exposed in the cause of truth. This was not, after all, an attack upon spiritualism, but a defence of spiritualism against fraudulent mediums and the gullible supporters who allowed them to operate. The growth of fraud did not negate the genuine manifestations that had occurred. There had been authentic spirit materializations, certainly when he had been the medium present, and possibly in the presence of the Fox sisters. But certainly in his case, spirits had appeared, not in the form that had now become fashionable, but in good light and while he had been in full view. Not all mediums were fraudulent, and there were many genuine mediums who had unfortunately felt the need to engage in fraud occasionally, but good light and properly controlled conditions could separate the true from the false. For example, he noted in a rare moment of generosity, 'the carefully-conducted experiences of Mr Crookes with Miss Cook were repaid with evidence giving undeniable certainty of the phenomenon'.[36]

As the book proceeded towards its conclusion, Mrs Guppy must have felt somewhat relieved to have escaped any obvious references to her. But that was not to last, as Daniel went on to dismiss the transportations of eels, lobsters and blocks of ice, on the basis that matter did not pass through matter. He then parodied one of her séances in which unlikely objects were asked for and appeared, conducted by an anonymous lady medium with ample 'facilities for concealment' within her dress. According to the scenario, she would note that 'at our last séance the dear spirits brought in some cabbages. Suppose they were to bring lilies of the valley this time, how nice that would be! Oh dear no! We must not ask for lilies of the valley. Let us think of something else.' At which point a sitter would say, '*I* would like lilies of the valley,' and the medium would hesitate, and say that the spirits might not bring them, and 'Why *will* you ask for such out-of-the-way things?' And then the sitter would insist, and declare that if lilies of the valley were brought, he would 'consider it a test'. And so they would arrive in the darkness, and be seen when the lights went up, and later a spiritualist journal would report that there had been a 'test séance' in which a sitter 'asked for some lilies of the valley, which the spirits instantly brought'.[37]

Such was the tenor of Daniel's book, and the reaction of spiritualists was immediate. A few rallied round, and stressed that his position was both honourable and necessary, but many friends were less than friendly and many supporters unsupportive. In fact, the reaction of most spiritualists was not so unlike that of the general public to his autobiography all those years before. It was reviewed in the spiritualist press and condescendingly dismissed as 'a superficial compilation without an original thought or inspired purpose . . . it is charmingly illogical'.[38] And just as critics of spiritualism had dismissed anonymous testimony in his autobiography as unreliable, so his attempt here to avoid naming individuals was used by spiritualists as a way of dismissing his allegations. He was accused of having 'gone about the world picking up hearsay scandals, not one of which [he] could substantiate, or give the names of those [he] accused'.[39] It was hardly the first time his facts had been disputed, but those who had accepted them previously were rather more reluctant to accept these.

Meanwhile, as spiritualists became sceptics, so sceptics became believers. W. B. Carpenter, that most sceptical of scientists, promptly accepted the word of the medium on precisely those facts that spiritualists disputed. Now convinced that Daniel was entirely trustworthy, Carpenter published a lengthy article that praised his honesty, and used his book to support his own theory that spiritualism was nothing more than imposture and delusion. Daniel's 'lilies of the valley' narrative was accepted unquestioningly as an explanation for the eclectic materializations of Mrs Guppy, and used to discredit Alfred Russel Wallace. At the same time, his exposure of full-form materializations was cited at length, and used to discredit the investigations of William Crookes. The fact that Daniel had endorsed Crookes's investigations with Florence Cook was, of course, not mentioned. 'I feel that the cause of Common Sense has been so greatly served by Mr Home's fearless exposure', Carpenter declared, 'that I would not here call in question his own belief in the phenomena.' Such was his sense of gratitude that he did not even attempt to explain Daniel's feats, though perhaps that was simply because Daniel had not provided him with an explanation. Instead, having accepted his sincerity, he merely expressed 'the independent judgement as to what is inherently probable, which [Mr Home] himself so freely passes upon the pretensions of others'.[40] Which is to say, in short, that he had no idea, but there remained some facts he continued to dispute.

The greatest of mediums had become the most effective of debunkers, and his most vocal scientific critic had refused to question his sincerity. The irony of the situation was not lost on Wallace, who wasted no time in criticizing them both. Daniel's accusations were 'never authenticated in any way, and appear to be in many cases pure imagination', yet Carpenter, having treated him as an impostor for years, now 'quotes him as an authority', and will 'consider him only as a victim of delusion . . . this is absurd'. Either Daniel was 'the vilest of impostors and utterly untrustworthy' or he was not, yet Carpenter 'accepts as true all the malicious stories retailed by this alleged impostor against rival impostors'. Spiritualists, of course, did not regard Daniel as an impostor: 'We believe that he is a medium . . . but this implies no belief in his integrity or his judgment.'[41] And so the most scientific of spiritualists denounced the testimony of the greatest of mediums, and accused the most sceptical of scientists of being gullible.

No doubt all this would have been confusing, if there was anybody left who had not already taken a side, but there was at least one consistent theme. For though most spiritualists were angry with Daniel, and though they accused him of jealousy and inaccuracy, none of them doubted his abilities as a medium. Whatever seeds of doubt he might have sown in their minds about the abilities of other mediums, and however much he had antagonized his rivals, no spiritualist and no medium ever accused him of having cheated. As for Carpenter, he had virtually absolved Daniel of fraud, and, as Wallace had pointed out quite clearly, if he was not a fraud then he had to be genuine. After all, perhaps Daniel might delude himself, but he could hardly levitate through the power of 'expectant attention', and even if his witnesses had been deluded, they had to have been deluded by somebody. The fact that Carpenter had seized upon the information in *Lights and Shadows* showed how useful he found such information, but these exposures of the methods of fake mediums shed no light on Daniel's own feats. Daniel may also have been a fake, which is no doubt what Carpenter really suspected, but whatever suspicions he had, he failed to provide any insight into how such fraud might work. And so, as spiritualists continued to regard Daniel as the greatest of mediums, sceptics were left to regard him, and perhaps only him, as an ongoing mystery.

This was the result of Daniel's final book, and perhaps that was precisely why he had written it. His unique reputation was secured, and acknowledged by those who resented the book as well as by those who had welcomed it. Crookes was so upset by the ammunition it had offered to his critics that, in the interests of civility, his wife wrote to Daniel about 'the awkward position he has been placed in'. He was 'irritated by the unfair attacks upon him, in which quotations in your book were so abundant, [which had allowed his enemies] to prove how easily he had been deceived'.[42] The exposures of fraud had left Crookes disillusioned with spiritualism. 'I am so disgusted with the whole thing', he later told Daniel, 'that if it were not for the regard we bear to you, I would cut the whole spiritualist connection.' And though he later acknowledged the fraudulence of other mediums he had tested, with Daniel he had 'never detected any trickery or deceit whatever', and he continued to publish notes on his séances.[43] Others agreed that Daniel's phenomena were 'the only things left to which I attach hope. All the other phenomena . . . except those accruing through you have been in the last degree unsatisfactory.'[44]

A year after the publication of *Lights and Shadows*, Charles Williams and his new partner were caught cheating by a group of spiritualists in Amsterdam. In his pockets were found all the necessary props and make-up for impersonating John King, including several yards of muslin and a false beard. Even then there were those who chose to blame this upon the work of evil spirits, and one believer even refused to believe it was fraud until 'John King' himself had been consulted. But many spiritualists found such a leap of faith too difficult, while nobody who was not a spiritualist even attempted the leap. 'From this episode', concluded an early historian of spiritualism, 'may be said to date the decline of Spiritualism in this country. Its later history is little else, indeed, than a history of similar exposures.'[45] Spiritualism did not die, of course, and psychical research was only beginning, but physical manifestations were largely dismissed as unworthy of investigation, and mental phenomena, such as clairvoyance and telepathy, became the psychic phenomena of choice.

As for Daniel, his own days were numbered, and soon he would know whether he had been telling the truth about spiritual survival. His emphasis had always been on the life that followed death, and it was after his death that his life would be reassessed. It was then that the rest of the world would decide for themselves whether he had been telling the truth, or whether he had indeed been the charlatan that so many suspected. And as his life came to be examined, allegations quickly emerged that he had been caught cheating after all.

15

Death and afterlife

The last years of Daniel Home were no less varied than those that had passed before. His circle of friends was rather smaller, as was his circle of enemies, but his range of acquaintances remained impressive, and he continued to meet the odd celebrity. 'Since I have been [in Paris]', he recorded in 1879, 'I have seen much of Mark Twain. He seems to have taken a fancy to me and is most enthusiastic.'[1] 'He is a very fine fellow', Twain confirmed, 'and makes warm and everlasting friendships with all sorts of people.'[2] The two great storytellers got on so well that Daniel translated parts of *A Tramp Abroad* into Russian, and sent a copy to the author, who was unable to read a word of it. 'It seems an excellent translation,' he nevertheless wrote to Daniel, 'at any rate it looks funnier than it does in English. If it has a defect it has escaped me.'[3]

But life was rarely so light-hearted, and Daniel's worsening tuberculosis began to take its toll. By 1882, this was made worse still by his concern for his son, Gregoire. The boy had been subjected to an unorthodox childhood, and over the years had been cared for by various spiritualist friends of his father. Daniel said surprisingly little about his only son, so one can only guess

249

what sort of upbringing he had. But given the constant financial problems, his father's bad health and fluctuating reputation, not to mention the regular visits of the spirits, it could hardly have been easy for Gregoire. He was now a young man and, it seems, living an unsavoury life. He had left the care of Daniel's friends and fallen in with the wayward son of another spiritualist whom Daniel detested. Daniel wrote to his friends, in frantic prose and erratic handwriting, begging them to save his son 'from the utter ruin that awaits him'. He was 'playing flunkey to a blackguard son of a clodhopper', a 'lad of 28, who was "as in a night mare" because he had left an old music hall strumpet'. And in this immoral environment Gregoire had been painting 'sexual pictures'.[4] Gregoire returned to the haven of his father's friends, but it was not long before they confessed that he was beyond their control. 'His conduct is simply scandalously wicked,' Daniel was informed, 'I fear it is a hopeless case.'[5]

Daniel 'suffered terribly the last few years', an intimate friend remembered.[6] According to his devoted widow, 'He suffered cruelly – long and cruelly' but when death came to him, we are assured that it came 'without a pang'. It was, she recalled, 'a sublime and tranquil death . . . [in which] the spirit had left imprinted on the face an expression of celestial happiness'.[7] Yet even the nature of his death was disputed, and his enemies told of a less pleasant departure, that after having 'suffered for years' he 'died a perfect wreck'.[8] Whatever the circumstances of his death, the first psychic drew his last breath on the 21 June 1886, and was buried at St Germain-en-Laye, alongside his infant daughter. That much was agreed upon, but after that, little was agreed upon again. And from that time, throughout the following decades, as the arguments over Daniel Dunglas Home persisted, his spirit remained silent, and has so ever since.

*

The End?

After Daniel's death came what was called 'the death-blow to spiritualism'. Kate and Margaret Fox, who as young girls had launched modern spirit communication, decided to give one last communication, and this time it was not from the spirits. They were now middle-aged women, living in squalor, and had been drinking heavily for several years. Kate had been arrested for drunkenness in New York, and her children had been taken away from her. Her sister was in a similarly desperate state, and in 1888 they walked into the New York Academy of Music prepared to confess their sins. On stage, Margaret announced to the audience that their spirit raps had indeed been fraudulent, produced by the methods those three wise men of science had claimed all those years ago. As she demonstrated how it was done, with clicking toe joints that could be heard throughout the hall, her sister sat in the box above, silently confirming all that was said. And as the sceptics nodded knowingly, the believers sat in disbelief. Later, however, as if such clarity was deemed inappropriate to a subject plagued by questionable testimony, Margaret retracted her confession, leaving both sides to argue about which of her statements was a lie.

Within a couple of years, both sisters were dead, while Mary Showers also descended into alcoholism, and continued to conduct séances while half-drunk. Florence Cook was unmasked again, and Annie Eva Fay went back to her stage career, confessing that she had no supernatural powers and going on to become the first Lady Honorary Associate of the Magic Circle. The new star of physical mediumship, Eusapia Palladino, convinced intelligent investigators that she could produce genuine spirit manifestations, but she was also caught cheating on several occasions, and admitted that she cheated whenever she could. The well-known fact that genuine mediums often cheated was consistently pointed out, and it remained as logical as it had always been, if no more convincing to the sceptically-minded.

Whatever the details reported by witnesses, it was simply too easy for critics to argue that if a medium had been caught faking phenomena, his or her 'genuine' phenomena were nothing more than fake phenomena that had not been detected.

And so the record of Daniel Dunglas Home continued to be hailed as the strongest evidence of spirits being able to manifest themselves in this world, and that psychic phenomena might be real. No psychic could compare with the man for whom the word was invented: for while so many mediums and psychics suffered the indignity of being exposed, if not of making an outright confession, there appeared to be a unique lack of evidence that Daniel had ever been caught cheating. There had been countless allegations, of course, by most of his enemies and much of the press, but precious little had rested on any solid evidence. There had been the conjectures of Sir David Brewster, but it was now clear that they had been entirely invented. There had also been the guesswork of Dickens and Mrs Linton, who felt that Daniel had climbed on top of the furniture in order to convince the audience of the *Cornhill* article. Yet the only actual evidence of fraud possessed by Mrs Linton was that Daniel had got the name of her deceased daughter wrong. So far, the most damaging accusation had been the letter of Dr Barthez, who had witnessed Daniel in Biarritz, but the letter had still not been published.

Nevertheless, there were many people who thought that Daniel had cheated, and unless he had been both genuine and fraudulent, that meant he had cheated consistently for twenty years. Throughout those years he had conducted séances for critics as well as sympathizers, and in conditions that often allowed for a good deal of investigation. In such conditions, one might expect that someone would have caught him out at some point. And so, shortly after his death, his record was examined again, as critics sought to discover proof of fraud, and sympathizers sought to demonstrate that there was none. It was then that Robert Browning was given his last chance to expose Daniel.

Browning had been the most hostile of Daniel's critics, and between stamping and cursing and foaming at the mouth he had indirectly accused Daniel of fraud in his poem, 'Mr Sludge'. In the poem he had also suggested an explanation for the mysterious spirit hand, that it was merely a glove at the end of Daniel's slipper. And it turned out that this was not merely poetic licence, for he had told others that this was actually the case. According to Nathaniel Hawthorn, Browning 'avowed his belief that [the spirit] hands were affixed to the feet of Mr Hume, who lay extended in his chair, with his legs stretched far under the table'. Another acquaintance had even heard 'from Browning's lips' that when a spirit hand had appeared, he had 'clutched at the apparition, and seized Home's naked, "obscene foot" . . . [whereupon] Browning literally kicked the impostor out of the house: whence he departed with one shoe off and one shoe on'.[9] If this were true, it seemed rather odd that Browning had not made it public, or even privately told others that he had caught Daniel cheating. However, he was now given the chance to make an official statement, and to record for posterity his evidence that Daniel was a cheat.

In 1889, during an investigation by the Society for Psychical Research, Browning was finally asked upon what basis his accusations rested. His response made no reference to the spirit hands, or to his having grabbed Daniel's foot. Indeed, the only evidence he provided was related to the appearance of spirit lights. It seems that he had heard a story from a lady, who had heard it from a couple, who said they had found Daniel 'experimenting with phosphorous on the production of "spirit-lights", which (so far as Mr Browning remembers) were to be rubbed round the walls of the room'.[10] For all his private accusations and public insinuations, the only evidence he actually had to go on was this piece of third-hand testimony, which he did not supply until he was asked, twenty-five years after the publication of his poem.

Nevertheless, it was still the best evidence available that Daniel was a fraud. And that in itself begged another question. For the people who dismissed the reports of Daniel's witnesses did so on the basis that testimony was unreliable. And if the first-hand accounts of so many witnesses could be dismissed as unreliable, then it might be asked how reliable were third-hand accounts from individuals no less biased? And it might be said that to dismiss the former while accepting the latter rather opened them up to the charge of hypocrisy. Browning may have been convinced that Daniel was a cheat, but his own evidence was not very convincing. If Daniel was watching from above, then he probably would have smiled, though soon he would have realized that the accusations were far from over.

The next allegation appeared that year, in *Popular Science Monthly*, reported by the pioneering American psychologist Joseph Jastrow. It was in an article that dismissed spiritualism as the product of deception and a lack of critical thinking, and no doubt to the relief of fellow sceptics, Jastrow included 'the confession of an exposed medium, Mr D. D. Home'. In this confession the medium admitted how he had dressed up in disguise and paraded before his sitters as a materialized spirit.[11] This was undoubtedly an incriminating statement, the only problem being that Daniel had never said this. It was, as it turned out, based upon a description that Daniel had provided in *Lights and Shadows*, and it concerned another medium entirely. As Jastrow must have got his information from the book, he must have been aware of this. At the very least, he had not been particularly thorough. And so it was Jastrow, paradoxically, who could be accused of deception or a lack of critical thinking.

The next accusation was more serious, however, for it came

from a man who had been at one of Daniel's séances. Indeed, it proved to be the strongest evidence yet that Daniel was a cheat, and it seemed to support Browning's theory about the spirit hands. The witness was anonymous, but he had attended a dark séance back in 1855. During that séance the outline of a spirit hand had appeared from below the edge of the table. He had noticed that the hand appeared at two main points, one 'corresponding to the length of Home's arm', and the other 'about the place of his foot'. He had also seen 'slight movements in the shoulder or upper part of Home's arm corresponding to the movements [of the spirit hand]'. And then he had seen a 'continuous connection' between Home's arm and the spirit hand, and with 'the trick so plain to my eyes, and the reverential and adoring expressions of the company', he had been 'seized with a strong impulse to laugh'. But his allegation was serious, for he claimed he had seen what hundreds of witnesses had not; in his view, the spirit hand was attached to Daniel, at times to his foot (as Browning had thought) and at times to his arm (where he had actually seen the connection).[12]

Finally, here was a witness who had caught Daniel cheating. Daniel's enemies should have been pleased, yet they found themselves in a difficult position, for this testimony was anonymous and thirty-four years old. Critics regularly pointed out that accounts of séances were unreliable, so they could not simply accept an anonymous thirty-four-year-old memory of a séance even if it suited them. Why did the witness not give his name, and why had he said nothing of his discovery since 1855? So when Frank Podmore published *Modern Spiritualism* in 1902, though he assumed that Daniel's feats were fraudulent, he had to concede that, despite this allegation, there was 'no evidence of any weight that [Daniel] was even privately detected in trickery'.[13]

Ironically, this then prompted the anonymous witness to

reveal himself: his name was Mr Merrifield, and it turned out that he was an acquaintance of Browning. Furthermore, he had now found some notes he had written at the time. The notes, professedly taken a few weeks after the séance, were so similar to his thirty-four-year-old account of it that investigators thought the correspondence 'very remarkable'.[14] Nobody ever suggested that Browning's acquaintance had faked the notes, but people were still left to wonder why it had taken so long for this incident to be reported, and why Browning himself had never mentioned this alleged exposure. After all, he had said nothing of this when asked for evidence that Daniel was a fraud. If he were aware of a genuine exposure, then why had he not said so? And if he were not aware of it, then why had his acquaintance not mentioned it to him (for he said he had specifically written to Browning about the séance with Daniel)? All these questions made the testimony suspicious, as testimony always is when it conflicts with what one already knows.

The letter of Dr Barthez, who had witnessed Daniel in Biarritz, was published in 1912. It had been written in 1857, and claimed that Daniel had used his foot to move a bell and tug at dresses. His theories were based on what another man (M. Morio) had seen, and though Barthez claimed that Morio himself recorded what had happened, that record has never appeared. Perhaps it never existed, and Barthez was indulging in wishful thinking, or perhaps it was written but was little more than Morio indulging in wishful thinking (or exaggeration, or maybe he was even the victim of expectant attention). Or was it indeed an accurate account of what happened, but was suppressed by those trying to avoid a royal scandal? All this was conjecture, of course, but fortunately Empress Eugenie was still alive to solve the mystery. According to those who asked her, she told some of them that the exposure had taken place, and others that it had not.[15] Needless to say, Daniel's critics cited her former remarks, while his supporters appealed to her denials, and both sides concluded that they had been right all along.

A few years later Harry Houdini attempted to debunk Daniel, and he did so with his usual blend of showmanship and dubious patter. 'It is quite unnecessary', he declared, 'to repeat the many proofs of fraud against Home.' And so, with the exception of one unsubstantiated allegation, he referred the reader to the writings of Frank Podmore, who he claimed had many other proofs of fraud (though Podmore himself had said quite the opposite). Nevertheless, Houdini maintained, 'many of his manifestations were discovered to be fraudulent and every one of them can be duplicated by modern conjurors under the same conditions'. He provided no new evidence, and offered no new methods, except for some guesswork about the Ashley House levitation (that will be considered below). But he did point out that the asylums were full of insane persons driven mad by spiritualism, and concluded that Daniel was 'a hypocrite of the deepest dye', and that such people 'are, for the most part, moral perverts'.[16]

The arguments have continued for the last century, and no resolution has been reached. The last significant contributor to the debate declared that he had come to 'startling new conclusions'. He pointed out that while other mediums 'were later proven frauds, this was never the case with Daniel Dunglas Home – *until now*'. To back up this italicized claim, he even wrote a whole chapter on the charges of fraud he had discovered, though it transpired that he had failed to discover any evidence that others had not discovered already. The case of the name of Mrs Linton's daughter was, he admitted, 'a relatively minor matter', and the accusations of Dr Barthez 'may well *not* be true'.[17] However, there had been a report that Home had been caught looking at some phosphorous, and Robert Browning had had 'feelings of fraud'. And if that did not amount to clear proof of trickery, there was also a second-hand report that, when

Daniel had been sculpting in Rome, sculpted hands had been seen in his studio. 'Although merely sculpting hands is *not* a fraudulent action per se,' the critic generously conceded, 'the use of such hands in a séance [to fake spirit hands] would be.'[18] And surely that is a point upon which all sides could agree.

These were the most notable charges of fraud against Daniel, as compiled by the most recent critic, with one significant exception. He seems to have thought, and it is hardly surprising, that the Merrifield account was the strongest evidence of fraud. There remains the mystery of why he did not tell Browning of it, and why he did not make it public until Daniel was dead. But if we accept it at face value, then what we have is an account written in 1855, in which a witness recorded how he saw Daniel fake a spirit hand. If we accept the suggested method, then the spirit hand (perhaps it was even a sculpted hand) had been connected to Daniel's person, at the end of his leg or (presumably) held in his own hand. After twenty years of scrutiny, that is the closest anyone got to catching Daniel in the act. But if it is a satisfactory explanation for what you have read so far, then there is absolutely no reason to read any further.

Post-mortem

What are we to make of Daniel Dunglas Home? It is true that there were many accusations of fraud, but most of them were entirely without base, and actual evidence for fraud was both rare and inconclusive. He might have been a cheat, but if he was, then he cheated successfully for two decades, before hundreds of witnesses in thousands of séances. Many of the witnesses were hostile to spiritualism, and many remained unconvinced by what they had seen, yet time and again they admitted that they were unable to explain what had happened. One could argue that this is not so different from watching a competent conjuror, but then Victorian conjurors were also unable to explain how his tricks were done. John Henry Anderson provided no clues, and 'One who is in the secret' clearly was not. Other conjurors did no better, suggesting that his levitation might be the result of elaborate stage apparatus or, perhaps, a gas-filled balloon. John Nevil Maskelyne, who succeeded Anderson as the most public conjuror-debunker of spiritualism, also attempted to debunk Daniel. But he could do little more than repeat the conjectures of Sir David Brewster, then focus on the Lyon versus Home case as evidence of deceit.[1]

Meanwhile, when Bosco (one of the greatest of nineteenth-century conjurors) was asked by a witness what he thought about Daniel's feats, he 'utterly scouted [i.e. dismissed] the idea of the possibility of such phenomena as I saw produced by Mr Home being produced by any of the resources of his art'.[2]

If Victorian conjurors were unable to explain what was going on, Victorian scientists fared no better. Faraday avoided him, and Darwin was too ill to test him, but those who took an interest were impressed with what they saw. William Crookes was so impressed that he carried out experiments specifically designed to rule out fraud, which ended in the announcement of a new force, and in Daniel becoming the first psychic. And while many did not accept this, when Crookes's critics attempted to dismiss his results, they could do little more than attack his credentials, question his competence, and misrepresent the experiments themselves. Whatever the Victorians thought of other mediums, however difficult they found the notion of psychic or super-natural phenomena, they were regularly forced to acknowledge the extraordinary range and nature of the feats that he performed, and the sheer quantity of performances, variety of audiences and openness of conditions in which they took place. Psychic, medium or charlatan, Daniel Dunglas Home was a uniquely mysterious individual for the Victorians.[3]

The question remains: What are *we* to make of Daniel Dunglas Home? He might have been a charlatan, but how can we be sure? We might begin by arguing that he must have been a charlatan, since his feats contravene the laws of physics. But that would be to place theory before evidence, and as theories are themselves based upon evidence, they must always be open to revision in the light of new or conflicting evidence. To argue that such things are impossible because our existing theories do not allow for them is to assume that the theories we construct are themselves reality. Of course, we could point out that there is overwhelming evidence that the laws of nature are correct, that while they are not reality themselves, they nevertheless reflect how the world really works. In addition to all the scientific evidence, we know from our own daily lives that gravity is a useful concept, and that people do not float in the air. And we might, in a fit of rhetoric, demand that anyone who disagrees jump out of the window and see what happens.

But what if they did jump out of the window, and what if they did not fall? And if somebody else witnessed such an event, what would we make of that? And this is not a hypothetical question, for it is essentially what Lords Adare and Lindsay reported at Ashley House. And even if they appear to be rather dubious witnesses, countless others reported tables that seemed to contravene the law of gravity. And if we are not convinced by them, then we might want to look at things a different way. The philosopher David Hume, argued against miracles not because they were impossible but because they were based on insufficient evidence. Hume was quite clear that if someone were to jump out of a window, there was no way of knowing for certain whether he or she would fall. The reason we expect the drop is that we have learned from experience that such things invariably happen when competing with gravity. But Hume would argue that while such things may have invariably happened in the past, that does not mean that they will always happen in the future. That said, in the case of miracles, there is such an overwhelming body of evidence that things fall rather than float, that testimony in favour of floating is bound to be unconvincing. As far as Hume was concerned, such extraordinary events require equally extraordinary evidence. But then Hume never had to deal with the testimony of Daniel's witnesses, and many who did felt that their evidence was indeed extraordinary.

Whatever philosophical position we take, the testimony remains, and we would probably prefer to have some explanation. And if these were not psychic or supernatural events, then how can we explain them? We may accept that Daniel's séance witnesses failed to catch him cheating, or at least failed to provide strong evidence that he had cheated, but that might simply show that he was very good at cheating. And if we wish to argue that he was capable of deceit, we might recall the incident in Florence, when he seems to have acted dishonestly by exploiting the generosity of friends in the matter of his expensive coat. He was also found guilty in court of having used his influence over Mrs Lyon to obtain large amounts of money. And though he never accepted monetary payment for his séances, he consistently depended upon hospitality, and accepted many gifts in the process. All of this might support the impression that he was capable, willing and motivated to deceive. But that would not explain how he deceived witnesses in the séance room. And so we return to the central question: how did he do it?

His feats were extraordinary and varied, but that does not mean they are without potential explanation. The raps might have been produced by the movement of joints, and the movement of small tables by unconscious muscular movement, or by surreptitiously using his feet. He may also have used his feet (or even a lazy-tongs) to move a bell or pull a dress with his toes, or otherwise simulate spirit contact. And who can say how many times a spirit touch might have been a naughty sitter secretly exploiting the situation for private amusement. The spirit hands may have been gloves at the end of his slipper, or some kind of fake apparatus connected to his arm. But then witnesses said that they shook the spirit hand, and 'felt it minutely', and even Edward Lytton, who remained deeply sceptical, had said that he could feel the fingernails. So perhaps, at times, the spirit hand was actually Daniel's foot. This might also explain why sitters reported the hand being fleshy, sometimes warm and sometimes cold, since the temperature of feet is obviously variable. And when, if we recall back in 1852, a journalist reported that the spirit hand 'ENDED AT THE WRIST', perhaps he was merely feeling the heel of the foot. After all, though Daniel was keen to point out that dark séances were unreliable, most of his own séances were fairly dark, for what Victorians regarded as good light was hardly what we are familiar with today. Sometimes it was little more than twilight, perhaps the embers of a coal fire, some gaslights, or a few candles burning. And often, though the séances began in better light, the spirits requested that the lights be dimmed.

The playing of an accordion might have been simulated by the use of a small mouth organ, concealed in the mouth and used in the knowledge that the human ear is unreliable in detecting direction of noise.[4] And the levitation reported in the *Cornhill*, when Daniel floated horizontally around the room, might have been nothing more than the result of his placing his boots on his hands, and holding his arms horizontal while leaning his head back. In the darkness described, it is possible that the silhouette against the window provided a convincing illusion. And when he was heard to rise higher in the air, and the mark on the ceiling later showed that he had risen, perhaps Mrs Linton was right in her guesswork, and he simply stepped on top of the furniture to give the illusion of height, and to provide the physical evidence of levitation.

These explanations may sound too simplistic, but the séances took place in the homes of respectable friends and acquaintances, and it would have been a dreadful display of manners for witnesses to investigate without the host's permission, especially considering that few of Daniel's hosts were in any doubt that he was genuine. When the witnesses checked under the table, they often did so at Daniel's request, and his charismatic manner – combined with a strong say in who was allowed to attend his séances – would have given him a significant degree of control. And, in the end, if conditions were particularly troublesome, he could always have announced that his powers were not with him, and waited until the conditions improved. In such circumstances, perhaps it is not so surprising that he was never caught cheating.

When one thinks of Lords Adare and Lindsay, this seems all the more relevant. Much of what they reported reads like hallucination, and added to the various forms of trickery that might have been used, there was always the possibility of suggestion or hypnosis. Considering the influence Daniel seems to have had over people such as Adare, with whom he lived and shared an intimate relationship, perhaps Adare's bizarre accounts were largely the product of his own imagination, directed by a friend who was in psychological control. Houdini suggested that the Ashley House levitation could have been nothing more than Daniel pretending to go out the window, but actually quietly crawling through to the adjacent room in the dark. He also suggested that Daniel might have swung between the windows using a wire, and that his horizontal exit and entrance through the second window might have been accomplished by nothing more than suggestion.[5] And possibly this is true, for both Adare and Lindsay seem to have believed unquestioningly in Daniel, and Wynne's testimony is interestingly vague. How many other witnesses with whom Daniel stayed might have been similarly under his influence, and been convinced of things that never really happened? This might explain the discrepancies in testimony among witnesses – a lack of consistency that could be the result of not having shared an objective experience, and of being in a mildly altered state of consciousness.

And what of the experiments of William Crookes, specifically designed to eliminate fraud, conducted in good light and witnessed by four observers, two of whom were Fellows of the Royal Society? How did Daniel affect the spring balance, and cause the accordion to play and float around inside the cage? The music might have been produced by a mouth organ, or perhaps by Daniel blowing through a secret tube connected to the accordion. This may not have been seen under the table, if the shadow was sufficient to prevent adequate observation. And perhaps he was able to move the table on which the board rested, and this in turn affected the spring balance. Perhaps he was not observed in this because he was an expert in misdirection, and with enough time to succeed in the experiment, he may have waited until attention levels dropped sufficiently. And the fact that he could always say the spirits had failed to communicate, and that he sometimes modified procedures when being investigated by Crookes, shows that he was always in control to some extent. Not to mention the fact that Crookes failed to report fraud with any of the other mediums he tested, and his conclusions regarding them suggest that he may have been quite easily fooled.

Most of these arguments have been made at one time or another, and all are consistent with evidence that exists.[6] When placed together, they may be sufficient to convince us that the mystery is not really so mysterious. It remains the case that all these explanations were rejected by witnesses, many of whom were aware of such theories, and some of whom were acknowledged experts in mesmerism. Perhaps they were so keen to believe the phenomena that their critical faculties were overcome, though that is another theory they rejected. But if we are happy to overrule the authority of witnesses, and choose to accept what might have happened, rather than what they themselves reported, then we have potential answers to most of what Daniel did.

But then is it really plausible that so many otherwise intelligent people could have been deceived by such blatant tactics over such a long period of time? Doubtless there were many who were desperate to believe, and witnesses such as Benjamin Coleman certainly do seem credulous. Yet many witnesses refused to believe that what they had seen was supernatural, so how can they be guilty of wishful thinking? And many others do not seem credulous at all: when Daniel visited Amsterdam he conducted séances for avowed sceptics, men who admitted that their primary purpose was to debunk his claims. They examined the table, with candles in hand, and went out of their way to avoid being influenced, with declarations of disbelief. And yet the table, large enough to sit fourteen people, moved about in ways they were unable to prevent. Try as they might, they were unable to find even the slightest suspicion of fraud. At least that is what we are told, according to eye-witness testimony. But then perhaps this was an extraordinary case of exaggeration or distorted memory, perhaps it was a hoax or an outright lie. Perhaps none of this even happened, and I have invented the whole story, for while it is true that I have cited all the relevant primary sources, perhaps I suspect that you will never check them. Such are the problems of testimony.

So what are we to make of Daniel Dunglas Home? When Home wrote his memoirs, a Victorian reviewer declared that if this is 'a true and honest book, it is one of the most important works ever presented to the world. But should the opposite be the case, then Mr Home is the greatest impostor that ever deluded mankind.'[7] For this critic, at least, the choice was simple enough: either Daniel was on an important mission, or else he was the greatest impostor in history. Personally, I do not think that these two things are incompatible, but that is only my opinion. So if you are able to choose between them, then there is absolutely no need to read any further.

Postscript

There were once two farmers who were neighbours and friends. Their farms were separated by a small dirt path. One day a stranger walked down the path, and the stranger was wearing a hat. The hat was red on one side and blue on the other, and as the stranger passed between the two farmers, he greeted them, turning neither left nor right. The farmers wished him a good day, and then began to talk. That was a fine red hat, said the first. It was indeed a fine hat, said the second, but it was blue, of course, not red. No, insisted the first, it was red. And so an argument began.

As both men grew more and more insistent, they remembered that the path was a dead-end, and so the stranger would have to return, and then they would settle the question. So they began to wager, and each was so certain that he was right, and so frustrated at the arrogance of the other, that it was not too long before they had bet their respective farms on the question of the colour of the stranger's hat.

And sure enough, when the stranger reached the end of the path, he turned around and began to walk back. But before he came within sight of the farmers, he also turned his hat around, so that each man would see the same side that he had seen before. As he passed between the two men, he again greeted them, turning neither left nor right, and the men replied, and each one smiled as broadly as the other. As I told you, said the first, the hat was red, and so I win the bet. Are you blind, said the second, it was blue, just as I said, and it is I who wins the bet. And so the argument grew and grew, and they began to fight, until finally the police became involved, and the men ended up in court. Families and friends attended the court, to hear what all the fuss was about, and people took sides and began to argue, and soon the whole community was divided. And as the proceedings descended into chaos, the stranger walked into the court, wearing the very same hat.

And he announced to all that he was the Trickster, and then he left, laughing aloud, and left them to themselves.[1]

The story of the Trickster takes many forms, and can be found in the mythologies of many cultures. The meaning of myths is a matter of debate, because myths are never explicit, and so we are free to read them in ways that make most sense to us. We are also free to ignore them, or to dismiss them as stories that are not true, but that would be to miss the point. For while there is no explicit point, there are ways of making sense of myths, and if we wish to make sense of the Trickster, we might say that his role is to upset our world, to remind us that things are not always as they seem, and that sometimes confusion is preferable to order.

Perhaps we need to be reminded that uncertainty is real and certainty an illusion. After all, is there anything of which we can be truly certain? And we might wonder whether confusion is reality, and that order is simply our attempt to make sense of it. For while there are laws of nature and scientific models that we exploit regularly and with confidence, these are laws and models we have created. They may describe the real world, but they are not reality itself. They are words to describe our ideas of how the world seems to be, ideas reliable enough to fly aeroplanes or to communicate on the Internet, or to predict that when certain substances are mixed, a certain reaction will follow. But how certain is such a reaction, for how often in a chemistry class did a predicted effect not happen as it was supposed to, and then we were told that we had done the experiment wrong? And perhaps we had indeed made a mistake, perhaps the test tubes were not properly cleaned, or the substances had oxidized, but then there are so many variables. And that is the point: precision is an ideal that is rare in the real world. Planes crash and computers crash, and when they do, it is attributed to human error, since the real world is supposed to operate according to universal laws.

But these laws have been formulated by human observation, not of the laws themselves, but of the world we can observe. Nobody has seen gravity; we have seen objects fall, and have seen them fall so often that we have concluded that this is a universal law. Newton did not observe gravity any more than he invented it, and he only discovered the law of gravity in the sense that he provided the theory. He did not discover it in the sense that one might discover a hole in one's sock, or even in the sense that Columbus is said to have discovered America. The law of gravity only exists in our understanding of how the world works. It does not exist in the sense that a falling apple exists. And if you are tempted to suggest that anyone claiming this should jump out of a window, then be aware that they would probably decline on the grounds that they also understand the world to work in that way. But that does not make the law of gravity real, it only makes it popular.

And even if you were to find someone who believed that he could fly, then he might actually jump out of the window, and that might be considered an experiment. And if previous experiments are anything to go by, you would probably win the argument. But that would still not make the law of gravity real, it would only make it a replication of previous experiments. And that is an important part of science, some would say the most important part. Theories are tested through repeated experiments, and if the results are not as predicted, then the theory might be falsified. So if someone jumped, but did not fall, the theory of gravity might be falsified. That, according to many scientists today, is what makes it science, for a theory that cannot be falsified cannot be considered scientific. But what would then happen if the man did not fall (or, to take a less dramatic example, if he was somehow able to alter the weight of a board in an experiment)? Would that falsify any scientific theory, or would the experiment be rejected? After all, there are so many variables, such as dirty test tubes or oxidization, or the possibility that the experimenter was mesmerized by a werewolf? What if the experiment was done wrong, and who is to determine that?

When Crookes declared he had discovered a psychic force through experiment, eminent members of the scientific community declared that he had done the experiments wrong. They did not witness the experiments, even though they were invited, nor did they explain adequately what was wrong with them; they simply rejected the testimony of the experimenter. And they did so for the same reason that many of us would, because such testimony is not enough for most of us to revise our world-view. The experiments may have been 'done wrong', but had Daniel failed in the experiments can there be any doubt that they would have been hailed as scientific proof that no such force existed? For that is precisely what happened elsewhere.[2] In that sense, the quality of the experiment was measured by its outcome, much as a chemistry teacher might recognize that an experiment has been carried out correctly when the appropriate result is obtained. And if it is not obtained, then the experiment is repeated until the desired result is achieved, and that is when we are told that we have done the experiment correctly. This is part and parcel of doing science: the reluctance to accept results that do not fit with existing theories.

There is, of course, much more to science, and no one would

question its technological success, but the notion that scientists are simply objective observers of the real world is not one to which scientists themselves would adhere. They do the best they can, which is better than most of us, but they are prone to agendas just like everyone else. The teaching of science, the funding of research, the publication of scientific knowledge, all these are shaped by personal, moral, social and political agendas; and in a different situation, scientific knowledge would be different. The world may be objectively real, but what we know about it is created by humans, accepted or rejected for a variety of reasons, and then there is the worry about 'human error'. And if science is the most successful means of gaining knowledge about the world, how much more problematic is history, where experiments cannot be carried out, and none but the most naive would pretend to objectivity. We do the best we can, but our knowledge of both past and present is no more than our best guess. Most people probably realize this, at the end of the day, yet throughout the day we generally forget, and spend most of our lives thinking we know more than we do, dismissing too easily those with whom we disagree. Perhaps we also trust authorities too easily, particularly when we like what they say, and so we reinforce our views and, if necessary, appeal to these authorities when we want to win an argument. And so, in turn, we reinforce both our certainty and their authority, and feel that much more comfortable in our views. Thus, we place our world in order, and feel more secure within it. And perhaps that is what the Trickster is trying to prevent.

We all try to make sense of our world by defining and organizing our experience. We observe events and we construct categories into which these might be placed. We do this so well that we rarely encounter an event that does not fit into one of our boxes, and so we go through life feeling confident about the categories that we have constructed. And soon these categories become our reality in language and in thought, and we see an object or event as one thing or another, and that is what passes for reality. But it is not reality, because reality lies behind these boxes we have built, and every now and then we are reminded of this. For sometimes we encounter an anomaly, an object or event that does not easily fit into one of our boxes, and then we are faced with a decision. We have the option of forcing the anomaly into one of our boxes, which allows us not to have to look at it any more. And we also have the option of enlarging one of our boxes, perhaps even creating a new box. But that is rather more troublesome, for then we have to reassess our overall world-view.

We can assume that Daniel was a charlatan, a conjuror of tricks rather than of spirits. We might have to admit that we do not really know how he did his tricks, and that no contemporary conjuror provided an adequate explanation. But there were theories, and they may sound more plausible than the idea of psychic or supernatural phenomena, and the remaining mystery could probably be explained by unreliable testimony. This is not quite an explanation, of course, unless we know how the tricks were done, and how the testimony came to be so unreliable.[3] But it is probably enough for most of us, and so the problem is dealt with. Or we may be more sceptical, and feel that we need to revise a box or two. If Daniel could deceive with such success, and provoke such extraordinary testimony, then perhaps our ideas of what magicians can do should be extended. And if witnesses can report such seemingly inexplicable events, and be so certain that they were not deceived in any way, then we might become more sceptical about testimony in general. And that might even change how we read the news or listen to others.

Then we might be even more sceptical, and wonder just how plausible deception and unreliable testimony are as explanations. Are we really prepared to accept that so many people could be deceived so often, and that what people say can be so utterly unreliable? Is that not extraordinary in itself, perhaps more extraordinary than the possibility that he might really have been psychic, or a genuine spirit medium?[4] After all, there have been countless reports of paranormal and miraculous events, and it might be more efficient simply to accept that such things can happen. We might then have to reassess how the world works, whether scientists have got it all wrong, and even whether religious answers might be more reliable. And that may lead us to question scientific authority more generally, or even change our way of life. All of which would be troublesome, possibly dangerous, and even unwarranted, since to call an event 'psychic' is no more of an explanation than to call it a trick. As Crookes pointed out, the term had no theory connected to it, it merely referred to an unknown force, and what sort of explanation is that? There have been people since who have provided theories about the paranormal, but these theories have not been validated adequately by experiment, so even professional parapsychologists do not know how such a force, if it does exist, actually works.[5]

A trick without an explanation, an unknown force without a theory, or perhaps the work of spirits; but does that tell us any more? It might be more appealing, and serve a useful purpose, providing us with the comfort of knowing we do not really die. But we do not know this, we can choose to believe, but to explain a floating table as the work of spirits is to do no more than provide another box. It is no more of an explanation than the psychic box, for if minds can be read, and matter can be moved without contact, then what is the need for the spirit hypothesis? The information Daniel got from the spirits could have been obtained from the minds of those present, and the spirit hands and floating tables could have been manifestations of an unknown natural force. If we wish to believe that spirits were behind this, that is our choice, but it is no more an explanation of the evidence than the alternatives.

So we have a choice of boxes, but if none of them is adequate, we might simply decline to use any of them. We could instead recognize that we do not always know what is going on, that perhaps we never know for certain. Our ways of seeing the world are not the world itself, and the boxes we use to define and organize experience are merely a way of ordering things. When faced with an anomaly, we can see it as a problem, as a source of confusion that upsets our comfortable world-view. Or we might use it to remind ourselves that reality is not so comfortable after all, that behind the boxes we have built lies a more complex universe, and therefore a sense of mystery that may never be removed. That, perhaps, is what the Trickster seeks to point out, and in that sense at least, Daniel Dunglas Home was a Trickster. Not a mythological figure, but a man of flesh and blood who upset the Victorians, forcing them to question their comfortable world-view, and making them wonder whether they really knew what was going on. Perhaps, at least in retrospect, that was his glorious mission. And even if he was the greatest impostor that ever deluded mankind, whose legacy is that of an unsolved mystery, that need not make him any less important. For what is life without wonder, or wonder without mystery, and a mystery with a solution would be no mystery at all.

NOTES

This is not the first biography of D. D. Home. The first, apart from his own, was written by his widow, who portrayed her late husband as a figure of infinite patience and honesty (Mme Home, *D. D. Home: his life and mission* (1888). Horace Wyndham's *Mr Sludge, the medium* (1937), on the other hand, denounced Home as a fake in rather sarcastic language. Jean Burton's *Hey-day of a wizard* (1948) was more balanced, though it was less concerned with the issue of whether Home was genuine or not. Otherwise, biographers have been openly one-sided. On Home's side (as their subtitles might suggest) were George Zorab's *D. D. Home the medium: a biography and a vindication* (tr. by B. Inglis, unpublished) and Elizabeth Jenkins' *The Shadow and the light: a defence of Daniel Dunglas Home the medium* (1982), both of which went to great lengths to clear Home of accusations of dishonesty. On the other hand, Trevor Hall's *The Enigma of Daniel Home: medium of fraud?* (1984) made an equally desperate effort to accuse Home of wrongdoing at every opportunity, even when there was no solid evidence, while Gordon Stein's *The sorcerer of kings: the case of Daniel Dunglas Home and William Crookes* (1993) was as critical in its language, if no more critical in its assessment of the evidence. Just as Home divided Victorian society, so he has split the opinions of biographers.

The fact is that one cannot write a worthwhile biography without providing the reader with a sense of the subject's motivation, and in Home's case, that is entirely dependent upon whether he was genuine or fraudulent. That is why other biographers have taken a line according to their own positions on the matter, and that is what I have done as well. My belief, as you have probably gathered by now, is that Home was a charlatan whose feats have never been adequately explained. Of course, I might be wrong, which is why I have avoided any explicit statement that he was a charlatan. Nevertheless, that is my belief, so that is the line I have taken. Naturally, I regard this as an eminently balanced view, but then I have yet to meet anyone who did not feel that his or her view was balanced. It is, however, a quite different view from most of Home's biographers, and so perhaps deserves a brief explanation.

I am not convinced, as Zorab and Jenkins were, that Home's feats were genuine, but that is a matter of more general beliefs about phenomena such as floating tables and human levitation, and the problems of eye-witness testimony. In short, I have encountered too many examples of deception and self-deception to be easily converted by historical evidence, and there are insufficient details (particularly about the conditions in which Home worked, and the competence of his witnesses) to convince me that he must have been a genuine psychic. However, neither do I agree with Hall (whose subtitle was 'The mystery of Britain's most famous spiritualist unraveled') and Stein (who, at times, claimed that Home was a proven fraud) that Home's feats have been adequately explained. That is a more straightforward matter of historical evidence, of adequate research and (what I regard as) appropriate interpretation. Neither of these writers provided convincing explanations for Home's most impressive feats, and both not only made unsubstantiated claims but also failed to include important evidence that was available to them.

There is, however, one thing of which I am convinced. In their eager attempts to defend Home on the one hand, or to condemn him on the other, previous biographers have (to varying degrees) ignored evidence that did not suit them and, as a result, have presented a rather one-sided view of a man who was, whether genuine or fraudulent, as complex as he was remarkable. As to whether he was actually genuine or fraudulent, that we shall never know, and so we can choose what to do with the evidence. Whether one regards Home's feats as unexplained depends upon how satisfactory one finds the available explanations, and there are different levels of explanation. At one level, there are the specific methods that have been suggested (which, in my opinion, do not satisfactorily deal with what the eye-witnesses reported). At another level, there is the general question of whether the eye-witness testimony is sufficiently reliable and detailed to rule out possible deception and self-deception (which, in my opinion, it is not). My own view, then, is that Home's feats remain unexplained, but they are not inexplicable.

However, I believe that whether one decides that they are inexplicable (by deception and self-deception), and therefore psychic or supernatural, depends upon how plausible one finds the idea of such phenomena. If I ever see a floating table, and come to the conclusion that it is a genuine levitation, I will have little trouble in regarding Home as a genuine psychic. After all, when one believes that such things can really happen, historical evidence that they have happened before is that much more convincing. And if someone ever provides a more convincing explanation for how Home achieved his more inexplicable feats, then I will be that much more convinced that he was indeed a charlatan. But until either of these rather unlikely events occurs, I suspect my view will remain as it is. I have read the arguments on both sides, and checked the primary sources they used, along with countless sources they did not use, and have come to the conclusion that Home was a charlatan whose feats have never been adequately explained. I choose to embrace the resultant mystery, not as evidence that such extraordinary psychic phenomena really exist, but as a powerful reminder that we should never be too comfortable with our own view of the world. Others, more confident in their world-view, are free to disagree. Indeed, I suspect they will (even as I write this, a few names immediately spring to mind). I look forward to some interesting (and a few rather familiar) discussions.

Meanwhile, if you wish to investigate further for yourself, here are the sources that I used. Be aware that many of the secondary sources are unreliable in various respects (e.g. inaccurate or unsubstantiated), and that the primary sources against which I checked them are occasionally difficult to access. Such is the challenge of historical research into matters of controversial and extraordinary characters.

Prologue

1 The journalist was Frank L. Burr, who later became editor of the *Hartford Times*. The account appears in Home's autobiography, D. D. Home, *Incidents in my life* (London, 1863), pp. 56–61. Twenty years later, Burr gave an account of this séance to the *New York Sun*, and in

1887, he wrote to Home's widow to confirm what he had seen (Mme Home, *D. D. Home: his life and mission* (London, 1921), pp. 20-22. The letters that appeared in this book, reporting as they did rather extraordinary events, were checked by the Society for Psychical Research, who concluded that they had been accurately represented by Mme Home (*Journal of the Society for Psychical Research* [henceforth *JSPR*], 4, 1889, p. 101).

1 The birth of a wizard

1 Home, *Incidents*, p. 3
2 Wyndham, *Mr Sludge*, p. 30. Wyndham claimed there was little evidence to support this claim, other than the fact that Home had been baptized 'Daniel Dunglas'. In fact, Wyndham is wrong on both counts. Home's birth certificate refers merely to 'Daniel Home'. On the other hand, the aristocratic connection is not without evidential support. According to John Dea, a retired paper-maker of Colington parish, who had family in Currie when William was there, it was 'a fact well known that he was a natural son of the late Earl of Home and was always spoken of by all as such' (SPR.MS28/139, Home collection, Cambridge University). Furthermore, I have checked the census, and it shows a Dea family in Currie at the time, suggesting John was related to neighbours (or at least acquaintances) of the Homes. For some reason, despite all the disagreement about Home's ancestral roots, neither he nor any of his biographers since have mentioned this testimonial. One of them, Trevor Hall, went out of his way to argue that this claim was false, as part of his general accusation that Home was untrustworthy, yet though he checked the Home papers, he failed to mention this particular piece of evidence (T. Hall, *The enigma of Daniel Home: medium or fraud?* (Buffalo, 1984)). Given Hall's tendency to point out the errors of others, it seems only fair that this omission on his part be noted. In the interests of balance, it might also be pointed out that one of Home's defenders, George Zorab, wrote a piece entitled 'Have we finally solved the enigma of D. D. Home's descent?', which contained countless errors, some of which were based upon no evidence at all (*JSPR*, 49, 1978, pp. 844-47).

3 The occupation of William Home has been guessed at before, but since his address is given in the census as Balerno Mill, and that mill rented out cottages to its workforce (V. Wilson, Kinleith Paper Mill, Currie: its workforce and effect on the community in 1880–1881), it seems fairly clear that he worked at the paper mill.

4 *New Statistical Account of Scotland (1845)*, pp. 541–57.

5 Mme Home, *The gift of D. D. Home*, pp. 211–12.

6 J. Burton, *Hey-day of a wizard* (London, 1948), p. 44.

7 *New Statistical Account of Scotland (1845)*, pp. 541–57.

8 Home, *Incidents*, p. 1.

9 Population figures for Portobello are taken from the 1841 Census, other figures refer to the parish of Duddingston as a whole.

10 Home, *Incidents*, p. 1.

11 M Lindsay, *The eye is delighted: some romantic travellers in Scotland* (London, 1971), pp. 225–6.

12 W. Scott, *Letters on demonology and witchcraft* (London, 1830).

13 Scott, *Letters on demonology*, p. 320.

14 *Chambers' Journal*, 1, 1832, 1 (4 Feb.), p. 1.

15 These articles are sprinkled throughout a single issue of the journal [*Chambers' Journal*, 1, 1832, 4 (25 Feb.)].

16 ibid.

17 D. Brewster, *Letters on natural magic* (Edinburgh, 1832).

18 *Chambers' Journal*, 1, 1832, 18 (28 Apr), p. 102.

19 *New Statistical Account of Duddingston (1843)*.

20 Robert Stewart, *Henry Brougham, 1778–1868: his public career* (London, 1985), pp. 308–16.

21 There have been various claims by Home's biographers about who left when, but none of them bothered to check the census. The Currie census of 1841 lists William (labourer) and Elizabeth Hume (both 30), Alexander (9), Mary Anne (6), William (5), and Adam Pennycuik (3), residing at 17 Kenleith Mill. It also lists a John Hume (labourer, 13) of 13 Balerno Mills Cottages, where the head of household is listed as McNeill (Elizabeth's maiden name). John was most likely the eldest son, who was living with Elizabeth's father in 1841. The Portobello census lists only one Cook family, and the wife's name is Mary (25), but as three children are also mentioned, none of them named Daniel, this is hardly likely to be the childless aunt who adopted him.

22 From *Martin Chuzzlewit*, cited in Jenkins, *Shadow and the light*, p. 6.

23 Letter from J. G. Woodward, dated 1895 (SPR.MS28/861, Home collection).

24 The former description was from Prof. Calvin Stowe to George Eliot (Charles Edward Stowe, *Life of Harriet Beecher Stowe*, London, 1889, p. 420). The latter is from Mme Home, *Life and mission*, p. 1.

25 Home, *Incidents*, p. 2.

26 Mme Home, *Life and mission*, p. 2.

27 Home, *Incidents*, p. 2–3.

28 ibid., p. 5.

29 ibid., p. 5.

30 Mme Home, *Life and mission*, p. 4.

31 Home, *Incidents*, 7; Mme Home, *Life and mission*, p. 4.

32 Home, *Incidents*, pp. 7–8.

2 The rise of a medium

1 Letter from Miss Ely, dated May 1851 [Mme Home, *The gift of D. D. Home* (London, 1890), p. 65].

2 Francis Gerry Fairfield, *Ten years with spiritual mediums: an inquiry concerning the etiology of certain phenomena called spiritual* (New York, 1875), p. 18.

3 ibid, pp. 7–10.

4 Podmore, *Modern spiritualism*, i, pp. 184–5.

5 ibid, p. 186.

6 ibid, p. 188.

7 Home, *Incidents*, p. 9. I have not seen the original account, but having checked countless other original accounts that Home cited, I have no doubt this is also an accurate representation of the original. Whether the original account is a reliable description of what actually happened, of course, requires a more difficult leap of faith.

8 That this Mr Hayden was W. R. Hayden, wife of the famous medium, was disputed by Burton (1948, p. 50), but maintained by Zorab (unpublished, p. 2). I am assuming that Zorab read Burton, and had some reason for disagreeing with her, though he provides no evidence.

9 Among these was George Bush, a Professor of Hebrew with a mixed reputation. According to Daniel, he was 'a profoundly learned man,

with a more open and child-like mind than often falls to the lot of those with so much worldly knowledge' (Home, *Incidents*, pp. 16–17). He was, more importantly, a Swedenborgian, a follower of the eighteenth century scientist and mystic who had claimed to converse with spirits a century before the birth of Modern Spiritualism. When Andrew Jackson Davis, the 'Poughkeepsie Seer', set the stage for the birth of Modern Spiritualism with his own spiritual writings, the spirit of Swedenborg was a major contributor from the other world, while George Bush was his biggest supporter in this one.

10 This account appears in several places, including A. Mahan, *The phenomena of spiritualism, scientifically explained and exposed* (London, 1855), p. 112.

11 Both Hare and Edmonds published books on spiritualism, and Hare subsequently gave a presentation to the American Association for the Advancement of Science. The extremely cold response he received – 'The fact was, the eminent man had gone insane; the meeting would not listen to him' – is describe in *English Mechanic*, 14, 1871, pp. 425–6.

12 This account is by Frank Burr, who published it in the *Hartford Times*. It appears in several books, the most accessible being: Home, *Incidents*, pp. 36–9; Podmore, *Modern spiritualism*, i, p. 245.

13 The quote comes from an anonymous pamphlet (*Spirit rapping in Europe and America* [1853], p. 121). The levitation is also described at this time in H. Spicer, *Sights and sounds of spiritualism* (London, 1853), p. 131. The form of these descriptions show that Home was not known to these authors other than through this levitation.

14 Mme Home, *Life and mission*, p. 78.

15 G. N Ray (ed.), *The letters and private papers of William Makepeace Thackeray* (London, 1946), iii, pp. 123–34.

16 The fee and expenses were offered in a letter from A. Gerald Hull (SPR.MS28/364). The rest is described by Daniel, and confirmed in a letter from W. J. Bauer (SPR.MS28/26).

17 This is confirmed in a letter from A. S. Jarves (SPR.MS28/370).

18 The authenticity of both the middle name, and the claim associated with it, has been a subject of much controversy. The main critic, Trevor Hall, went into somewhat tedious detail to argue that, since

Dunglas did not appear on the birth certificate, the name and the associated claim was an invention of the medium. Hall supports his argument by claiming that Home did not use it until much later in life, though he failed to point out that there were several earlier references to the middle name, including a letter addressed to 'Daniel Dunglass Home' from L. Aurelia Ely, Lebanon, dated 29 June 1851 (Home collection, SPR.MS28/179). On the claim that Home's father was the natural son of the tenth earl of Home, see note 3.

3 The reception in London

1 S. Nenadic, 'Illegitimacy, insolvency and insanity: Wilkie Collins and the Victorian nightmares' in A. Marwick (ed.), *The Arts, Literature, and Society* (London, 1990), pp. 6–7.

2 For a more detailed image of dark London, and Jack the Ripper in particular, see: J. Walkowitz, *City of dreadful delight: narratives of danger in late-Victorian London* (London, 1992), pp. 15–39, 191–228.

3 R. Noakes, 'Cranks and visionaries: science, spiritualism and transgression in Victorian Britain', (unpublished thesis, Cambridge University, 1998), p. 21.

4 [W. B. Carpenter], 'Electro-biology and mesmerism', *Quarterly Review*, 93, pp. 501–57.

5 'Faraday on table-moving', *The Athenaeum*, 1853 (2 July), pp. 801–3.

6 This appeared in *The Leader*, 12 January 1853 (cited in Podmore, *Modern spiritualism*, ii, p. 5), and is described in J. H. Anderson, *The magic of spirit rapping* (London, c. 1854).

7 Anderson, *Magic of spirit rapping*, p. 88.

8 F. Podmore, *Robert Owen: a biography* (London, 1923), p. 602.

9 Jenkins, *Shadow and the light*, p. 73.

10 Mrs Gordon, *The Home Life of Sir David Brewster* (Edinburgh, 1870), pp. 257–8.

11 Mme Home, *Life and mission*, p. 24.

12 Robert Lytton, *Letters from Owen Meredith to Robert and Elizabeth Barrett Browning* (Waco, 1936), pp. 109–12.

13 F. Kenyon, *Letters of Elizabeth Barrett Browning* (London, 1897), ii, pp. 196, 201; L. Huxley (ed.), *Elizabeth Barrett Browning: letters to her sister, 1846–1859* (London, 1929), p. 218.

14 B. Miller, 'The Séance at Ealing', *Cornhill Magazine*, 169, 1957, p. 318.

15 It 'did not melt in my clasp, but eluded it by a sudden and brisk withdrawal, as that of a skilful human being might do . . . and I c[oul]d feel, at times, the nails . . . Mr H. went twice into trance, and gave us a sort of "inspired lecture" — but what he said was really great twaddle'. Lytton, *Letters*, pp. 109–12.

16 Huxley, *Elizabeth Barrett Browning*, pp. 201–21.

17 Miller, 'Séance at Ealing', pp. 317–18.

18 *JSPR*, 11, 1903, pp. 11–14.

19 H. Allingham & D. Radford, *William Allingham: a diary* (London, 1907), p. 101.

20 Huxley, *Elizabeth Barrett Browning*, p. 219.

21 Allingham & Radford, *Allingham*, pp. 101–2.

22 Dingwall, *Some human oddities* (New York, 1962), p. 107.

4 The Wizards of the North

1 Frost, *Lives of the conjurers*, p. 251.

2 E. A. Dawes, *The great illusionists* (Secaucus, 1979), p. 110.

3 Biographical details have been taken from: E. P. H[ingston], *Biography of Professor Anderson: sketches from his note-book* (c. 1865); Frost, *Lives of the conjurers*; 'The Wizard of the North: life story of John Henry Anderson', *The People's Journal* (Glasgow, printed serially, 1901); J. B. Findlay, *Anderson and his theatre* (Shanklin, 1967); and Dawes, *The great illusionists*.

4 This is, at the moment, the general view among historians of magic, based on the earliest known print of the trick being of Anderson in the late 1830's (M. Christopher, *Panorama of prestidigitators: magic through the ages* (New York, 1956), p. 18.

5 C. Pecor, *The magician on the American stage, 1752–1874* (Washington, 1977), pp. 186–97.

6 Ibid., p. 188.

7 Ibid., pp. 195–6.

8 R. Jay, *Jay's journal of anomalies* (New York, 2001), pp. 83–94.

9 Ibid., p. 89.

10 *Times*, 7 July 1853, p. 8; 11 July 1853, p. 8, 14 July 1853, p. 8, 19 July 1853, p. 8, 25 July 1853, p. 5.

11 Anderson, *Magic of spirit-rapping*, pp. 68–74.

12 *Yorkshire Spiritual Telegraph*, 1, 1855, p. 9.

13 Frost, *Lives of the conjurers*, pp. 251–2.

14 The details of the show are described in an advertisement in *The Times*, 3rd September, 1855, p. 6.

15 Ibid. pp. 252–3.

16 Anderson, *Magic of spirit-rapping*, pp. 89–90.

17 *Spiritual Magazine*, 5, 1864, p. 503.

18 *Morning Advertiser*, 3rd Oct 1855, p. 4.

19 Coleman's letter appeared on the 4th Oct., p. 4, Cox's letter on the 5th Oct., p. 4.

20 Brewster's reply appeared in the 12th Oct, p. 4. That, and the ensuing correspondence appeared on the letters pages of the *Advertiser*, and much of it is reproduced in detail in Home, *Incidents*, p. 240ff.

21 This part of the debate took place in the *Advertiser* between 20th Oct and 9th November, but is not reproduced in Home's autobiography.

22 See, respectively: Sir Charles Isham in the *Spiritual Herald*, 1, 1856, p. 17; Thomas Barlee in the *Yorkshire Spiritual Telegraph*, 3, 1857, p. 20; and 'Verax' in the *Morning Advertiser*, 12th Oct 1855, p. 2.

23 *Morning Advertiser*, 1st Nov. 1855, p. 4.

24 H. Morley, *The Journal of a London Playgoer* (London, 1866), p. 109.

25 Ibid., pp. 110–12.

26 'The Wizard of the North: life story of John Henry Anderson', p. 49.

5 Scandal and loss in Florence

1 Huxley, *Elizabeth Barrett Browning*, p. 237.

2 Mme Home, *Gift of D. D. Home*, p. 97.

3 Home, *Incidents*, p. 86.

4 Huxley, *Elizabeth Barrett Browning*, pp. 237, 262.

5 Burton, *Hey-day of a wizard*, p. 86.

6 Jenkins, *Shadow and the light*, p. 62.

7 Home, *Incidents*, p. 93.

8 Huxley, *Elizabeth Barrett Browning*, p. 241; Kenyon, *Letters*, ii, p. 226. Letters between Hiram Powers and the Rymers in 1856 tell of how Home said 'horrible things' about two of the Trollopes and certain

other unnamed parties. They also refer to several selfish acts that led to the Rymers disowning Home, refer to Home himself in extremely negative language, and describe behaviour suggestive of fraud during séances. Indeed, Powers was convinced that he cheated at times (though not all the time), and doubts that he suffered from any chronic illness. Copies of these letters, which are held at the Smithsonian Archives of American Art, Washington D.C., were sent to me by Doug Harlow after the final proof had been sent for printing.

9 Kenyon, *Letters*, ii, p. 226.

10 P. Neville-Sington, *Fanny Trollope: the life and adventures of a clever woman* (London, 1997), pp. 350–2. The book was entitled *Fashionable Life: or Paris and London (1856)*.

11 Home, *Incidents*, p. 86.

12 The quotes are from Arthur Conan Doyle, who read the letters (A. Conan Doyle, *The Wanderings of a Spiritualist* (London, 1921), p. 172). Conan Doyle seems to have heard of these letters after writing to Rymer's son, who replied as follows: 'Home turned out, by his conduct, a great disappointment, and was evidently much adversely discussed by the members of the English and American colony in Florence, and the correspondence above-mentioned refers to his conduct and also his manifestations. Both [T. A.] Trollope and [Hiram] Powers discredited him, and came to the opinion that he resorted to trickery whilst they honestly admit that some of the manifestations could not be explained' (letter from Vernon Rymer to Conan Doyle, dated 5 November 1920). Many thanks to George Locke at Biblion for allowing me to read this.

13 Huxley, *Elizabeth Barrett Browning*, p. 262.

14 Home, *Incidents*, p. 93.

15 The story is related by John Bigelow, who met Dickens in Boston, who told him what Anthony Trollope had told him several years earlier. According to this story, when Daniel had been in Florence, he had tried to eavesdrop on conversations in order to gain information surreptitiously, so Trollope had deliberately fed him the wrong information, which Daniel had duly communicated at a séance later that evening. (John Bigelow, *Retrospections of an active life* (New York, 1913), iv, p. 121).

16 Huxley, *Elizabeth Barrett Browning*, p. 262.

17 Home, *Incidents*, p. 93.

18 Mrs Browning had heard of the year's suspension by early March (Huxley, *Elizabeth Barrett Browning*, p. 241).

19 Mme Home, *Life and mission*, p. 42.

20 *Westminster Review*, 13, 1858, p. 42.

21 Huxley, *Elizabeth Barrett Browning*, pp. 248–9.

22 Mme Home, *Life and mission*, p. 43.

23 Huxley, *Elizabeth Barrett Browning*, p. 263.

24 Cited in Zorab, *D. D. Home*, p. 50.

25 Ibid., p. 51.

26 F. A. Wellesley, *The Paris Embassy during the Second Empire* (London, 1928), pp. 111–12.

27 Kenyon, *Letters*, ii, pp. 266–7.

28 Burton, *Hey-day of a wizard*, p. 107.

29 Lord Edmond Fitzmaurice, *Life of Lord Granville, 1815–1891* (London, 1905), i, p. 230.

30 Wellesley, *Paris embassy*, p. 112.

31 E. Barthez, *The Empress Eugenie and her circle*, p. 138.

32 The Minister's threat to resign is noted by Jenkins, *Shadow and the light*, p. 80, though she gives no reference. A note by Brian Inglis in his translation of Zorab's *D. D. Home* gives the source for this claim as R. Sencourt, *The Life of the Empress Eugenie* (London, 1931), pp. 106–7, but this is not true. The actual claim is made by Octave Aubry (Octave Aubry, *Eugenie, Empress of the French, translated by F. M. Atkinson* (London, 1939), pp. 136–8) though he confuses it with a later allegation of exposure by M. de l'Isle, and he adds that the Minister thought Home a spy. That other rumours of Home being a spy existed is claimed by E. Dingwall, *Some human oddities* (London, 1947), p. 121.

33 Princess Caroline Murat, *My Memoirs* (London, 1910), p. 274

34 Brussels *Independence*, April 1857, cited in a letter by Frederic Lees to the *Westminster Gazette*, 27 February 1899, p. 4.

35 The conversation was heard by Home himself in 1857, shortly after his departure from France (Mme Home, *Life and mission*, pp. 65–6).

36 Home, *Incidents*, pp. 103–5. Meanwhile, the British press provided an alternative account of his reasons for leaving. It was said that he had conjured up the spirit of Socrates, 'the white and flowing beard, the bald head and crushed nose were unmistakable', and then that of Frederick the Great, King of Prussia, his 'head surmounted by the

little traditional cocked hat'. But Daniel's response had been 'to turn deadly pale . . . [and] the perspiration rolled in great drops from his forehead'. The tension had been broken, however, when the spirit had given out 'a loud and uncontrollable laugh', and Daniel had realized he had been deceived by some sceptical pranksters wearing a false beard and a borrowed hat. According to this story, 'he disappeared, and the next day we heard, without astonishment, of his sudden departure from Paris' (Home, *Incidents*, pp. 112–13).

37 This was also the understanding of the British Ambassador – 'He has now gone to America, to bring his sister, a girl of nine, who, he says, is more wonderful than himself, and who is to be educated here at the Empress's expense' (Wellesley, *Paris embassy*, p. 111).

38 Wyndham, *Mr Sludge*, p. 68.

39 Dingwall, *Some human oddities*, pp. 109–10.

40 Barthez, *Empress Eugenie*, pp. 137–42.

6 Diagnosis in Biarritz

1 Home, *Incidents*, p. 108.

2 The incident was not even mentioned by Mme Home. When one compares the amount of space she gave to refuting other charges of imposture, this might be regarded as a little unusual.

3 Barthez, *Empress Eugenie*, pp. 164–167.

4 For evidence of early rumours of this exposure, see: *Westminster Gazette*, 18 Febrauary 1899, p. 3 (letter from W. J Stillman); Count Perovsky-Petrovo-Solovovo, Some thoughts on D. D. Home, *Proceedings of the Society for Psychical Research* [henceforth *PSPR*], 1930, p. 247; Dingwall. *Some human oddities*, p. 120.

5 G. Zorab, 'Test sittings with D. D. Home at Amsterdam (1858)', *Journal of Parapsychology*, 34, 1970, pp. 47–63.

6 Home, *Incidents*, p. 124.

7 Zorab, 'Test sittings', pp. 56–7.

8 Home, *Incidents*, p. 106.

9 Lytton, *Letters*, p. 146.

10 Wyndham, *Mr Sludge*, pp. 85–6. The story is based upon the writings of the Comte de Viel-Castel, and referred to in Dingwall, *Some human oddities*, p. 121.

11 Huxley, *Elizabeth Barrett Browning*, p. 293.

12 Dingwall, *Some human oddities*, p. 121.

13 Pisanus Fraxi [H. S. Ashbee], *Centuria Librorum Absconditorum* (London, 1879), p. 412.

14 Pisanus Fraxi [H. S. Ashbee], *Catena Librorum Tacendorum* (London, 1885), p. xiv.

15 Kenyon, *Letters*, ii, p. 280. According to Horace Wyndham, the lady was Madame Bediska, relative of the Russian Consul (Wyndham, *Mr Sludge*, p. 92).

16 Lytton, *Letters*, p. 146. This letter to Browning is signed '29th April '56', but the postmark is 4 May 1858, and the content of the letter confirms the latter date to be correct.

17 Huxley, *Elizabeth Barrett Browning*, p. 293.

18 The story is recounted by Dumas in *Adventures in Tsarist Russia* (Westport, 1975), pp. 33–48. Home's amusement at the story is recalled by Mme Home, *Life and mission*, p. 62.

19 Home, *Incidents*, p. 129.

20 Ibid., p. 219.

21 Ibid., pp. 131–2.

22 *Town Talk*, 16th Oct. 1858, p. 282.

7 The Cornhill Exchange

1 *Spiritual Magazine*, 4, 1863, p. 336.

2 Letter from Mrs Webster (Mme Home, *Life and mission*, p. 213).

3 Mme Home, *Life and mission*, p. 96.

4 The circulation was around 80,000 (A. Ellegard, *Darwin and the general reader* (Gotheburg, 1958), p. 372).

5 [R. Bell], 'Stranger than fiction', *Cornhill Magazine*, 2, 1860, pp. 211–24.

6 Home, *Incidents*, p. 154.

7 G. H. Lewes, who had so enthusiastically reported how he had led the spirits to denounce Mrs Hayden as an impostor, publicly stated that he believed the facts were as described, but he attributed them to trickery (though he failed to explain how any of it was done) (*Blackwood's Edinburgh Magazine*, 87, 1860, pp. 381–95). A fellow sceptic, John Delaware Lewis, described how he had detected the medium Mrs Marshall in fraud, and offered to test Daniel. '[T]his is

a fair challenge', the *Literary Gazette* observed, 'which Mr Home would do well to accept; as on a non-acceptance an unfavourable construction must necessarily be placed' (*Literary Gazette*, 8 September 1860, pp. 180–1). The challenge, however, was not taken up, and no doubt some unfavourable constructions were the result. Curiously, the *Spiritual Magazine* subsequently reported both the Lewis article and the comment in the *Literary Gazette*, but deleted Lewis' challenge to Home from the extract (*Spiritual Magazine*, 1, 1860, p. 437). It seems unlikely that Home would not have known about the challenge, but it was never taken up, and neither the challenge nor the failure to respond received further attention.

8 See, for example: *Punch*, 18 August 1860, p. 63; *Fraser's Magazine*, 66, 1862, pp. 521–22.

9 Cited in *Spiritual Magazine*, 1, 1860, p. 438.

10 [R. Chambers], *On testimony: its posture in the scientific world* (London, 1859).

11 Brewster, *Letters*, p. 11.

12 J. C. Bucknill & D. H. Tuke, *A manual of psychological medicine: containing the history, nosology, description, statistics, diagnosis, pathology and treatment of insanity* (London, 1858), p. 123. A similar point is made in J. Pritchard, *A treatise on insanity and other disorders affecting the mind* (Philadelphia, 1837), p. 16.

13 See, for example: *Fraser's Magazine*, 60, 1859, p. 630; *North British Review*, 34, 1861, p. 123; *British Quarterly Review*, 36, 1862, p. 416.

14 This was claimed by E. R. Lankester, FRS, an eminent zoologist and critic of spiritualism, and reported with frustration in the *Yorkshire Spiritual Telegraph*, 1, 1856, p. 169.

15 This particular quote comes from *The Spiritualist*, 2, 1871, p. 13, though the sentiment was certainly around earlier.

16 In regard to J. S. Rymer's accounts of Home's séances, Robertson wrote: 'These are strong facts, and it is allowing a great deal to say that we think Mr Rymer to be in earnest in stating his belief in them. For ourselves, we entirely disbelieve them'. Indeed, he suggested Rymer read a college textbook describing 'those immutable laws which the unchanging God has impressed, once for ever, on his creation' so that he might come to share the writer's 'disbelief of those imaginings which tell us of their violation in moving tables' (*Journal of Mental Science*, 4, 1857, pp. 385–6).

His subsequent conversion, three years later, is described, with a degree of satisfaction, in the *Spiritual Magazine*, 1, 1860, p. 342.

17 On Elliotson's change of mind, see: *Spiritual Magazine*, 5, 1864, p. 216; *Morning Post*, 3 August, 1868, p. 3.

18 *Saturday Review*, 12 January 1856, p. 194. A similar point was made in the *Athenaeum*, 2 February 1867, p. 150.

19 C. Weld, *Last Winter in Rome* (London, 1865), pp. 179–81. According to Weld, when Thackeray was in New York, he 'saw a large and heavy dinner-table . . . rise fully two feet from the ground'. This is rather more impressive than what Thackeray himself recorded, but if it is what Thackeray recalled, rather than an exaggeration by Weld, it might explain his defence of 'Stranger than fiction'.

20 *Spiritual Magazine*, 2, 1861, pp. 63–6.

21 *Medium and Daybreak*, 2, 1871, p. 325.

22 'Katerfelto', 'Spirit-rapping made easy; or how to come out as a medium. By one who is in the secret', *Once A Week*, 6 Oct 1866, pp. 403–7.

23 'Katerfelto', 'Spirit-rapping made easy. No. II. The Cornhill narrative and the performances of Mr Home', *Once A Week*, 27 Oct 1866, pp. 489–94.

8 Versions of events

1 Ibid., p. 94.

2 The article was entitled, 'The fins and wings of war-ships: undamageable propellers'.

3 The séance is described in Home, *Incidents*, p. 193.

4 G. S. Layard, *Mrs Lynn Linton: her life, letters and opinions* (London, 1901), p. 174.

5 Home, *Incidents*, p. 143.

6 Layard, *Mrs Lynn Linton*, pp. 169–74.

7 M. House (ed.), *The letters of Charles Dickens* (Oxford, 1965), vii, p. 651.

8 Ibid., p. 657.

9 Burton, *Hey-day*, p. 142

10 House, *Letters of Dickens*, ix, p. 311.

11 [Mrs Lynn Linton], 'Modern magic', *All The Year Round*, 28 July 1860, pp. 370–4.

12 *Times*, 13 Mar. 1862, p. 6.

13 *Spiritual Magazine*, 3, 1862, p. 45.

14 *Spiritual Magazine*, 3, 1862, p. 90.

15 *Spiritual Magazine*, 3, 1862, pp. 91, 147–50.

16 *Spiritual Magazine*, 3, 1862, p. 294.

17 *Spiritual Magazine*, 3, 1862, p. 153.

18 For example, 'A séance with Mr Foster', *Spiritual Magazine*, 6, 1871, pp. 66–70.

19 W. Crookes, 'Spiritualism', p. 322.

20 G. Cantor, *Michael Faraday: Sandemanian and scientist: a study of science and religion in the 19th century* (Basingstoke, 1991).

21 The correspondence was subsequently published in the *Pall Mall Gazette*, and reprinted in the *Spiritual Magazine*, 3, 1868, pp. 259–60.

22 Home, *Incidents*, p. 199.

23 Ibid., p. 212.

24 Mme Home, *Life and mission*, p. 104.

25 Home, *Incidents*, p. 215.

25 Mme Home, *Life and mission*, p. 105.

27 Ibid, p. 108.

28 The publishing deal was negotiated by the political economist, Nassau Senior, who had been bewildered by what he had seen at Daniel's séances (Zorab, *D. D. Home*, p. 104).

29 Home, *Incidents*, ii, p. 21.

9 *An International Incident*

1 *Athenaeum*, 14 March 1863, pp. 351–3.

2 D. D. Home, *Incidents in my life*, 2nd series, pp. 24–5; *Cornhill Magazine*, 7, 1863, pp. 706–19.

3 [C. Dickens], 'The martyr medium', *All the Year Round*, 4 April 1863, pp. 133–5.

4 House, *Letters of Dickens*, x, p. 239. Dickens told the Earl of Carlisle that he had 'some considerable reason, derived from two honourable men, for mistrusting [him]' (House, *Letters of Dickens*, ix, p. 284).

5 [D. Brewster], 'Pretensions of Spiritualism', *North British Review*, 39, 1863, pp. 174–206.

6 His authorship of the anonymous article was revealed in Gordon, *Home Life*, pp. 454–55.

7   Jenkins, *Shadow and the light*, p. 36.

8   Home, *Incidents*, ii, p. 191.

9   [H. L. Mansel], 'Modern Spiritualism', *Quarterly Review*, 114, 1863, pp. 180.

10 *Literary Times*, 21 March 1863, cited in Home, *Incidents*, ii, p. 37.

11 *Times*, 1863, April 9, pp. 4–5. The Times had heard that Daniel had been caught cheating, that a well-known and respectable gentleman had discovered a handkerchief at a séance, and had claimed that Daniel used this to simulate the sensation of being touched by the spirits. The rumour cited concerned Richard Monckton Milnes, subsequently Lord Houghton. There was no evidence, however, that Milnes had made such a charge. So Daniel wrote to *the Times*, denying the charge, and challenging his accusers to come forward, which ended that particular matter (*Times*, 16 April 1863, p. 12).

12 *Quarterly Review*, 114, 1863, pp. 196–8. The basis of this allegation was an article in *All The Year Round* which had accused a gentleman 'trumpeted about London as the most wonderful of all the wonderful mediums ever wondered at' (*All The Year Round*, 7, 1863, p. 608). While the Quarterly Reviewer concluded that this meant Home, this is highly unlikely since Dickens and the French conjuror Robin were stated to have been present, and there is no reference anywhere else to suggest that either Dickens or Robin ever attended a Home séance. Given the prominence of the former as a critic, and of the latter as a performer of spiritualist exposés, it seems inconceivable neither would have mentioned this at some point. The procedure described by Dickens sounds more like Charles Foster, who arrived in Britain that year and rapidly rose to prominence. However, he was caught cheating almost as rapidly, and returned to America.

13 *Spiritual Magazine*, 4, 1863, p. 81.

14 A lecture on spiritualism by an unknown spiritualist in the south of England resulted in 'the indignant assembly denouncing his statements as sheer blasphemy and the language of a lunatic'. The meeting had been chaired by a somewhat sceptical magistrate, one Captain Noble, who wrote to the *Sussex Advertiser* that 'Home is as rank an impostor, I verily believe, as ever lived'. Unlike so many of Daniel's critics, however, Captain Noble provided his name and address, a decision that he no doubt quickly regretted. Daniel wrote to him to say he himself would

bring a libel action, forcing a rapid and somewhat embarrassing public apology 'in large type'. Noble took the 'earliest opportunity of withdrawing the charge', providing the 'fullest apology', indeed 'every apology' for his 'unjustifiable assertion [which] I so much regret'. It had been 'unfairly formed . . . [and] I now express my readiness to make any retraction equally public, and shall with pleasure clothe it in any appropriate form which you may deem satisfactory to your own honour'. The relevant letters were published in the *Sussex Advertiser* on 23 March and 14 April, 1863 (*Spiritual Magazine*, 4, 1863, pp. 219–20).

15 T. L. Hood, *Letters of Robert Browning* (London, 1933), pp. 182–3.

16 *Spiritual Magazine*, 5, 1864, p. 62.

17 Weld, *Last Winter in Rome*, 1865, p. 176.

18 *Times*, 12 January 1864, p. 6.

19 *Spiritual Magazine*, 5, 1864, p. 96.

20 *Spiritual Magazine*, 5, 1864, p. 64.

21 *Spiritual Magazine*, 5, 1864, pp. 171–2.

22 Home, *Incidents*, ii, pp. 83–4.

23 *Human Nature*, 4, 1870, p. 532.

24 *Spiritual Magazine*, 5, 1864, p. 319.

25 I have somehow lost the source of this quote, but have no doubt that it will turn up eventually. However, I appreciate that you are possibly the only person in the country who has bothered to read through these notes, and feel that you deserve better. So, if you really want to know where the quote comes from, do get in touch, as I'll probably have located it by then.

26 Home, *Incidents*, ii, pp. 87–88.

27 Later, when in opposition to Disraeli, Bright and Gladstone were compared by *Punch* to 'the political Davenport brothers', because they had tied themselves in knots, and were unable to extricate themselves. However, *Punch* noted that, unlike the Davenports, the opposition performed outside a cabinet, and that they could command a larger show of hands (*Punch*, 54, 1868, p. 222).

28 N. Hawthorn, *Passages from the French and Italian note-books* (London, 1883), p. 296.

29 Wyndham, *Mr Sludge*, pp. 94–5.

30 Edward McAleer, *Dearest Isa: Robert Browning's letters to Isabella Blagden* (Austin, 1951), p. 160.

31 Paul Landis (ed), *Letters of the Brownings to George Barret* (Urbana, 1958), pp. 257–8.

10 Mr Sludge and the Davenport Brothers

1 *Spiritual Magazine*, 5, 1864, pp. 540–41.
2 It has often been said that the Davenports never claimed to be real spirit mediums, but that was only their general public position. In fact, they did privately tell spiritualists that their demonstrations were spirit manifestations (*Spiritual Magazine*, 5, 1864, pp. 508–9).
3 *Spiritual Magazine*, 5, 1864, pp. 493–519.
4 Cited in *Spiritual Magazine*, 5, 1864, p. 501.
5 R. Kudarz, 'Magic and magicians – past and present in Australia and New Zealand', *M.U.M.*, 9, 1919, p. 13.
6 *Lancet*, 2, 1864, p. 420.
7 *Spiritual Magazine*, 5, 1864, p. 561.
8 *Spiritual Magazine*, 5, 1864, p. 556.
9 The Davenports' career has been described in various places, the most recent being Jim Steinmeyer's wonderful *Hiding the Elephant: how magicians created the impossible and learned to disappear* (London, 2004).
10 *Spiritual Magazine*, 5, 1864, p. 522.
11 Podmore, *Modern Spiritualism*, ii, p. 61.
12 *Spiritual Magazine*, 1, 1860, p. 461.
13 *Medium & Daybreak*, 2, 1871, p. 56.
14 *Spiritual Magazine*, 3, 1862, p. 273.
15 *Spiritual Magazine*, 4, 1869, p. 173.
16 *Spiritual Magazine*, 7, 1879, p. 31.
17 *Spiritual Magazine*, 5, 1864, p. 503.
18 The relationship between Daniel and Benjamin Coleman seems to have been mysteriously acrimonious. Following a soiree, at which the two had been present, Coleman wrote to Daniel (letter dated 5 December 1865) as follows: 'I was much surprised that you should have forced me to take your hand last evening as you and I can never be on friendly terms again. I therefore wish you to understand that the proposal made by yourself, and accepted by me three years ago, I hold to be binding, and that my motives for desiring that "we should meet as strangers" are now stronger than ever' (SPR.MS 28/99).

Alas, I have been unable to discover what happened three years earlier to provoke this.

19 For example, see Matthew Sweet's excellent *Inventing the Victorians*, pp. xv, 13–14.

20 Home, *Incidents*, ii, p. 27.

21 McAleer, *Dearest Isa*, p. 214.

22 This is the assumption made by Kenyon, *Letters*, ii, p. 388.

23 Allingham & Radford, *Allingham*, p. 101.

24 Home, *Incidents*, ii, p. 95.

25 Mme Home, *Life and mission*, pp. 131–3.

26 Letter to T. A. Trollope (Trollope, *What I remember*, pp. 158).

11 *The Wizard and the widow*

1 Jay, *Jay's journal*, p. 91.

2 Jenkins, *Shadow and the light*, p. 160.

3 Home, *Incidents*, ii, p. 139.

4 Ibid., pp. 126–8.

5 *The Sphinx*, 43, 1944, p. 19.

6 According to Mrs Lyon's testimony, she first met Home on the 3rd, rather than the 2nd, indeed they disagreed on almost everything. However, I begin with Daniel's version of events, so have chosen this date for the moment.

7 Home, *Incidents*, ii, p. 227.

8 Ibid., pp. 213–26.

9 McAleer, *Dearest Isa*, pp. 272–3.

10 *Times*, 23 May, 1868, p. 8.

11 Home, *Incidents*, ii, p. 206.

12 Ibid., p. 207.

13 *Scotsman*, 25 April 1868, p. 4.

14 *Times*, 28 April 1868, pp. 10–11.

15 *Times*, 25 April 1868, pp. 10.

16 Home, *Incidents*, ii, p. 278.

17 Ibid., pp. 196–7, 272.

18 Jenkins, *Shadow and the light*, p. 281.

19 *Pall Mall Gazette*, 18 May 1868, p. 2.

12 Rising to Adare

1 *Experiences in Spiritualism with D. D. Home* was reprinted in the *PSPR*, 35, 1924, pp. 1–285. The specific extracts here were identified by Trevor Hall as evidence of Home's close relationship to Adare (Hall, *Enigma*, pp. 128–9).

2 Hall cites this as evidence of Adare's suggestibility (ibid., p. 129).

3 Hall cites this as evidence of Lindsay's suggestibility (ibid., pp. 129–30).

4 *Report on Spiritualism of the London Dialectical Society* (London, 1873), p. 229.

5 Ibid., p. 279.

6 Ibid., pp. 207–14.

7 Ibid., pp. 214–15.

8 Ibid., p. 193.

9 Ibid., p. 223. Ironically, perhaps, Mrs Marshall claimed that this was nonsense, denying such activities ever took place at her séances (*Athenaeum*, 28 October 1871, p. 557).

10 ibid., p. 204. This optimistic statement was made by Sgr. Diamani, whom Daniel himself later described as 'either insane or a knave' (SPR.MS28/289).

11 Ibid., p. 6.

12 *Athenaeum*, 28 October 1871, pp. 556–7.

13 *Contemporary Review*, 27, 1876, p. 286.

14 Mme Home, *Life and mission*, pp. 169–70.

15 *Fraser's Magazine*, 15, 1877, p. 135.

16 *Fraser's Magazine*, 16, 1877, p. 697.

17 *Times*, 26 December 1872, p. 5.

13 The first psychic

1 Mme. Home, *Life and mission*, pp. 35–6.

2 *Scotsman*, 29 January, 1870, p. 6.

3 Ibid.

4 *Edinburgh Evening Courant*, 31 January 1870, p. 5.

5 C. Colegrove, *The European sphynx: or, Satan's masterpiece. Louis Napoleon the personal anti-Christ and the man of sin. The coming of the Lord at hand* (Buffalo, New York, 1866).

6 *Spiritual Magazine*, 5, 1870, p. 561.

7 *Athenaeum*, 23 March 1870, p. 552.

8 Faraday had made this point years earlier, in a lecture on the conservation of force, and had been heavily criticized by a colleague (*Athenaeum*, 28 March 1857, p. 398).

9 W. Crookes, 'Spiritualism viewed by the light of modern science', *Quarterly Journal of Science*, 7, 1870, pp. 316–35.

10 W. Crookes, 'Experimental investigation of a new force', *Quarterly Journal of Science*, 8, 1871, pp. 339–49.

11 *Birmingham Morning News*, cited in *The Spiritualist*, 1, 1871, p. 189.

12 W. Crookes, 'Some further experiments in psychic force', *Quarterly Journal of Science*, 8, 1871, pp. 471–93.

13 *Nature*, 29 February 1872, p. 343; 7 March 1872, pp. 363–4.

14 *Glasgow Herald*, 13 September 1876, cited in J. Palfreman, 'Between scepticism and credulity: a study of Victorian scientific attitudes to Modern Spiritualism', R. Wallis (ed.), *On the margins of science* (London, 1979), p. 224.

15 W. Crookes, 'Some further experiments', pp. 479–80.

16 Ibid., p. 82.

17 Joseph Larmor, *Memoir and scientific correspondence of the late Sir George Gabriel Stokes* (Cambridge, 1907), p. 362.

18 W. Crookes, *Researches into the phenomena of spiritualism* (London, 1874), pp. 31–2.

19 The bizarre discussion took place in the letter pages of *English Mechanic* during November and December of 1871.

20 Crookes, 'Some further experiments', p. 492.

21 [W. B. Carpenter], 'Spiritualism and its recent converts', *Quarterly Review*, 131, 1871, pp. 301–53.

22 W. Crookes, *Researches into the phenomena called spiritual* (London, 1874), p. 66.

23 Ibid., pp. 47–56.

24 Ibid., pp. 73–80.

25 The initial letter was from Henry Dircks. Dircks had co-created the illusion known as 'Pepper's Ghost' that had been demonstrated at the Polytechnic Institute in Regent Street, and that had been loosely compared to Home's spirit manifestations. In reply to Dircks's letter, which claimed that '[n]o really scientific man believes in

Spiritualism', letters cited the Dialectical Society investigation and the experiments of Crookes, and pointed out that Crookes and Varley and Wallace were clearly 'scientific men'. When Dircks responded that two or three names among so many was negligible, A. R. Wallace was only the most eminent of those who supplied the names of several other scientific men who attested to the phenomena of spiritualism, and stressed the scientific nature of investigations into such phenomena (letters to *The Times*, 27 December 1872 to 6 January 1873).

26 *Edinburgh Evening Courant*, 7 August 1871, p. 4.

27 *Evening Standard*, 15 January 1872, p. 4.

28 Gordon S. Haight (ed.), *The George Eliot Letters* (London, 1955), v, p. 253.

29 Francis Darwin (ed.), *More letters of Charles Darwin* (London, 1887), ii, p. 443.

30 Darwin's letter to Galton is in the archive at the Dittrick Medical History Center, and a scanned copy was kindly sent to me by Jennifer Nieves. Galton's correspondence is published in K. Pearson, *The Life, letters and labours of Francis Galton* (London, 1924); pp. 64–66.

31 The quote is given in Burton, *Hey-day of a wizard*, p. 215, alas without a reference. The most likely source in Burton's limited bibliography is Nathan Dole, *Tolstoi*, 1911, but I have been unable to find a copy anywhere in the UK.

14 The last word

1 *Cornhill Magazine*, 7, 1863, p. 717; *Fraser's Magazine*, 77, 1868, p. 365.

2 *Westminster Review*, 98, 1872, p. 462.

3 Lord Amberley, Experiences in Spiritualism, *Fortnightly Review*, 15, 1874, p. 90.

4 *Fraser's Magazine*, 71, 1865, pp. 259–60.

5 *Fraser's Magazine*, 4, 1871, p. 515. The argument that Christianity proved the miracles rather than vice versa had been made by Locke. Indeed, W. B. Carpenter cited Locke as he stressed the effect of personal belief on testimony (*Contemporary Review*, 27, 1876, p. 295). Thomas Arnold had also argued the point in the 1830's with reference to mesmeric phenomena (A. Winter, *Mesmerized: powers of mind in Victorian Britain*

(Chicago, 1988), p. 271). The stress upon internal evidence was also made in mid-Victorian periodicals (e.g. *Fraser's Magazine*, 71, 1865, p. 32; *Fraser's Magazine*, 71, 1865, pp. 259–60; *British Quarterly Review*, 58, 1873, p. 169; *Cornhill Magazine*, 30, 1874, p. 39).

6 *Spiritual Magazine*, 2, 1867, p. 51.

7 *Spiritual Magazine*, 6, 1871, p. 88.

8 *Spiritual Magazine*, 1, 1873, pp. 279–81.

9 *Spiritual Magazine*, 6, 1871, pp. 289–90.

10 *Echo*, 8 June 1871, cited in Podmore, *Modern spiritualism*, ii, pp. 81–2.

11 *Spiritualist*, 15 June 1871, p. 172.

12 *Medium and Daybreak*, 2, 1871, p. 106.

13 *Spiritual Magazine*, 6, 1871, p. 299.

14 [Carpenter], 'Spiritualism and its recent converts', p. 349.

15 One of these was Charles Blackburn, the Manchester merchant who had witnessed Mrs Guppy's arrival, and found the idea of Herne and William's involvement so absurd. This was hardly surprising, since if Blackburn had suspected Herne of being a fraud, he would not have been financing his mediumship.

16 Owen, *The darkened room: women, power and spiritualism in late Victorian England* (London, 1989), p. 59.

17 Owen, *Darkened room*, p. 66.

18 Ibid., p. 48.

19 Ibid., p. 66.

20 Letter to Home from Nelson Holmes (SPR.MS28/316).

21 Owen, *Darkened room*, p. 71.

22 R. Brandon, *The spiritualists: the passion for the occult in the nineteenth and twentieth centuries* (London, 1983), p. 106.

23 Letter from Crookes to Home (SPR.MS28/130).

24 *Spiritual Magazine*, 4, 1876, p. 472.

25 Darwin, *Life and letters*, iii, p. 187.

26 Letter from Home to 'John' (SPR.MS28/313).

27 Letter from Holmes to Home (SPR.MS28/316).

28 Letter from Kate Fox-Jencken to Home (SPR.MS28/379).

29 Letter by Home (SPR.MS28/280).

30 Mme Home, *Life and mission*, p. 221.

31 *New York World*, 6 April 1876.

32 This was Dumas *fils* (Mme Home, *Life and mission*, p. 222).

33 Ibid.

34 D. D. Home, *Lights and shadows of spiritualism* (London, 1877), pp. 301–5.

35 Ibid., p. 298.

36 Ibid., pp, 349–50.

37 Ibid., pp. 352–3.

38 *Human Nature*, 11, 1877, pp. 204–21.

39 Letter by Home (SPR.MS28/282).

40 Carpenter, 'Psychological curiosities of spiritualism', *Fraser's Magazine*, 16, 1877, pp. 541–64.

41 Wallace, 'Psychological curiosities of skepticism: a reply to Dr Carpenter', *Fraser's Magazine*, 16, 1877, pp. 694–706.

42 R. G. Medhurst & K. M. Goldney, 'William Crookes and the physical phenomena of mediumship', *PSPR*, 54, 1964, pp. 121–22.

43 W. Crookes, 'Notes of séances with D. D. Home', *PSPR*, 6, 1889, pp. 98–127.

44 Mme Home, *Life and mission*, p. 217.

45 Podmore, *Modern spiritualism*, ii, p. 112.

15 Death and afterlife

1 Letter by Home (SPR.MS28/284).

2 F. Anderson, L. Salamo, & B. L. Stein (eds.), *Mark Twain's Notebooks and Journals* (Berkeley, 1975), ii, p. 306.

3 Mme Home, *Life and mission*, p. 223.

4 Letters by Home (SPR.MS28/288; SPR.MS28/289).

5 Letter from Samuel Carter Hall to Home (SPR.MS28/236).

6 *JSPR*, 6, 1894, pp. 177–78.

7 Mme Home, *Life and mission*, pp. 229–30.

8 H. Houdini, *A magician among the spirits* (New York, 1972), p. 49.

9 Hawthorn, *Passages*, p. 296; letter from F. Greenwood to the *Westminster Gazette*, 24 February 1899, p. 3; see also H. Addington Bruce, 'Mr Sludge the medium', *Journal of the American Society for Psychical Research*, 39, pp. 131–2.

10 *JSPR*, 4, 1889, p. 102.

11 J. Jastrow, The psychology of spiritualism. *Popular Science Monthly*, 34, 1889, p. 727.

12 *JSPR*, 4, 1889, pp. 120–21.

13 Podmore, *Modern spiritualism*, ii, p. 230.

14 *JSPR*, 11, 1903, pp. 76–80.

15 Count Perovsky–Petrovo-Solovovo, 'Some thoughts on D. D. Home', *PSPR*, 39, 1930, pp. 247ff.

16 Houdini, *A magician among the spirits,* pp. 38–49, 243.

17 G. Stein, *The sorcerer of kings: the case of Daniel Dunglas Home and William Crookes* (Buffalo, 1993), p. 99. This concession was made in response to an article that argued against the validity of the alleged exposure (E. Osty, 'D. D. Home: new light on "the exposure at the Tuileries"', *Journal of the American Society for Psychical Research*, 30, 1936, pp. 77–93). Osty's article, however, was itself misleading, not least in that it was based primarily on the testimony of a lady who had not even been present at the séance in question.

18 Stein, *The sorcerer of kings,* p. 104.

Post-mortem

1 See chapters 4 and 5 of J. N. Maskelyne, *Modern Spiritualism: a short account of its rise and progress, with some exposures of so-called spirit media* (London, 1876).

2 London Dialectical Society, 1873, p. 278.

3 The extent and significance of the mystery surrounding Home's feats during his own time is described in P. Lamont, 'Spiritualism and a mid-Victorian crisis of evidence', *Historical Journal*, 47, 2004, pp. 897–920.

4 It has in fact been claimed that a number of small one-octave mouth organs were found among Home's effects [e.g. M. Gardner, *The New Age: notes of a fringe watcher* (Buffalo, 1988), p. 177; J. Randi, *The Supernatural A–Z,* (London, 1995), p. 159]. The source of this claim was William Lindsay Gresham, who told James Randi that he had seen these mouth organs in the Home collection at the Society for Psychical Research. As Michael Coleman has pointed out, Gresham's own writings on Home make no such claim, though this may be because the finding took place later, 'around 1960' according to Randi's recollection (*JSPR*, 61, 1996, p. 352). Perhaps more importantly, however, no such mouth organs were subsequently

found in the collection, and neither the list of contents nor those familiar with the collection provide any support for Gresham's claim that they had been present (*JSPR*, 61, 1996, p. 128; *JSPR*, 62, 1997, p. 96). Indeed, Eric Dingwall catalogued the collection on its arrival at the SPR, and it is difficult to imagine either that he would not have noticed, or that he would not have made it public.

5 Houdini, *A magician among the spirits*, p. 48. Houdini's statement sounds as if he has confused events (i.e. that Home went out of the window of the first room, then entered, or appeared to enter, by the window of the next-door room), when the reverse was reported by Adare and Lindsay. There has been a host of attempts to solve the mystery of Ashley House, the two general theories being either that Home crossed between the windows by physical means (swinging, stepping or jumping), or else that the event was largely the product of suggestion. Given the reliance upon the eye-witness testimony of Adare and Lindsay, any objective evidence would be valuable. With this in mind, Archie Jarman visited Ashley House prior to its demolition in 1970, measured the distance between the balconies, and found them to be (as Lindsay had stated) 7 feet 5 inches apart (A. Jarman, 'How D. D. Home got his feet off the ground', *Alpha*, October 1980, p. 12). Later, however, Trevor Hall (who not only knew Jarman, but referred to his visit to Ashley House, and actually thanked him for helping supply information about the building) went in search of his own objective evidence. Rather than refer to his friend's measurements, Hall had an architect estimate the distance between the windows (based upon a photograph of Ashley House), which led to the conclusion that the window ledges were only 4 feet 2 inches apart (Hall, *Enigma*, pp. 115–20). As both Jarman and Hall concluded Home could have crossed between the balconies (either by swinging on a rope, or by holding on to the balustrade), it is unclear why Hall ignored Jarman's measurements. Nevertheless, it goes to show that even the 'objective' evidence is disputed. As for the various interpretations of the rather conflicting eye-witness testimony, it has been debated by all the usual suspects, and many others, with a regularity that obscures the more important point that this was never the most impressive of Home's recorded feats in the first place.

6 From the preceding two notes, it should be clear that there has been an ongoing and often confusing debate about the plausibility of various explanations for Home's feats. The inadequacy of the explanations in Home's own time is clear (Lamont, 'Spiritualism and a mid-Victorian crisis of evidence'), but later summaries of possible explanations can be found in F. Podmore, *The Newer spiritualism* (London, 1910) and, more recently, in Hall, *Enigma of Daniel Home* and Stein, *Sorcerer of kings*. Needless to say, most of these explanations have been challenged with reference to evidence appearing in countless sources already cited above, but critical reviews of Hall (*JSPR*, 53, 1985, pp. 45–6; *Zetetic Scholar*, nos. 12/13, 1987, pp. 154–9) and Stein (*JSPR*, 40, 1984, pp. 45–50), along with responses in subsequent issues, will give you a flavour of the problem. If you wish to read a strong argument against the key 'normal' theories (and, therefore, for the genuineness of Home's phenomena), see: S. Braude, *The limits of influence: psychokinesis and the philosophy of science* (Lanham, 1997), pp. 63–93. After that, you will have to examine the countless primary and secondary sources, most of which have been provided in these notes, then make up your own mind. My own reasons for not being convinced by the evidence were given in P. Lamont, 'How convincing is the evidence for D. D. Home?', Proceedings of the 42nd Annual Convention of the Parapsychological Association, Palto Alto, 1999, pp. 166–79. However, because it was part of a study of British history, the paper only deals with British séances (so does not include, for example, the Amsterdam séances, which are described in Zorab, 'Test sittings'), and it amounts to no more than a justification for my personal position, briefly stated in the introduction to these notes. My only advice would be that, if you encounter anyone who claims that the issue is clear and the problem resolved, do not believe them.

7 *Literary Times*, 21 March 1863, cited in Home, *Incidents*, ii, p. 37.

Post-script

1 This story is based upon a Nigerian myth about the Trickster God, Edshu. Recently, George Hansen has provided a detailed discussion of the relationship between the trickster and psychic phenomena in his fascinating *The trickster and the paranormal* (Xlibris, 2001). My point

here is a simple one, and quite different from the argument in George's book (which, in my opinion, more parapsychologists should read).

2 Crookes, *Researches*, p. 16.

3 An enormous amount of research has been done on the unreliability of eye-witness testimony, but the most appropriate reference is: R. Hodgson & W. Davey, 'The possibilities of mal-observation and lapse of memory from a practical point of view', *PSPR*, 4, 1887, pp. 381–495. This pioneering and sometimes amusing study is recommended reading for anyone interested in testimony about séance phenomena.

4 It should be pointed out that neither Hodgson & Davey nor anyone else since has produced testimony of the sort that Home's witnesses provided.

5 There have been several theories of how *psi* (the term used to described both the ostensible phenomena and the possible underlying mechanism) works, but no consensus exists within parapsychology about which is the most useful, or best supported by experimental results. However, academic parapsychology is presently little concerned with the magnitude of phenomena that Home reportedly produced. In the quest to counter the many criticisms of sceptics, and given the obvious controversy that surrounds such claims, academic parapsychology has increasingly avoided individuals who claim to have such impressive paranormal abilities, and instead focused upon rigorous experiments to test *psi* ability among the general population. The debate about whether such a force exists continues, and it often seems as if it will never end, but the evidence suggests that, if it does exist among the general population, it amounts to no more than a significant deviation from what one would expect by chance. Several individuals, who have claimed to possess stronger paranormal abilities, have been tested by a variety of scientists and other interested parties, but the results with them have been, to say the least, inconclusive. Many who believe that such abilities exist continue to regard Home as the most impressive psychic to date.

INDEX

A

accordion playing 85, 89, 121–122, 123–124, 203, 204, 215, 218, 221, 264, 266

Adare, Wyndham Wyndham-Quinn, Lord 182, 183–187, 189, 190, 199–200, 262, 265

Experiences in Spiritualism with Mr D. D. Home 187–188

Aide, Hamilton 197

Albert, Prince Consort 61

Alexander II, Tsar 101, 102, 103, 164

All the Year Round (journal) 126, 169, 170, 292n12

Amsterdam sittings 93–96, 141, 267

Anderson, John Henry 52–53, 54–56, 58–59, 150, 154, 160, 169

and 'Aztec Lilliputians' 60 61

death 171

and exposure of spiritualism 59–60, 61–65, 70, 111, 118, 154–155, 260

meeting with Home 167, 169–171

Royal Opera House performances and fire 72–73

Anderson, Lizzie 155, 156, 164–165, 168

Arnold, (Sir) Edwin 153–154

Ashley House, Westminster 183, 184

Home's séance 185–187, 188, 190, 192–194, 258, 262, 265

Athenaeum 137, 192–193, 201

Athenaeum Club 45, 48

Atlas 87

'Aztec Lilliputians' 60–61, 169

B

Balerno Mill, Currie 6, 11

Bancroft, George 34

Barnum, P. T. 14, 160

Barthez, Dr François 89–90, 91–93, 121, 131, 253, 257, 258

Beardslee (medium) 27

I

THE RISE OF THE INDIAN ROPE TRICK

Peter Lamont

'A short, sharp little book . . . wonderfully
entertaining' *The Times*

It has been called a conjuring feat, but nobody has been able
to discover how it is done. It has been called impossible, yet
many have claimed to have seen it with their own eyes. But
the thing about the Indian rope trick is that it isn't Indian,
it doesn't involve a rope, and it isn't a trick. From the
Victorian fascination with the East to the Magic Circle,
from Chicago and London to the beaches of India, in this
acclaimed book Peter Lamont describes how a simple hoax
grew into the world's most famous mystery, assisted on its
way by those in search of fame and fortune, and by others
whose aim was to destroy it in defence of the West.

'Beguiling . . . A magical read'
Observer

'The truth here is more bizarre than even the most
outlandish fiction . . . Full marks for entertainment'
Guardian

'A riveting yarn, full of quirky stories and wisdom
about our need for mystery'
Daily Express

Abacus
0 349 11824 8

Now you can order superb titles directly from Abacus

☐ The Rise of the Indian Rope Trick   Peter Lamont   £7.99

The prices shown above are correct at time of going to press. However, the publishers reserve the right to increase prices on covers from those previously advertised, without further notice.

────────────────── ⬭ABACUS⬭ ──────────────────

Please allow for postage and packing: **Free UK delivery.**
Europe: add 25% of retail price; Rest of World: 45% of retail price.

To order any of the above or any other Abacus titles, please call our credit card orderline or fill in this coupon and send/fax it to:

Abacus, PO Box 121, Kettering, Northants NN14 4ZQ
Fax: 01832 733076   Tel: 01832 737527
Email: aspenhouse@FSBDial.co.uk

☐ I enclose a UK bank cheque made payable to Abacus for £ . . . .
☐ Please charge £ . . . . . . to my Visa/Access/Mastercard/Eurocard

Expiry Date ☐☐☐☐   Switch Issue No. ☐☐

NAME (BLOCK LETTERS please) . . . .
ADDRESS . . . .

. . . .

. . . .

Postcode . . . . Telephone . . . .
Signature . . . .

Please allow 28 days for delivery within the UK. Offer subject to price and availability.

Please do not send any further mailings from companies carefully selected by Abacus ☐